THE UNIVERSITY OF
WINCHESTER

Martial Rose Library
Tel: 01962 827306

To be returned on or before the day marked above, subject to recall.

D1334451

Standardization, Ideology and Linguistics

Standardization, Ideology and Linguistics

Nigel Armstrong
University of Leeds, UK

Ian E. Mackenzie
Newcastle University, UK

palgrave
macmillan

First published 2013 by
PALGRAVE MACMILLAN

Palgrave Macmillan in the UK is an imprint of Macmillan Publishers Limited, registered in England, company number 785998, of Houndmills, Basingstoke, Hampshire RG21 6XS.

Palgrave Macmillan in the US is a division of St Martin's Press LLC, 175 Fifth Avenue, New York, NY 10010.

Palgrave Macmillan is the global academic imprint of the above companies and has companies and representatives throughout the world.

Palgrave® and Macmillan® are registered trademarks in the United States, the United Kingdom, Europe and other countries.

ISBN 978-0-230-29675-6

This book is printed on paper suitable for recycling and made from fully managed and sustained forest sources. Logging, pulping and manufacturing processes are expected to conform to the environmental regulations of the country of origin.

A catalogue record for this book is available from the British Library.

A catalog record for this book is available from the Library of Congress.

10 9 8 7 6 5 4 3 2 1
22 21 20 19 18 17 16 15 14 13

Printed and bound in Great Britain by
CPI Antony Rowe, Chippenham and Eastbourne

Einen Satz verstehen, heißt, eine Sprache verstehen.
Eine Sprache verstehen, heißt eine Technik beherrschen.

Ludwig Wittgenstein

Contents

List of figures and tables

Figure

Tables

Abbreviations

ACC	Accusative case marked by the Spanish preposition *a* (known as the prepositional accusative)
AUX	Auxiliary verb
CDE	Corpus del Español (Davies 2002–)
COCA	Corpus of Contemporary American English (Davies 2008–)
CORDE	Corpus diacrónico del español (Real Academia Española, undated (a))
CREA	Corpus de referencia del español actual (Real Academia Española, undated (b))
DP	Determiner Phrase (equivalent to 'Noun Phrase' as found in earlier models)
EPP	An abstract feature that attracts another constituent such as a subject or an object (see note 13 to Chapter 4)
EETS	Early English Text Society (http://users.ox.ac.uk/~eets/)
FEM	Feminine
FRANTEXT	Base textuelle FRANTEXT (http://www.frantext.fr/)
INF	Infinitive
MASC	Masculine
NEG	Negative marker
OV	Object-Verb (word order)
PLU	Plural
PP	Prepositional Phrase
RP	Received Pronunciation (hyper-standard variety of British English)
SING	Singular
SUBJ	Subject
SUBJUNC	Subjunctive
VO	Verb-Object (word order)
VP	Verb Phrase
v^*P	Transitive verb phrase together with its left periphery (see note 12 to Chapter 4)

Introduction

The issues studied in this book

In this book we explore some of the ways in which standardization, ideology and linguistics are connected. Standardization in language has received a fair amount of scholarly attention, and in Chapter 1 we undertake a conspectus of the various ways in which the phenomenon has found expression and been theorized. Standardization is of course the manifestation of an ideology, and we consider here, as well as its effects on speakers in general, those which press upon the practitioners of linguistics, both in the 'theoretical' branches and in sub-disciplines relying on empirical methods.

An ideology is a set of shared beliefs that, while partial, presents these as the objective way of looking at things, or at least as 'received wisdom' where 'received' has the usual sense of 'generally accepted'. While it is perfectly obvious that the Milroys' 'ideology of the standard' (Milroy and Milroy 1999) is a term referring to the view that favours a dominating or hierarchical situation, not only in language but in the ordering of society, the counterpart of this ideology, that which opposes standardization, has no one name that comes very readily to mind, at least in linguistics. This state of affairs can perhaps be explained, in part at least, by reference to the time interval that commonly precedes the adoption of a social change. It may be that much change follows the so-called S-curve pattern, comprising a slow onset or 'lag phase' followed by a rapid or 'log phase' where the majority of elements are affected, in turn followed by a further gradual phase where the residual elements may or may not fall in line with the majority that have undergone change. The S-curve model was first applied in linguistics by Chen (1972) to account for exceptions to sound change; the motivation behind this model is not wholly clear, but Chen suggests (1972: 474) that 'as the phonological innovation gradually spreads across the lexicon [...] there comes a point where the minor rule gathers momentum and begins to serve as a basis for extrapolation.' The cumulative S-curve is a model applied to other forms of social change such as product adoption and the diffusion of technology, and commonly refers to adopters rather than the objects of adoption. Certainly the notion is intuitive, and awareness of its effects is widespread among laypersons; for instance, Gertrude Stein remarked informally, apropos of modernism in the arts, 'for a very long time everybody refuses, and then almost without a pause everybody accepts'.

The model is more complicated where an ideology is in question, for one of the essential features of ideologies is that they work at an unconscious level. In this they differ both from products that are the object of conscious adoption, like MP3 players, but also from 'memes' like linguistic variants, where diffusion seems to take place more intuitively. We discuss this in more detail in Chapter 1, but in general it seems implausible that people should adhere to an ideology while recognizing it as such. We shall explore in what follows some of the consequences of the implicit adoption in theoretical linguistics of the ideology of the standard. These include, but go beyond, the rather well-known rejection by Chomsky and his followers of the acceptability of certain 'non-standard' forms, and the consequences of this rejection for the robustness of their theories.

The obvious corollary of an acceptance of the ideology of the standard is that its rejection offers a standpoint from which criticism can be directed by those concerned to demonstrate the distorting effects of standardization in everyday language use and perhaps in linguistics too, as does J. Milroy (2001). But beyond this is an element of subtlety that sees a lack of readiness on the part of those who study variation and change in language from a speaker-oriented viewpoint to consider closely what we called above the counterpart of the ideology of the standard. It is quite plain that standardization and its associated ideology, in its primary form rather than as an object of reflection by scholars, has a long attestation, so that sufficient time has passed for this ideology to become apparent as such, and to attract criticism. The obvious point here is the presence since around 1945, although of course foreshadowed well before then, of the ideology that opposes the standard and what lies behind it. The readiest term for it is perhaps 'egalitarianism'. Mention of it is by no means new; anyone who has read a sample of British novels published in the late 1940s and early 1950s will have encountered references to 'levelling down', and this period was of course marked by socialist measures designed to promote equality, like high marginal taxation rates, a nationalization programme and the widespread introduction of social welfare schemes that previously had been patchy. The then Prime Minister, Clement Attlee, remarked at the time that levelling down for the few meant levelling up for the many. Few today would deplore the achievements in relative social and economic equality brought about by the welfare programmes introduced in recent times in the advanced economies. Egalitarianism remains none the less an ideology, and we are in any event interested here in tracing its effects in culture, not economics or politics. The fact that equality, and one of its opposites, elitism, are delicate subjects should not discourage investigation. In his *Dictionnaire philosophique* Voltaire attacks received wisdom in the following terms:

> Quelqu'un répand dans le monde qu'il y a un géant haut de soixante et dix pieds. Bientôt après, tous les docteurs examinent de quelle couleur doivent être ses cheveux, de quelle grandeur est son pouce, quelles dimensions ont ses ongles: on crie, on cabale, on se bat. Ceux qui soutiennent que le petit doigt du géant n'a que quinze lignes de diamètre font brûler ceux qui affirment que le petit doigt a un pied d'épaisseur. «Mais, messieurs, votre Géant existe-t-il? dit modestement un passant. – Quel doute horrible!' s'écrient tous ces disputants; quel blasphème! quelle absurdité!» Alors ils font tous une petite trêve pour lapider le passant; et après l'avoir assassiné en cérémonie, de la manière la plus édifiante, ils se battent entre eux comme de coutume au sujet du petit doigt et des ongles.[1] (Moland/ Voltaire 1877–85: 87)

The image of the giant evokes the contemporary cliché of the elephant in the room. The existence of the ideologies of interest here is not in question, clearly; what Voltaire's formulation captures more comprehensively is the tendency to focus on the minutiae of a phenomenon while ignoring its totality; and to accept received wisdom.

Standardization and the linguist

This linkage was identified tellingly in J. Milroy's (2001) article entitled 'Language ideologies and the consequences of standardization'. Milroy argues that linguists of most persuasions are susceptible to the influence of the standard ideology, and we examine this influence upon theoretical linguistics in some detail here. In particular, we suggest that many of the grammaticality judgments on which linguistic theorizing relies do little more than recapitulate the normative dynamic of the standardization process. Criticisms directed by a sociolinguist against those who focus on idealized abstractions are hardly surprising, but Milroy in his article taxes variationists too as suffering from 'the consequences of standardization'. One of these is a tendency to regard the standard as a benchmark against which other varieties are measured. This is not necessarily reprehensible; it may be convenient methodologically to use this approach, since standardized situations tend to have only one standard variety. Again, a sociolinguistic enquiry that seeks to extrapolate change from variation may well be interested in the assimilation by the legitimate variety of non-standard forms, such that a comparison in these terms is integral to the enquiry. Milroy's criticisms go deeper than this, however. Use of the standard as a benchmark, in comparison with which other varieties are measured, can easily lead to a distorted description; thus a non-standard variety may be characterized as having 'copula deletion' where in fact absence of copula is the default state. Characterizations of this type seem implicitly to assume deviation from the standard. But the more fundamental criticism of Milroy's that concerns us here has to do with an ideology prevailing in linguistics that may have the effect of discouraging enquiry. He remarks (p. 548) that 'to undertake a study of an urban variety for its own sake was, until as late as the 1960s, a grave risk to any young scholar in Britain'; the present authors hope to run no such risk, but the point stands that any ideology, perhaps especially one that is currently prevalent, has a weight and momentum of its own that can discourage examination.

Structure of the book

This book is organized as follows. Chapter 1 gives an overview of standardization in some of its forms as linguists have theorized them. Chapter 2 considers the issue of grammaticality as defined by theoretical linguistics within the context of the standard ideology, while Chapter 3 examines the phenomenon of so-called 'prestige constructions' (Sobin 1997), together with the associated notion of hypercorrection, within the same framework. Chapter 4 considers language change, broadly in the light of the opposed parametric and speaker-based approaches to the subject. In Chapter 5 we examine the thesis that much current linguistic change constitutes a form of anti-standardization, a process that tends towards a levelling of the distinction between standard and non-standard. In Chapter 6 we look at anti-standardizing tendencies in contemporary France, arguably the European country in which the notion of the standard language is crystallized at its most extreme.

Notes

1. A report is spread that there is a 70-foot-high giant. Soon doctors argue about what colour his hair must be, how big his thumb is, how long his nails are: there is shouting, plotting and fights. Those who believe that the giant's little finger is only 12 lignes in diameter burn those who say it is a foot wide. 'But, gentlemen, does your giant exist?' asks a passer-by modestly. 'What an appalling lack of faith,' scream the arguers, 'what blasphemy, what absurdity!' They then agree a brief truce so that they can stone the passer-by; and after ritually killing him, in the most edifying manner, they go back to fighting among themselves over the giant's little finger and his nails.

1
The nature of the standard

In this chapter we attempt to characterize the essential features of standard languages. In the interests of clear exposition we set out these features below in separate sections, although it will be seen that they overlap. These features of the standard refer to the following attributes: the standard as an ideology, which includes beliefs about its beauty, logical nature and efficiency; the socially dominant variety; the overlay acquired subsequent to the vernacular; the synecdochic variety; that which is regionless. We then look at some examples of folk-linguistic perceptions of the standard, before considering more closely the essential characteristics of ideologies as they concern us here.

1.1 The standard as an ideology

Milroy and Milroy (1999) suggest that a standard language is an abstraction, or more specifically, since all languages are abstractions, an ideology. The terms 'standard' and 'non-standard' are of course used by specialists in an ostensibly value-neutral sense, even if this specialized use of these terms does not match with their everyday currency; but normative terms like 'sub-standard', among many others, are frequent among linguistically naive speakers who have absorbed the 'ideology of the standard' (Milroy and Milroy 1999), which sees the standard as the only language worthy of the name, and the associated non-standard varieties as imperfect approximations to it. One view current in sociolinguistics sees standardization as a form of cultural oppression, most obviously by the upper classes, and indeed it is hard from this viewpoint to see the social advantage accruing to most speakers through their acceptance of the ideology of the standard. The notion of this ideology also explains style variation, which is linguistic accommodation determined by social situation; very few speakers enjoy such linguistic security that they can neglect to adapt their speech to someone of different social status, and this is the root of stylistic or situational variation. L. Milroy (2003: 161) cites Silverstein's (1979: 193) definition of language ideologies, which is as follows: they are 'sets of beliefs about language articulated by users as a rationalization or justification of perceived language structure and use'. The view we adopt in this book is that standardization is the expression of a broader ideology, to do with a hierarchical, as opposed to an egalitarian, view of how society should be ordered. From that perspective, the sets of beliefs alluded to in Silverstein's definition of language ideologies can be understood as 'second-order' ideologies, such that, in a fairly obvious way, the standard borrows prestige from the power of its users. Less obviously perhaps, the perceived invariance of the standard derives too from the hierarchical viewpoint that opposes change.

It should be pointed out in this connection that the oppressive view of social and linguistic hegemony highlighted above neglects the importance of 'culture', in the sense of the individual's subjective experience. It has been assumed until fairly recently that social class is generally the major element that determines social structure and that drives changes in it. The more recent development in cultural studies known as the 'cultural turn' lays stress on the difficulty of disentangling the various social and economic elements in any cultural phenomenon under examination – the phrase is calqued on the earlier 'linguistic turn' applied to positivist philosophy, and refers to a turn to, or emphasis on, the study of culture in disciplines that attempt to theorize social and cultural history. The cultural turn is in contrast to, say, a 'vulgar' Marxist approach (Eagleton 1991) that lays stress on the economic as underlying the social, and on an 'objective' view of any given situation as against the 'false consciousness' that may be held to afflict a social class. Clearly, however, economic, social and cultural elements and effects can scarcely be separated out in a hierarchical way, for instance in the rather crude Marxist 'base–superstructure' model according to which the cultural and social merely express the economic (we recognize that other Marxist approaches have greater subtlety). The 'vulgar' view cannot be supported in any strong sense, since the perspective of an individual or community on their socio-cultural experience forms an integral part of that experience, and cannot be overridden by any 'objective' viewpoint, as no cogent argument supports the theorist's claim to that privilege. The point need not be laboured any further, beyond saying that the complex congeries of factors that determines a speaker's response to the pressure of standardization is resistant to any straightforward analysis. Speakers' responses are in any event not of a piece, either with each other or with their behaviour; it is well known that working-class speakers pay (or paid) lip service to the standard while using their vernacular in the local networks which are meaningful to them. We shall have occasion to consider this global–local opposition when we come to examine the role of ideology more closely, below.

The schematic and static view of the standard, which for clear exposition ignores the fact of standardization as a process, reifies and opposes the standard language (or languages) and non-standard varieties. The process of cognition that interprets the abstract as real seems to be common: social class, for example, is a conceptual organization of the reality of inequality (Cannadine 1998: 188), but like many concepts it undergoes widespread objectification, 'moulding our perceptions of the unequal social world'. It is certainly true that all attempts to define the essential characteristics of the standard are opposed by the facts. We shall later consider Dennett's 'intentional stance', which takes the argument a stage further. Lodge (2004: 207) lists the 'set of beliefs' current in France about the standard language as comprising three: the ideal state of the language is one of uniformity; the most valid form of the language is to be found in writing; the standard is inherently better than the adjacent non-standard varieties (more elegant, clearer, etc.). French is standardized to an exceptionally high degree, in the related senses of its relative lack of variation, and in the internalization by its speakers of an unusually normative reflex of the ideology of the standard, so that the French situation illustrates the standardizing principle in a particularly vivid form. We now discuss in turn these characteristics.

The etymology of *standard* seems to be ultimately from Frankish *stand-hard 'steadfast' or 'unwavering', but in practice standard languages, like their associated non-standard dialects, are neither fixed nor monolithic. If we define standardization as the suppression of difference, we can see the process at work most obviously in its application to products like electrical components, in the sense of the reduction of variation to the limits of the practical. The everyday use of the word reflects this: when one talks of a 'standard' plug, the sense conveys universal application. The manufacturing goal is realistic, but the analogy with language breaks down instantly because non-standard linguistic variants can re-emerge endowed with different social capital, and the standard language can 'legitimize' elements formerly perceived as non-standard. When we come to consider language change, we shall see that much recent change is opposed to the standard, which is a moving target as well as an elusive one. An equally valid conceptualization of standard languages as being subject to continuing, multi-dimensional pressures, as well as exerting them, can be achieved by thinking in terms of Bourdieu's (1982) neo-Marxist perspective, from which the concept of *la langue légitime* or *autorisée* expresses quite cogently the legitimate and dynamically legitimating properties of standard language varieties. These properties are capable of inciting their speakers to engage in a continual process of assimilating arbitrary linguistic forms, in the interests of conferring on these forms a legitimacy that assures the capacity to maintain social distinctions. As J. Milroy remarks (2001: 532), the idea of the standard as invariant cannot in any case be equated with its prestige: 'it is not sensible to apply the notion of prestige to sets of electric plugs, for example, although they are plainly standardized, and many things that are unstandardized, like hand-made suits, may actually be the ones that acquire prestige.' The latter attribute stems from the prestige enjoyed by those who speak or write the standard. Divergence from the standard as manifested in spelling and pronunciation is in any case practised in what might be called the 'hyper-standard', as we shall see in the following chapter. A further sense of 'standard', as Milroy points out, is related to a level of achievement, as in *examination standards* and similar phrases. The sense here is therefore of a normative goal to be aimed at. But it is plain from the informal remarks of some normativists that certain standard features are regarded as shibboleths, and that these promote the gate-keeping function of the legitimate variety. The *Concise Oxford Dictionary* defines a shibboleth as a 'test word or principle or behaviour or opinion, the use of or inability to use which reveals one's party, nationality, etc.' Among well-known shibboleths in lexis are *lavatory* and *napkin* as against *toilet* and *serviette*. Kingsley Amis (1991: 245), novelist and self-appointed normativist, remarked in the course of a criticism of the use of *relevant* as synonymous with *meaningful* or *interesting*, that the usage is 'very unpopular [...] in some quarters. I'm all for it; it's a useful or even infallible sign that the writer is a victim of appalling herd-instinct [...]'. Even allowing for Amis's jocular intention, the quotation hints at the double-edged attitude that deplores innovation while welcoming it in the measure that it upholds the gate-keeping function just alluded to.

Along with and against the capacity of the standard to absorb and legitimize change goes an attitude among its speakers that sees language change as unwelcome, a view that is commonly shared by laypersons, as is shown by Amis's remark. The opposition in this regard between emotion and reason is deep-rooted. A lexical change currently in progress in English is the pluralization of *behaviour*. Even a professional linguist who is aware that Shakespeare used *behaviours*, and that processes of this type are perfectly possible and indeed common across languages, may feel distaste at the innovation. This perspective is understandable if we accept that many people dislike change and tend also to adhere to a 'golden-age' mentality, especially perhaps as they grow older. However, an oblique reflection of this attitude, cleansed of its judgmental character, may unwittingly enter the discourse of linguistic analysis. In the extract below, for example, Kroch (2001: 699) refers to syntactic change in terms which, while not intended in a negative sense, nevertheless presuppose a dichotomy between an assumed default state of quiescence and the interruption thereof:

> Language change is by definition a failure in the transmission across time of linguistic features. Such failures, in principle, could occur within groups of adult native speakers of language, who for some reason substitute one feature for another in their usage, as happens when new words are coined and substituted for old ones; but in the case of syntactic and other grammatical features, such innovation by monolingual adults is largely unattested. Instead, failures of transmission seem to occur in the course of language acquisition; that is, they are failures of learning.

There is no implication here that language change is in any way dysfunctional – the term 'failure' is not to be understood in a moral or similar sense. On the other hand, the tacit assumption is that change is the marked state and thus something that needs to be accounted for – in this case by postulating imperfect acquisition during infancy (see 4.2). At various points in this book we will have cause to observe that many of the apparently neutral tenets of modern linguistics owe more to the ideology of standardization than linguists would typically be prepared to admit.

It is obvious enough from a functional linguistic point of view – that is, one that lays stress on efficiency of communication and tends to discuss linguistic phenomena in terms of a tension between the desire for economy on the one hand and for clarity and expressiveness on the other – that language variation and change are undesirable, if only because, at an intermediate stage, the two processes introduce competition between two or more exponents, and hence 'noise' or 'junk' into the system. The functional view is one that surfaces in one form or another in much, and arguably most, linguistic discussion. Even Labov, in an extended discussion (2001: 3–6) of the negative consequences of language change, remarks (p. 3) that: 'the continued renewal and far-ranging character of linguistic change is not consistent with our fundamental conception of language as an instrument of social communication.' The key phrase here is 'social communication', and by it Labov appears to mean something like clear and harmonious communication, since his account of language change as dysfunction stresses outcomes such as the difficulty of learning foreign languages (in a wider perspective that includes change across language families as well as within languages); conflict between generations, in the form of irritation experienced by (especially) older members of a speech community at incoming forms, and in derision directed by younger speakers against older features; and difficulties over spelling, caused by sound changes that have left behind them opaque forms like English *bight*, *drought*, *draught*, etc.; this is of course true across languages generally. More serious is the case of language varieties where mutual intelligibility is compromised by variation and change: as Milroy (1992: 34) states: 'there is no doubt that [communicative] breakdowns arising from the different [grammatical] structures of divergent dialects are quite common'. Regarding the widespread negative perception of language change, Labov remarks (2001: 6): 'some older citizens welcome the new music and dances, the new electronic devices and computers. But no one has ever been heard to say: "It's wonderful the way young people talk today. It's so much better than the way we talked when I was a kid".'

The second element of the standard language in Lodge's classification, that sees the most valid form of the language in writing, reflects perhaps a perception that planned language is preferable to unplanned, accompanied of course by a failure to recognize that the one cannot fairly be compared to the other. The result is a tendency to judge speech by the criteria applicable to writing. The following extract from a French 'complaint letter' is not untypical:

> Je viens d'écouter avec exaspération ce matin une émission [...] ponctuée de plusieurs 'hein' par minute, de répétitions, 'le-le-le', 'c'est-c'est-c'est' ou 'ces-ces-ces' [...][1]

The fact that written language can be planned and polished means that an author is able to achieve effects that are harder to bring off in speech, and that a reader can appreciate these at leisure. It is also of course possible to fix writing to some extent. So much is obvious, but the third of the elements identified by Lodge, the inherent beauty, logicality, etc., of the standard, is based on a surprisingly elementary misconception that is allied to the mismatch between speech and writing. The view that the standard is inherently better than associated non-standard dialects finds expression in various overlapping ways: the standard can be thought as more beautiful; as more suitable for literary expression; as better adapted to conveying abstraction; or, in a functional view, as a useful lingua franca.

The view of the pronunciation of the standard as more beautiful than non-standard varieties of the same language was stated in striking form by Wyld, as follows (1936):

> If it were possible to compare systematically every vowel sound in Received Standard [i.e., RP] with the corresponding sound in a number of provincial and other dialects, [...] I believe no unbiased listener would hesitate in preferring Received Standard as the most pleasing and sonorous form, and the best suited to be the medium of poetry and oratory.

It is an axiom of perceptual dialectology, the sub-discipline that studies the reactions of non-linguists to dialects other than their own, that listeners unacquainted with a dialect system are incapable of making 'aesthetic' judgments of this kind. Listeners acquainted with a dialect system may find RP pleasing and sonorous; they may also find it remote and affected. The direct counterpart to Wyld's praise of the standard pronunciation is represented by quite common statements of the type heard to this day: 'I think the Yorkshire accent is sloppy', for example. Impressionistic linguistic judgments of pronunciation are often expressed in terms like 'sloppy', 'flat', etc. An accent manifestly cannot be sloppy or flat, since these terms have no verifiable phonetic reference (any more than 'sonorous' has in this context), so that judgments on language of this type are really social judgments, in this case perhaps the expression of disapproval of uneducated speakers.

Wyld, a socially highly placed historian of the English language, remarked of pronunciation that relies on spelling that 'careful speech is always vulgar', and would berate his students for not using upper-class, non-orthographic pronunciations such as 'weskit' for *waistcoat*, or 'forrid' for *forehead*. Wyld's judgment in this case is overtly social, and it seems surprising in view of this that he felt the need to make out an aesthetic case for preferring RP to the regional and social accents. Yet there is no occasion to call Wyld's good faith into question; his views are of a piece in conflating a social with an aesthetic judgment. The incongruity we now perceive stems from his status as a linguist; admittedly, it is only fairly recently that non-prescriptivism became the norm in linguistics. We saw, however, in relation to the Kroch quotation, that the grip of the standard ideology can apply itself in subtle ways.

The view that sees the standard as the most suitable literary medium is based, as has often been pointed out, on the confusion between system and use. In this argument we can discard the postmodern view that refuses to recognize any literary canon, and suggest that some writers are more successful than others in their use of standard speech or writing to achieve the effects they wish to bring off. Since aesthetic judgments are notoriously subjective, the point can however better be illustrated by reference to the view, still prevalent in France, that the French language is characterized by logic and clarity, as summarized in Rivarol's well-known tag which appeared in an essay published in 1784: 'what is not clear, is not French'. As Lodge points out (1998: 23–31), the corollary of this view is that the structure of French is somehow closer to the 'language of thought' or 'mentalese' than that of other languages. The second part of Rivarol's proposition shows plainly that his discourse was nationalistic: 'what is not clear is still English, Italian, Greek or Latin'. Clearly, the proposition that any given language variety is inherently more logical than another is not worth quarrelling with; equally clearly, some users of language are more capable than others of employing logic, irrespective of the variety being used, as Labov's celebrated polemic on Black English Vernacular (1972a) was designed to illustrate. It appears quite plainly therefore once again that arguments in support of the standard on the grounds just discussed are really social.

As Milroy and Milroy remark (1999: 14–15), arguments aimed at demonstrating the superiority of the standard are nowadays articulated more subtly, in general using a functionalist discourse which is specious but makes no claims regarding the superiority of the standard in aesthetic terms, let alone as the property of superior persons. It may be that this latter view still finds expression outside of highly visible contexts, but the standard is now generally presented as the most suitable literary and intellectual medium, or the most convenient as a general vehicle of expression, or at least comprehension, across a community that is organized in a complex way. That education takes place in the standard has become axiomatic: an anecdote that is well known in sociolinguistics concerns an English academic who on one occasion gave a lecture in RP, and on another in his regional accent (of Birmingham, in the received version of the story). The first lecture was praised for its authority, logic, clarity, etc., while the second was criticized for its lack of these qualities. We shall see below that the standardization process requires the dominant variety to 'elaborate' or extend its functions further as time goes on.

The functionalist view that emphasizes unambiguous communication is seen most clearly in discourse that attacks lexical innovation or malapropisms like *mitigate* for *militate*, *infer* for *imply*, and many others. The promotion of the standard punctuation proceeds on the same grounds, resulting in conventions such as the one that hyphenates compound modifying phrases when they are used attributively but not when they are used predicatively. According to this principle, one should write *fair-haired children*, but *children who are fair haired*; *over-familiar examples*, but *examples that are over familiar*. This rule can be called arbitrary or conventional, since ambiguity is unlikely – supposedly ambiguous examples like *a man-eating tiger* as against *a man eating tiger* might be thought to be for amusement only, but the example of *eats, shoots and leaves* shows plainly that discourse of this type is taken seriously by its proponents. The arbitrariness of linguistic forms in this perspective is not of course the same as Saussure's *arbitraire du signe*, which emphasizes structure over form and assumes the socially neutral aspect of language. The functionalist argument is allied to the aesthetic and logical arguments in confusing system and user; it may well be that an accent that is more or less unmarked regionally has a better chance of being widely understood, but the overarching issue is that clear communication depends on a careful marshalling of the successive movements of the text, and their perspicuous expression. Users of the standard are not necessarily better equipped to do this than those who habitually express themselves in other varieties.

1.2   The socially dominant variety

Haugen's general model of standardization states in clear form the historical process whereby one variety among others achieves the status of the standard through an overlapping process of selection of the norm, acceptance of function, codification of form and elaboration of function (and maintenance of both), as in the schema illustrated in Figure 1.1.

We can understand selection in the more or less Darwinian sense of natural selection, adapted to social conditions, as Haugen's figure indicates,

	Form	Function
Society	Selection	Acceptance
Language	Codification	Elaboration

Figure 1.1   Haugen's model of standardization (1972: 110)

since selection is ranged in the society–form matrix. The obvious point here relates to the linguistically arbitrary selection of a given variety, expressed in the jocular phrase that a language is a dialect with an army and a navy. But as Judge points out (1993: 7) in connection with the *Edit de Villers-Cotterêts* of 1539, frequently cited as an early example of a piece of linguistic legislation, 'for a law relating to language to be followed it must conform with general opinion'. Thus the edict, promulgated by François I, explicitly substituted French for Latin as the language of legal and other official business; but this initiative is better understood as recognizing and regulating a state of affairs that had already largely come about as a result of various social developments: 'French' in the sense of the Île-de-France variety was the language of the court and was geographically central, plague and famine had seriously depleted the number of those capable of writing Latin, and so on. The categories set out in Haugen's model are porous, clearly, since selection relates to linguistic form as well as to the social function of that form.

Codification of the selected norm results from the decisions – sometimes arbitrary – concerning which linguistic elements are acceptable for inclusion in the standard and which are to be excluded. In less squeamish times these decisions were openly social, and even moral; thus standard seventeenth-century French was defined as a Parisian class dialect, of the royal court or certain parts of it: 'la plus faine partie de la Cour', in the celebrated phrase of Vaugelas (1663, Préface II: 3). The term *faine* is connected with the seventeenth-century concept of the *honnête homme* and the urbanity required of him (Lodge 2004: 151–4). Lodge renders *faine* as 'sensible' and points out that *honnête* translates as something like 'respectable' or 'honourable', so that there is present in the prescription of Vaugelas an element of moral judgment too. The more dissolute elements of the Court were therefore excluded. A similar sense of rectitude is detectable in the motto of Spain's principal normative authority, the Real Academia Española, founded in 1723: *Limpia, fija y da esplendor* 'Cleanses, defines and gives splendour'. Owing perhaps to the characteristic English suspicion of state intervention, the English language never had a national language academy. However, an analogous ideological driver to that animating codification on the continent is detectable in Swift's 1712 'Proposal for Correcting, Improving and Ascertaining [sc. standardizing] the English Tongue', where the assumed linguistic model is the language of the 'learned and polite'.

Regarding acceptance, Haugen (1972: 109–10) points out that 'a standard language that is the instrument of an authority, such as a government, can offer its users material rewards in the form of power and position'. In this commonsense view, speakers have an incentive to learn the standard if their social mobility is enhanced thereby. From a modern or contemporary viewpoint, the term 'acceptance' seems euphemistic and implies the more or less coercive imposition of the standard, most obviously through compulsory schooling. This is no doubt because of an anachronistic tendency to impose upon earlier epochs the modern nationalistic view, which expects political and cultural boundaries to coincide and lays much stress on the relationship that citizens have to the centralizing State as well as to their fellow-citizens, in uniformity of behaviour. Even the recent imposition of the standard through universal compulsory schooling, dating from 1880 or so, can be regarded as a pragmatic instrument of industrial mobilization as much as a means of social or cultural oppression.

There appears by contrast to have been little concern in earlier times to impose the standard language on the larger populace via schooling, and this reflects the rigidly hierarchical view prevalent at the time which deplored social mobility. As Lodge points out in regard to the French case (1993: 213), which in many respects is the starkest, the State was 'at best indifferent to the language used by the mass of its subjects, at worst very ready to exploit the advantages it gained from the linguistic exclusion of the peasantry from economic and political power'. Lodge (ibid.) cites an *intendant* called d'Etigny, an official of the *ancien régime* roughly equivalent to the contemporary *préfet*, who in 1759 expressed in a telling formulation the pre-revolutionary attitude to language planning. The underlying attitude is of course divide-and-rule, expressed through the total discouragement of social mobility:

> Je ne crois pas qu'il soit nécessaire de faire de grands raisonnements pour prouver l'inutilité des régens [instituteurs] dans les villages. Il y a de certaines instructions qu'il ne convient pas de donner aux paysans; rien n'était si commun lorsque je suis arrivé dans cette généralité que de voir des enfants de petits laboureurs, vignerons, même de journaliers, abandonner leurs villages pour chercher à sortir de leur état, soit en apprenant à écrire pour pouvoir entrer chez les procureurs et dans des bureaux, soit en se donnant au latin pour devenir avocats ou prêtres, ce qui peuplait le pays de fainéants et de mauvais sujets qui, en diminuant le nombre des cultivateurs, augmentait celui des gens inutiles et sans ressources pour la société.[2]

The revolutionary Jacobin position cited by Lodge is very different:

> Le fédéralisme et la superstition parlent bas-breton; l'émigration et la haine de la République parlent allemand; la contre révolution parle italien et le fanatisme parle basque. Brisons ces instruments de dommage et d'erreur [...] La monarchie avait des raisons de ressembler à la tour de Babel; dans la démocratie, laisser les citoyens ignorants de la langue nationale, incapables de contrôler le pouvoir, c'est trahir la patrie, c'est méconnaître les bienfaits de l'imprimerie, chaque imprimeur étant un instituteur de langue et de législation [...] Chez un peuple libre la langue doit être une et la même pour tous.[3]

The Jacobin formulation emphasizes the civic duty laid upon citizens of participation in the republican process, rather than the promotion of social mobility through education. A prominent feature of the revolutionary and post-revolutionary period was therefore the State's will to impose centralization on all citizens. The linguistic aspect of this was expressed in the motto: *La langue doit être une comme la République* 'The language must be one like the Republic', or more briefly, *République une, langue une*. The French language came to be closely identified with national identity, and correspondingly, regional languages (Breton, Alsatian, Catalan etc.) were associated with disloyalty to the Republic. The example of France is especially vivid and unambiguous in showing a highly explicit link between nationalism and the imposition of the standard, in contrast to the attempts of certain scholars to demonstrate connections that are latent and a matter of later interpretation, like Swift's proposal, mentioned above, set in the context of the uneasy relations between England and Scotland that marked the eighteenth century, and hence an emerging sense of English national identity. Whatever the underlying social conditions, it is undeniable that this period saw the major standardizing initiatives in English.

It is intuitive, though empirically problematic except in very general terms, to trace a broad association between the socio-political or cultural conditions prevailing in a certain country and the nature of the associated standardizing discourse. This reflects the difficulties of reconstruction and evidence that attend any historico-sociolinguistic enterprise; and indeed those attending our understanding of the present. In the case of France, the nationalism argument sketched above seems to hold when applied to the Revolutionary period, but needs more nuance in reference to the timing of the great codification drive of the seventeenth century. Rickard (1992: 104) suggests an association as follows:

> The seventeenth century, and particularly the second half of it, was to be an age of increasing control and regimentation of the language, reflecting the increasingly tight control of an increasingly despotic regime over every aspect of the national life, beginning with the Court.

A comparison of the language of Shakespeare (1564–1616) and his near-contemporaries in France, like Racine (1639–1699) or Corneille (1606–1684) shows the evident fact that French writers of that time were taking heed of normativists like Vaugelas, and indeed the differences between the French of that period and the contemporary formal written variety are remarkably few, as has often been pointed out. According to Rickard (1992: 107), Vaugelas's *Remarques sur la langue françoise* were 'discussed and debated in the [literary] *salons*, and were on the whole taken seriously by authors, who began to revise their works in the light of Vaugelas' book'. This observation is hard to reconcile with that made previously about the 'despotic' character of the codification of French at that time. It suggests rather that in the context of the admitted despotisms of Richelieu and Louis XIV, and of the intervening *Frondes* that can be assumed to have increased upper-class solidarity, a group of influential grammarians were able to stimulate and maintain a widely held debate over the best norms to follow in French usage, to the extent indeed of actually changing practice. This seems fortuitous, at least in its precise timing.

It is impossible to draw a wholly valid comparison between Shakespeare's 'extravagant genius', in Seamus Heaney's phrase, and the restrained classical tragedy of Racine and Corneille, but from the perspective of the different rates of progress of codification in the two countries, it is noticeable that Shakespeare's writings are peppered with features that are now proscribed: double negatives, preposition copying in interrogatives and relative clauses, and non-agreement between subject and verb, are perhaps some of the most striking. To state the obvious, namely that standardization was initiated earlier and more successfully in France, does not help us to present a coherent explanation of the later success of the English self-appointed grammarians who expelled features like multiple negation from the canon. In all probability, in some instances at least, the effect of such grammarians was simply to consolidate an outcome upon which individual speakers in the relevant social grouping had already converged, codification in this case being 'organic' rather than driven by a salient authority (see the discussion of self-editing on p. 31).

In the present day, we can suggest that standardization operates in a largely impersonal context, on a maintenance basis since the initiation phase is long past, through the agency of mass media like education, and with a mostly unacknowledged gate-keeping function that controls access to a largely 'professionalized' or tertiary workforce where some measure of educational achievement is a qualification for entry. This contrasts sharply with the initiation phase where literacy concerned the few and where the codification debate took place in a relatively cohesive community.

Overall, the difficulty of accounting for the rise of standardization is closely linked to that which attends its definition, on account of the plurality of factors – aesthetic, personal, functional, political, some in alliance, some in tension – which have contributed to its past and current manifestations.

1.3   The synecdochic variety

In linguistic communities that have a standard language we can say rather schematically that the standard is taken by many if not most speakers to be the language variety that subsumes all the others. This is reflected in the terms 'language', opposed to and inclusive of 'varieties' or 'dialects', and there is a parallel here with the various terms used to refer to culture – the bare term 'culture' remains available to denote 'high' culture and every other form, while marked terms like 'popular culture' are needed for reference to the hyponyms in the set. From this viewpoint the phrase 'standard dialect' is an oxymoron, although some linguists do use it, seemingly with ideological intent (see Trudgill *passim*). Joseph (1987: 2) calls this situation 'synecdochic', in reference to the rhetorical trope that takes the part for the whole. The image corresponds with reality in that it conveys Haugen's 'elaboration of function', which dictates that the standard should be capable of functioning as a means of expression in a wide range of domains, and indeed the history of standardization shows the encroachment of the standard into most if not all areas of public activity.

The view of the standard that sees the part as subsuming the whole is also of course a reflection of its dominance, and this reflects the fact that synecdoche typically takes the operative or dominant part as representing the whole, as in *The Crown* used to refer to the UK head of state. To take the example of English, those who speak a standardized variety of the language, i.e. by using the standard grammar and vocabulary but having a regional accent in some measure, are quite clearly a small minority – between 7 and 12% in Trudgill's (1990: 3) estimate – but the power they wield is disproportionate. This is recognized in many informal comments, not only in the linguistic literature: the Victorian novelist George Gissing (1892a: 157) has a passing reference to 'that little world that deems the greater world its satellite'. More starkly, a comment by Evelyn Waugh (1964: 215), a novelist frequently charged with snobbery, accords to the standard accent the status of what one might call the unmarked variety: writing of his days as a schoolmaster, he remarks that 'the private schools lay open to anyone who spoke without an accent'. The similar view that 'Standard English is [...] "normal English": that kind of English which draws least attention to itself over the widest area and through the widest range of usage', is the more striking because propounded by the linguist Randolph Quirk (1964: 95), the widely respected promulgator of non-prescriptive attitudes to language, in an otherwise judicious treatment of the subject. The proposition that Standard English is 'normal' implies either a statistical or a prescriptive judgment, neither of which is tenable in any branch of linguistics taking heed of empirical data. The latter part of Quirk's formulation recalls that of Lord Chesterfield on male attire: 'A man of sense carefully avoids any particular character in his dress.' Synecdoche is once again in question here, and we can suggest that the connection with this and the unmarked character of the standard is that the synechdochic variety stands for all varieties; this means that it dominates all varieties, as a superordinate subsumes its hyponyms. The next step is that this domination is in turn hegemonic, as it is in the nature of hegemony to present itself as unmarked or 'naturalized'. These observations highlight the fact that the terms 'standard' and 'non-standard', when applied to English, are to a certain extent ostensive, as discussed previously, for in everyday usage behaviour that is described as non-standard is simply that which is not sanctioned by majority practice, so that to eat cheese for breakfast is non-standard: in other words, unusual but not reprehensible. In this acceptation the term 'standard French' is more in line with everyday usage, as it is spoken by at least 70% of the population. At the same time it is difficult to align this use of the term with the sense of standard as 'prestigious', since prestige has more or less, by definition, a limited distribution.

1.4   The standard overlying the vernacular

Garmadi (1981: 64–72) distinguishes between what she terms the '*norme*' and the '*sur-norme*' 'supra-norm' where the *norme* refers to a core lect, primary in terms of order of acquisition and more or less common to all members in a speech community, although admitting of some degree of overlap, while the *sur-norme* corresponds to a supralectal overlay acquired at a secondary stage by an elite who have achieved a high degree of literacy. Garmadi's distinction is framed as follows:

> Norme: '[série de] contraintes effectives garantissant le fonctionnement satisfaisant de tout système linguistique en tant qu'instrument de communication.'

> Sur-norme: '[...] un système d'instructions définissant ce qui doit être choisi si l'on veut se conformer à l'idéal esthéthique ou socioculturel d'un milieu détenant prestige et autorité, et l'existence de ce système d'instructions implique celle d'usages prohibés.'[4]

It is quite clear that this definition of the '*sur-norme*' draws upon the notion of codification discussed above, with the exclusion of prohibited usage that implies, as well as on the aesthetic ideal of the standard. If we equate the '*norme*' with the vernacular, Garmadi's conception is essentially a functionalist one that sees it as an effective instrument of communication. This functional view, highly characteristic of the French approach, ignores the sociolinguistic value of the vernacular, defined by Milroy (1987a: 57) in the three related senses of the first variety to be acquired, that most likely to be used in unmonitored speech, and the most localized. It would be unwise to conclude from the above definitions the simplification that Garmadi implies, at least for all languages, but the example of French variable phonology does illustrate the possibility that standard languages may contain elements which, while being structurally redundant, serve to signal social distinction. The French vowel system shows this particularly clearly.

The standard system has six mid-vowels, as follows: /e/ ~ /ɛ/, /ø/ ~ /œ/ and /o/ ~ /ɔ/. The pair /e/ and /ɛ/ contrast in open syllables and it has been pointed out (Armstrong 1932: 85) that an intermediate variant in an unstressed syllable is common in this context. Gadet (1989: 92–4) has an analysis that suggests a simplification of the standard set of oral vowels from twelve to seven, pointing out that the system is vulnerable in view of the low functional yield of the mid-vowels. The vowels /e/ and /ɛ/ have in principle a high functional yield, most frequently in their distribution in inflectional suffixes on verbs in the -*er* class (infinitive, future, conditional, present, perfect and imperfect forms all have mid-vowel realizations); but Gadet points out what is indisputable, that their role in conveying the relevant semantic feature is subsidiary to that played by syntax. It certainly seems commonsensical to assume that context will almost always provide cues where a vowel neutralization might be in danger of compromising the sense.[5] The other two mid-vowel sets, /ø/ ~ /œ/ and /o/ ~ /ɔ/, are much less functionally productive, and indeed have a distribution in open and closed syllables that is close to being complementary. In particular, the vowels /ø/ ~/œ/ famously contrast in just two minimal pairs (*jeûne* 'fast' ~ *jeune* 'young'; *veule* 'spineless' ~ *veulent* 'want-3.PLU').

(Gadet 1989: 89) describes the overall vowel system in French as 'including some variables which [...] are not functionally indispensable'. The elements in the maximal twelve-vowel system, redundant in this linguistically functional view, continue however to serve a sociolinguistic purpose, as indeed is typical generally of 'conservative' elements in a linguistic system. This is facilitated in part by the fact that the functionally redundant elements in the twelve-vowel system have orthographic correlates, which are not equally accessible to all speakers. The French <â> grapheme, corresponding in theory to a retracted articulation [ɑ] of the phoneme /a/, is the most immediate example of the clear representation in spelling of a functionally redundant element.

On the other hand, the back variant [ɑ] is non-standard or regional in the pronunciation of /a/ in words like *pas* pronounced as [pa], [pɑ] or [pɒ], the standard realization being [pa]. Many young speakers frequently have the back vowel in sequences like *je sais pas*, *j'y vais pas*, etc., realized as [ʃɛpɑ], [ʒivɛpɑ]. This has a curious socio-stylistic effect that seems to be used with special communicative intent, such as conveying a degree of condescension on the speaker's part perhaps, or apathy. At the same time a few older, more conservative, speakers retain [ɑ] as a phoneme in pairs like *patte* 'paw' ~ *pâte* 'pastry', and as a variant in the suffix -*ation*, as do some rural speakers. Like the recessive nasal vowel [œ̃], [ɑ] has a limited lexical distribution, and as Coveney points out, 'the very low frequency in the lexis of the back vowel /ɑ/ has led to its demise among most SF [supralocal French] speakers' (Coveney 2001: 188). Thus even in French, where the regional vernacular component is less noticeable, the standard–vernacular relation is not easy to conceive straightforwardly in complex–simplex terms. This is no doubt true *a fortiori* of languages retaining a substantial social-regional vernacular element; for instance, much variation in British English has to do with alternation between two sets of complex systems, rather than reduction in the complexity of the standard phonology.

The notion of standardization as creating a linguistic overlay on the vernacular is also apparent in Chomsky's assertion that 'much of [the standard literary language] is a violation of natural law' (Olson and Faigley 1991: 30). In relation to language, the concept of 'natural law' is a challenging one, as it implies the existence of default patterns which external intervention – notably in the form of standardization – can disrupt. Chomsky's Universal Grammar would presumably be a repository of natural law, but it is not necessary to subscribe fully to the concept of UG in order to recognize that some features of standardized languages would not be as they are if standardization had not taken place. Certainly, artificial by-products of standardization may enter the chain of normal transmission and thus become naturalized, as it were. Lyons (1981: 51), for example, observes that *and I* formulations (*John and I are leaving tomorrow, between you and I* etc.) are 'now so common in the speech of middle-class and upper-class speakers of Standard English in England that they must have been learned naturally in the normal process of language acquisition by perhaps the majority of those who use them'. But this does not nullify the fact that the *and I* construction represents a striking exception to the general pattern in English whereby conjuncts are inaccessible for nominative case.

Whatever (if anything) natural law in the linguistic domain may ultimately be, it is probably wise to refrain from assuming that ever greater economy or simplicity are its guiding principles. For qualitative properties of the system such as these are not, as a rule, cognitively accessible to individual speakers and thus they cannot play a causal role in the processes of change that shape a given language variety (see 4.5). Any difference in complexity between a standard and a non-standard variety must therefore be a random outcome rather than one pre-determined by a natural law. This would apply even where the difference in complexity results from analogical levelling, for while the latter process embodies simplification and may indeed be more characteristic of language that is not weighed down by the ideology of stasis – that is, non-standardized language – it is not in itself a force of nature. Analogy arguably defines the working space for linguistic innovation – given that innovation does not take place *ex nihilo* – but it is wholly implausible to imagine that a determinate analogical change results from analogical pressure acting through large numbers of individual speakers at the same time. Convergent innovative linguistic behaviour across a speech community must ultimately be a social trend, reflecting the dynamics operative in the language ideologies in which the innovation is embedded (again, see Chapter 4).

Arguably this can be observed in the widespread adoption of the transparently deverbal sense of *oversight*, as in *without the persistent oversight of government bodies* (Matthews 1991: 53). In this example, the speaker assumes an analogical relation between the *oversee → oversight* derivation and the *see → sight* pattern. Writing in the early 1990s, Matthews was able to express surprise at this, stating that when a government body makes an oversight 'it is, if anything, a failure in 'overseeing'.' Twenty or so years later, Matthews's observation would now most likely be met with bemusement. It seems plausible to suppose that the spread of this innovation is related to the fact that it is linked to salient positive images, such as televised meetings of the various oversight committees in the US House of Representatives. By the same token, the innovation could easily have failed if its indexical value had not favoured its diffusion. Thus analogical innovation is subject to the whim of the linguistic market-place like any other innovation, and any simplification that arises as a result is contingent rather than pre-ordained.

1.5   The standard as supralocal

A further characteristic of the standard, and one that is reasonably robust, refers to regionality; if dialects are more or less by definition localized, or regional, or social-regional, then the standard is relatively regionless. The distinction between standard and vernacular is of course ancient, and for many centuries in Europe opposed Latin and local languages or dialects. Trudgill (2002: 162), perhaps a little controversially, proposes the following sequences which he asserts are all examples of 'standard English':

Father was exceedingly fatigued subsequent to his extensive peregrination.

Dad was very tired after his lengthy journey.

The old man was bloody knackered after his long trip.

If we assume that these sentences mean more or less the same thing, then the dimension along which they vary is clearly that of style. Trudgill argues that although the third sentence is informal, it is not 'non-standard' because it is capable of being uttered, or certainly understood, by any native speaker of British English. Trudgill suggests therefore that the dominant variety should be styled 'Standard English' with capitals, on the analogy of 'Yorkshire English', etc. Trudgill's line of argument is perhaps, as we suggested above, ideological in character. It is also perhaps contentious, given that some analysts assume that the standard language should include formality as a defining characteristic. Scholars of sociolinguistics are however accustomed to distinguish sharply between dialect and style, and it is undeniable that the three sentences shown above, while differing in their vocabulary along the style axis, would be identifiable in social-dialect terms through pronunciation features. The definition of the standard as regionless is therefore one that applies to some cultures but not others, and in English, to pronunciation rather than lexis. The regionless character of the standard is in some respects like its synecdochic quality, as it is related to the elaboration of its function.

1.6 Folk-linguistic judgments

In Chapters 2 and 4 we look at how certain elements of the standard ideology are covertly involved in theorizing by professional linguists. Of equal interest here is the internalization of the ideology of the standard by the linguistically uninstructed. We considered above a typical example of the 'complaint tradition', whereby 'ordinary' speakers set themselves up as custodians of the standard. The following quotation is taken from a study of traditional architecture, written by a specialist of the subject (Brunskill 1981: 22):

> The older among us, at least, can distinguish between vernacular and polite speech. Speaking in the vernacular, a person deals with concrete matters with the aid of a limited and backward-looking vocabulary of words picked up from here and there and put together without much thought for grammatical rules, and in a manner which, as dialect, is taken to belong exclusively to a limited district or region. Using polite speech his socially superior neighbour deals in abstractions with the aid of a forward-looking vocabulary of words, some newly culled from Latin or Greek roots, organised with strict grammatical correctness and in a manner which is shared with all others of the same select group wherever they may be found.

The parallel drawn is interesting here because of the normative terms used, and the concepts underlying them, notably the idea that vernacular speech is not rule-governed. The golden-age mentality referred to previously is expressed in the first sentence. The other characteristics of the vernacular alleged, its localization and archaic tendency, are by contrast well grounded, at least in traditional or rural dialectology; indeed, one of the contributions of sociolinguistics, or 'urban dialectology' as it is sometimes called, has been to systematize the everyday intuition that urban vernaculars are the chief sources of language change. The further element of interest in this passage is that the views are expressed by a writer who is linguistically naïve but who can nonetheless be presumed to have a fair level of education. Lodge remarks (1998: 25) that 'distinguished professors of French in Britain' are or were not immune from the ideology of the standard, albeit in the related form that sees French as logical. The following extract is from Ritchie and Moore (1914: 4), the authors of several textbooks of translation:

> In translating English prose into French we shall often find that the meaning is not clear and definite [...] Looseness of reasoning and lack of

logical sequence are our common faults [...] The French genius is clear
and precise [...] In translating into French we thus learn the lesson of
clarity and precision.

It is possible to interpret this passage as stating that French writers are more
logical than English, a stereotypical view and hardly a defensible one. The
other interpretation is that the authors view French itself as inherently more
logical than English, the position which was discussed previously. In either
case, it is of interest to our present argument that distinguished professors
of French, who unlike Brunskill might be presumed to possess some of the
metalinguistic concepts we have been discussing here, have internalized the
nationalistic aspect of the standard ideology.

1.7 The role of ideology

It is uncontroversial to state that a standard language is the expression of
an ideology, and in view of the centrality to our purposes of the latter concept, this merits exploration. That the issue is complex is illustrated by the
amplitude of the list given by Eagleton (1991) in one of his two book-length
treatments of the subject, even if several of the 16 senses of ideology he lists
are fairly closely related. Eagleton's formulation (1991: 2) that 'ideology, like
halitosis, is [...] what the other person has' captures in an amusing way the
undoubted truth that individuals tend strongly to regard their own world-
view as objective or neutral, indeed may not notice it, while perceiving bias
in that of others. An adherence to an ideology does not however rule out all
insight into its possession; this is apparent from the fact that speakers are
quite capable of prefacing a contentious remark with 'call me old-fashioned,
but...' or something similar. The preference for one's own point of view may
be allied to a more fundamental human trait: as Hobbes expressed the matter
long ago, 'such is the nature of men, that howsoever they may acknowledge
many others to be more witty or more eloquent or more learned, yet they
will hardly believe that there be any so wise as themselves, for they see
their own wit at hand and other men's at a distance' (*Leviathan*, chapter
13). In this perspective ideology is the expression, on the one hand of a
fairly innocuous kind of egotism that is fundamental to human nature, and
on the other of individual temperament. It is indeed sometimes suggested
that adherence to the conservative or progressive ideologies is a matter of
temperament; according to this stereotype, conservatives are notoriously
gloomy while progressives are sanguine.

The meaning of ideology listed by Eagleton that is closest to our present
concern is 'ideas which help to legitimate a dominant political power',
though again, those who set themselves in opposition to the dominant
political group may label their own set of views an ideology, perhaps
recognizing intuitively the normative character of all ideologies, further

discussed below. An additional important attribute of a dominant ideology is its 'naturalizing' function: the hegemonic state of affairs is presented as being rational, or dictated by common sense, or objective. We have seen this reflected in the view of the standard language as the unmarked variety, and the most efficient variety for communicative purposes. It is not difficult to demonstrate that a commonsense standpoint is in fact a loaded one; for instance, earlier views that saw certain social groups as irremediably inferior are now, happily, largely superseded, but these were accepted at the time as rational views. The commonsense view in this argument is simply one that is commonly accepted, and the proponents of the dominant ideology might be concerned to see this perception gain and maintain widespread consent. This does not imply cynicism; for instance, Wyld's remarks, cited above, were presumably held by him quite sincerely. His view of things was an aristocratic one, and one reason we regard it as an ideology is that competing views are available. In this hypothesis the Ancient Roman conception of slavery was not an ideology, since at that time and place no other view opposed it.

Ideologies offer, therefore, competing world-views, and the principal, overarching ones are currently to do with how power should be distributed. A reference to someone's ideology of painting would sound odd unless understood in a context that related an aesthetic theory to the promotion of the interests of some social group. That said, contemporary aesthetic theories are situated in this framework, since egalitarianism now extends beyond conceptions of social justice into other spheres of activity. A further crucial point, obvious enough but worth stating because central to our investigation, is that ideologies are, as hinted above, *normative*: they propose a view of the world, or an aspect of the world, as it should be. Even ostensibly non-normative ideologies, like religions having the aim of seeing things *sub specie aeternitatis*, lay a charge upon their adherents to follow a pattern of behaviour. In Western societies the two main opposing ideologies, or at least those that concern us here, might be defined as pro- and anti-hierarchical, or elitist and egalitarian. Both views are rich in contradiction and fallacy, and each is partial, in both (connected) senses of the word: in taking into account only a selection of the facts, and in adopting a *parti pris*. But as stated above, the dominant ideology will tend to disguise its normative intent as common sense. It is difficult to determine which ideology is currently dominant, and in a sense the question is futile since neither the elitist nor the egalitarian ideology enjoys total currency in any community. The two are moreover interlocked in that judgments on standard or non-standard types of behaviour are made with reference to a structured system that comprises both, and where *tout se tient*. This is well illustrated by Honey's example of southern Irish accents (1991: 131), of which he remarks: 'standing outside the British social system, they are relatively classless.' The remark needs considerable qualification, but does come close to capturing the general point just made: where an accent falls outside a structured system or frame of reference of the type described above, judgments in standard versus non-standard terms are difficult to make.

The normative character of ideologies appears to be underpinned by a more basic psychological trait, what Dennett (2006: 109–14) calls the 'intentional stance'. The essential concept is not new; Dennett cites Hume (1777) to the effect that 'we find human faces in the moon, armies in the clouds; and by a natural propensity, if not corrected by experience and reflection, ascribe malice and good-will to every thing, that hurts or pleases us'. In other words, we attribute intentionality to persons, animals, conceptual systems like ideologies and even things. It is no doubt a childish trait to attribute intentionality to inanimate objects, but in attenuated form the habit persists into adulthood and finds expression in more or less formulaic phrases like 'this stupid thing has stopped working', or jocular pseudo-theories of the hostility of the inanimate world. Dennett suggests that this tendency may be biologically adaptive; in the context of evolutionary psychology, it seems likely that survival strategies designed to promote reproduction, foraging and defence against predators will be enhanced by an intentional stance, or what is sometimes called a 'theory of mind'. As Dennett points out, the latter term is unsuitable in the measure that our conjectures about other minds are generally intuitive and not best described as consciously framed 'theories'. The intentional stance has far-reaching consequences; no reflection is needed to see that things can have no intentions, even if we retain a childish stratum in our psychology that holds this vestigial view, but a little more is required to realize that intentionality is also ruled out of conceptual systems and their cultural expression. The 'conspiracy theory' mentality fails to recognize this, or at least sees intentionality in a simpler way, but of greater interest here is the less extreme and more widely shared tendency to see intention exemplified in the proponents of an ideology. For our present purposes, this means of course ideology as it finds (quasi-unconscious) expression in variable language. Speakers most likely have no *conscious* awareness that they are expressing an ideology when they speak, while their hearers in contrast seem capable of identifying it. The classic sociolinguistic findings of Labov (1966) on self- and other-reporting revealed, among other things, that speakers having the most non-standard pronunciation tended to judge other, similar speakers most severely in terms of the standard ideology. What this seems to show is that a sample of speakers in New York City in the early 1960s had internalized the standard ideology, but that this was at odds with their everyday social practice, as constrained no doubt by the local network in which their social practices took place. Linguistic variation – and hence change – can thus be viewed broadly as 'phenomena of the third kind', i.e. systems attributable to human effort but not directly to human intentions (see p. 125).

L. Milroy (2003: 161) remarks that 'language ideologies may be viewed as a system for making sense of the indexicality inherent in language, given that languages and language forms index speakers' social identities fairly reliably in communities.' We suggest again, following Silverstein (1979), that language ideologies are second-order phenomena that express overarching ideologies. Further, in the local versus non-local framework developed by Milroy, one can conceptualize the adherence in Martha's Vineyard (Labov 1963) by young male speakers to the Chilmark fishermen's norms as the local expression of the wider opposition we are exploring here. This assumes of course that the opposition between the hierarchy and equality ideologies is the 'master conflict' that subsumes all others. Other local studies that emphasize contrasting modes of localized social practice, like Eckert's (2000) in Belten High, can be seen in the same way. These are in contrast to the traditional oppositions between class, gender, ethnicity, etc., commonly used to analyse variation. It must be said nonetheless that some phenomena remain hard to explain from this viewpoint; perhaps most notably the 'sociolinguistic gender pattern' that commonly sees female speakers importing non-local and non-standard variants into communities and legitimating them through their use.

1.8 Conclusion

We have examined from various viewpoints the notion that standard languages are socially dominant varieties that have succeeded in establishing their dominance on various non-social grounds to do with aesthetics, logic, rationality and efficiency, at least in the contemporary period when arguments overtly claiming social superiority are no longer acceptable. Labov (1972b: 130–2) suggests that speakers use language variably in a speech community, but paradoxically share the same 'norms'. By these are meant evaluative norms, such that speakers revere the standard and disprize their own speech, while still using their non-standard speech. This is allied to Houdebine's (2003) notion of the *imaginaire linguistique* 'linguistic imagination'. It is of course unclear how widely this generalization still applies, forty years later; Labov's questionnaire results showed the traditionally insecure lower-middle classes to be most subject to this mismatch between behaviour and evaluation, the classes above and below them less so. The results showed also that informants were more capable of evaluating the linguistic production of other speakers (in relation to the standard) than their own. The sociolinguistic concept of 'covert' or unacknowledged prestige was designed to cope with the recognition by working-class speakers of the parallel validity of non-standard norms. We consider at various points in this book whether these generalizations still hold.

Of equal interest to us here is the adherence to the ideology of the standard, illustrated above, by the well-educated, and especially those who might be thought to have shaken free of the ideology. The paradox whereby sociolinguists write and speak the standard has often been pointed out, and on the publication of Honey's *Language is power* (1997) the issue gave rise to a flurry of polemic. Honey taxed certain prominent sociolinguists with hypocrisy in decrying the standard while at the same time employing it and deriving from that employment an agreeable and remunerative career. Whether or not Honey's criticisms are well founded, the debate does illustrate in miniature the influence of the standard, which pervades, as we shall see, 'chairborne' or theoretical branches of linguistics, as well as those that draw on empirical data.

Notes

1. I have just this morning heard with exasperation a programme punctuated by several *um*s and *uh*s per minute, repetitions, *the-the-the*, *it's-it's-it's* or *those-those-those*.
2. I don't think it is necessary to put forward complex arguments to demonstrate the pointlessness of teachers in the villages. There are some lessons that it is better not to give to peasants; nothing was commoner when I first arrived in this district than to see the children of small farmers, wine growers or even casual labourers leave their villages to try to escape their condition, either by learning to write so as to be able to work for the local prosecutor or in an office, or by taking up Latin in order to become lawyers or priests, which populated the country with do-nothings and bad subjects who, by diminishing the number of farmers, increased that of people who are useless and unproductive for society.
3. Federalism and superstition speak *Breton*; emigration and hatred of the Republic speak German; the counter revolution speaks Italian and fanaticism speaks Basque. Let us break these instruments of damage and error. The monarchy had its reasons for resembling a Tower of Babel; in a democracy, to leave citizens ignorant of the national language and incapable of exercising power is a betrayal of the fatherland, it is to ignore the benefits of the printing press, because each printer is a teacher of the language and of legislation. Among a free people, the language must be one and the same for everyone.
4. Norm: series of effective constraints guaranteeing the satisfactory function of any linguistic system as a means of communication. Supra-norm: a system of instructions that define what must be selected if one wishes to conform to the aesthetic or socio-cultural ideal of a social group that commands prestige and authority, and the existence of this system of instructions implies the existence of prohibited usages.
5. Coveney (2001: 77) discusses a counterexample, of a speaker in his Picardy corpus having a pronunciation mid-way between *j'aurai* 'I will have' and *j'aurais* 'I would have', where the intermediate /e/ or *e-moyen* caused genuine difficulty in context in determining whether the future or conditional was intended. However, such cases of potential confusion are in practice uncommon.

2
Grammaticality

2.1 Introduction

It used to be the case that grammatical discourse was an overtly ideological activity, in the sense that an explicit part of linguistic description consisted in recommending certain patterns of usage and disparaging others, largely as a function of their indexical value. As we indicated in 1.1.2, the work of the celebrated seventeenth-century French grammarian Vaugelas can be seen as a paradigm example of this approach. In the preface to his *Remarques sur la langue françoise*, Vaugelas states that 'mon deffein en cét Oeuvre eft de condemner tout ce qui n'eft pas du bon ou du bel Vfage' (Vaugelas 1663: Préface, VII, 1).[1] The concept of *le bon Vfage* invoked by Vaugelas persists to the present day, most notably by supplying the title of the most widely consulted normative grammar of Modern French (see Grevisse 1986). Originally, however, it was explicitly linked to the social elite. Thus for Vaugelas it was, as stated in Chapter 1, 'la façon de parler de la plus faine partie de la Cour' (Préface, II: 3).[2]

On the face of it, modern linguistics could not be further removed from this ethos. This can be seen immediately in the introductory textbooks, which invariably contain a section devoted to asserting that linguistics is value-neutral rather than normative. Lyons (1981: 47–54), for example, has eight pages under the title *Linguistics is descriptive, not prescriptive*, while Fromkin, Rodman and Hyams (2010: 13) write as follows:

> To the extent that the linguist's description is a true model of the speaker's linguistic capacity, it is a successful description of the grammar and of the language itself. Such a model is called a **descriptive grammar**. It does not tell you how you *should* speak; it describes your basic linguistic knowledge.

Here we catch a glimpse of one of the basic assumptions of modern linguistics, namely the belief that a speaker's linguistic knowledge or 'competence' should be modelled with scientific detachment. The model thus constructed is called a grammar, in a specifically modern sense of the term.

Given this conceptualization of 'grammar', modern linguistics discriminates between 'grammatical' or 'well-formed' linguistic strings and those that are ungrammatical. However, unlike the pronouncements of normative authorities such as Vaugelas, the process of deciding what is grammatical and what is not is ostensibly a value-neutral exercise. According to Radford (2010: 388), '[a]n expression is grammatical if it contains no morphological or syntactic error, and ungrammatical if it contains one or more morphological or syntactic errors.' The term 'error' here is not to be understood in a value-laden sense, but rather as denoting something that cannot be generated by the rules of the grammar.[3] An interesting question that this approach raises is what the basis is – in the absence of any normative reference point – for determining the rules of the grammar. The usual assumption is that 'native speaker intuitions' are the final arbiter. Radford (2010: 384), for example, states that '[i]n syntax, the term "empirical evidence" usually means "evidence based on grammaticality judgments by native speakers".' What this means is that native speakers are invited to indicate whether a given linguistic string is grammatically acceptable or grammatically unacceptable for them. The rules of the grammar are inferred from these data, the target being a model that generates all and only those strings that are grammatical (as defined by native speaker intuition).

The basic approach just outlined has been criticized on methodological grounds. Adli (2005), for example, proposes that graded grammaticality judgments should be elicited from speakers rather than the conventional dichotomous assessment just described. Elsewhere, Schütz (1996) carries out a very detailed study of the utility of grammaticality judgments, highlighting a range of potential problems in relation to their collection and the use to which they are put. In the present chapter, while recognizing the validity of such critiques, we abstract away from methodological issues in order to focus on the concept of grammaticality itself. Our argument will be in essence that, far from being an empirical primitive, grammaticality is merely a projection of standardization. After addressing this in general terms, we present two illustrative case studies: one relating to impersonal reflexive constructions in Romance and one relating to long *wh* movement, primarily in connection with English but also involving consideration of French and Spanish.

2.2 Grammaticality by fiat

As a way of approximating to the core issues, we can consider the way in which native speaker judgments may interact with the standard ideology. A very straightforward case of this is highlighted by Lyons's observation (1977: 380), made in relation to corrigibility, that '[it] may well be that the native speaker is basing his judgment of unacceptability and his corrective procedure upon some normative rule that he has been taught at school or elsewhere.' Few linguists would, for example, accept a native intuition that a sentence with a split infinitive was ungrammatical as evidence that such sentences actually *were* ungrammatical, although there presumably are native speakers who would make that claim. Similarly, while at least some native speakers would fervently deny that formulations like *There were less people than I expected* or *Me and John broke a window* represent correct English, no serious linguistic analysis actually takes such judgments at face value. Thus some native speaker intuitions are deemed valid while others are discounted. On what basis are invalid grammaticality judgments filtered out?

In the kind of cases just considered, the fingerprints of normative tinkering can readily be detected and hence the deviant grammaticality judgments can be safely discarded. Away from such cases, however, the decisions of linguists as regards what constitutes a legitimate grammaticality judgment do not appear to be based on any solid criterion. Consider, for example, the following remark from Roberts (2007: 65, note 22):

> Many readers will recognize [*I didn't see nothing*] as the non-standard equivalent of [*I didn't see anything*]. This shows that non-standard varieties of English have negative concord. Therefore, if negative concord is determined by a parameter, we conclude that non-standard English and Standard English have at least one different parameter value and therefore are different grammatical systems [...] The normative notion that it is illogical to interpret sentences like [*I didn't see nothing*] as containing a single negation reflects ignorance of the nature of negative concord on the part of grammarians, rather than ignorance of logic on the part of speakers of non-standard English.

Notwithstanding its supportive attitude, as regards their logicality, the above quotation assumes that formulations like *I didn't see nothing* (in the sense of *I didn't see anything*) simply do not belong to Standard English. While no explicit justification for this assumption is given, the tacit premise appears to be that formulations of this type are rejected as ungrammatical by many native speakers of English. However, given that some native speakers would implicitly treat such formulations as grammatical, by actually using them in their own speech, it is legitimate to ask why grammaticality judgments that reject these formulations are admissible as evidence about Standard English but judgments that endorse them are not. The admissibility or otherwise of a grammaticality judgment regarding Standard English cannot be based on the social category of the individual supplying the judgment, as Standard English is not in principle limited to any particular demographic (though obviously one may expect to encounter it more regularly in some social groupings than in others). In reality, the reason why Standard English is unaffected by a judgment that treats *I didn't see nothing* as grammatical is simply that negative concord *is* ungrammatical in Standard English. This basic fact is recorded in all the manuals and is taught at school (typically in the form of a prohibition on 'double negatives'). What this illustrates is that standard languages are largely defined by ostension and not – except perhaps in cases where precedent is unclear – by native speaker intuitions. In relation to a standardized language, then, grammaticality is in principle independent of individual speakers and inheres instead in a corpus of shared public knowledge. From this perspective, the linguist who reconstructs the standard grammar is modelling something that is at least partly a cultural artefact. There is of course nothing wrong with that, but it may be unwise to make far-reaching claims about the human mind on this basis.

The foregoing 'externalized' character of grammaticality as it applies to the standard is associated with an important difference between the latter and adjacent non-standard varieties. The usual assumption is that the standard is not qualitatively distinct from non-standard varieties, except in the ideological sense that each occupies a characteristic position in the relevant language ideology. This is apparent in the above quotation from Roberts, where the relevant difference between Standard and non-standard English is presented as no more than a difference in abstract parameter settings. The same belief is detectable in the following quotation from Fromkin, Rodman and Hyams (2010: 441):

> No dialect, however, is more expressive, less corrupt, more logical or more regular than any other dialect or language. They are simply different.

This is a laudable position to adopt, and certainly it forswears the overt ideology embraced by the normative grammarians of bygone centuries. Nevertheless, the implicit vision of an array of grammars, each equivalent to each of the others, is not one that corresponds to reality. For, a standard language is not a direct manifestation of the phenomenon of language. Standardization implies human intervention to achieve specific results, one of which is unambiguous demarcation, in the sense that what belongs to the standard and what does not become clearly established. Salient authorities such as Vaugelas appear to play a role in this process,[4] but it seems likely too that individual speakers are involved, through self-editing. The latter phenomenon can be viewed as a linguistic correlate to Stockholm syndrome, arising whenever the notion of correct usage achieves prominence in the speech community.[5]

Non-standardized speech varieties are quite different in this regard, because by definition the usage they embody has not been codified. There is no such thing as a standard form of Cockney English, for example. Rather, Cockney features will be variably apparent in the speech of certain individuals and they will most likely coexist, to varying degrees depending on the speaker, with features that are characteristic of Standard English rather than being peculiar to Cockney English. In general, non-standard linguistic features are manifested as variable rules, meaning that their usage alternates with the corresponding standard variant. This is true even for shibboleths such as negative concord. Labov (1972c: 806), for example, reports that in what he terms Black English (BE), negative concord alternates with the standard pattern involving negative polarity:

> Any speaker is potentially capable of omitting the rule [of NEGCONCORD], and so producing sentences with *any*. He hears the standard form, and can interpret it, and in his careful speech he usually shifts away from the 100 percent use of NEGCONCORD. Even in casual speech many adults have shifted away from the BE vernacular and lost consistency in NEGCONCORD. And most importantly, consistent use of NEGCONCORD is the characteristic of core speakers of BE in their peer-group interaction. Marginal members of the peer-group culture and isolated individuals ('lames') do not show consistent NEGCONCORD.

The above captures a characteristic property of non-standard speech varieties, which is that the categorical use of non-standard grammatical features in these varieties is almost always confined to core interactions. Outside of these, speech is to varying degrees contaminated by the grammar of the standard. This core–periphery dichotomy sets non-standard speech apart from standardized speech, because the latter, at least in its idealized conception, is grammatically homogeneous.

Given this basic asymmetry, non-standard speech cannot be modelled in exactly the same way as standard speech. One possibility would be to describe the relevant non-standard variety in terms of multiple grammars, one that is like the grammar of the standard – in respect of the feature in question – and one or more that are different. This is the kind of approach proposed by Kroch (1994, 2001) for modelling syntactic variation during language change. He states categorically (2001: 720) that:

> [g]iven the assumptions of generative grammar, variation in syntax which corresponds to opposed settings for basic syntactic parameters must reflect the co-presence in a speaker or speech community of mutually incompatible grammars.

Alternatively, speakers of the non-standard variety could have a grammar that allowed optionality between an operation generating the relevant non-standard feature and one generating the corresponding standard feature. Either way, the type of model required for the non-standard variety differs from that needed to characterize the standard. In this way, we see that the standard variety of a language is not on an equal footing with non-standard varieties. It has properties that distinguish it from the latter and, indeed, from non-standardized language generally (see also the discussion at the beginning of Chapter 4).[6]

In fact, the minimal properties that characterize standard languages – homogeneity and a clear sense of what belongs and what does not – are also properties of grammars, at least under their modern conception as sets of structural rules from which the admissible sentences of a language can be inferred. The possibility of representing a standard language in the form of an abstract grammar is thus built into the standard itself. That is to say, a standard language is susceptible to modelling in the form of a grammar precisely because the standard has been deliberately moulded in the image of a grammar. As we have seen, however, in the case of non-standardized language the grammar concept can only be applied derivatively, because here the inherent variability of the phenomenon to be modelled means that any grammar posited must actually be a multiplicity of grammars (or, alternatively, its rules must be systematically variable). Thus the grammar concept itself, in its modern sense, and the notion of a standard language are inherently linked. Indeed, it is arguably the case that the application of the grammar concept to non-standardized language is only made possible by a conceptualization of the latter in terms of standardized language.

It is legitimate to ask ourselves, then, what the import is of the terms 'grammatical' and 'ungrammatical' when these are used within the framework of a non-standard linguistic variety. As a way of approaching this question, consider an arbitrary morphological or syntactic variable that has a standard variant α and a corresponding non-standard variant β, the latter associated with a given non-standard speech type Δ (this could be Cockney English, say, or *français populaire*). In this scenario, three things are clear:

(i) sentences containing α are grammatical in the standard language;
(ii) sentences containing β are ungrammatical in the standard language;
(iii) sentences containing β are grammatical in Δ.

Now if we encounter a sentence containing α in the speech of a speaker of Δ, is this sentence grammatical or ungrammatical? The view discussed above, according to which all varieties, including the standard, are in a symmetrical relationship to one another, would imply that such a sentence is ungrammatical, in exactly the same way that a sentence containing β is ungrammatical in the standard. But that view assumes that the boundaries of Δ – that is, which sentences are legitimate within Δ and which are not – are clearly defined, just like those of the standard variety. In practice, this is never the case among non-standardized speech modes. Rather, the boundaries of any given non-standard variety are fluid and, as we saw above, they typically overlap with the standard language, both at the level of the community overall and within the speech of individuals. Moreover, speakers who use non-standard features cannot be relied on to classify sentences containing a standard feature instead of the corresponding non-standard one as ungrammatical. Indeed, given the popular view that the standard language is the repository of correct speech, speakers tend to automatically assume that standardly grammatical sentences *are* grammatical,[7] regardless of their own linguistic practice. This latter point is not just a methodological issue, but instead reflects the nature of grammaticality in what J. Milroy (2001: 530) calls 'standard language cultures'. For both of these reasons, then, non-standard speech varieties do not provide clearcut criteria of grammaticality. An analyst can of course construct an idealized 'grammar' for such a variety by excluding from its description any standard features that conflict with features deemed to be characteristic of the non-standard variety. But the circular nature of that process is immediately obvious. In this regard, it is worth noting that while linguists quite freely use formulations like 'grammatical in northern working-class English', one encounters less frequently the converse formulation 'ungrammatical in northern working-class English'.[8] Here we see an implicit recognition of the boundary problem just alluded to, whereby the exclusion of an item from a non-standard corpus on the grounds that it is ungrammatical in relation to an idealized version of the relevant speech variety is essentially arbitrary.

In fact, an analogous consideration applies to the claim that a string is 'grammatical' in a non-standard variety, but this is obscured by the fact that the predicate 'is grammatical in' is systematically ambiguous between the senses 'is acceptable in' and 'is an output of the grammar of'. It is only the latter meaning that requires the ancillary existence of a grammar, in the sense of an exhaustive set of structural rules. In other words, when we hear a formulation such as 'is grammatical in northern working-class English' we understand this as meaning simply that the relevant feature occurs in northern working-class English, rather than that there is a grammar of northern working-class English that exhaustively defines the possible linguistic strings of that speech variety and that the string in question can be generated from that grammar. Notice that unlike in the case of the standard, whose boundaries have been demarcated (to some extent arbitrarily) by the process of standardization, an exhaustive grammar of a non-standardized variety is not possible without the application of some arbitrary selection process. As was observed above, in standard language cultures, the speakers of non-standard varieties also typically have access to the standard language, and features of the latter thus intrude into their own speech. The exact proportions of standard and non-standard that define the resultant blend will vary from speaker to speaker, so that any non-standard model that purports to describe a communal variety, whether this model takes the form of a single grammar with variable rules or a multiplicity of grammars used variably, will necessarily involve a degree of arbitrary stipulation.

We thus see that whereas a standard language can be modelled as a grammar because its content has been arbitrarily demarcated, a non-standard speech variety cannot be so modelled – at least not without arbitrary stipulation – precisely because it has not been standardized. There is, then, no grammaticality without standardization, at least if grammaticality is taken to imply the existence (or possibility) of a non-arbitrary grammar. Therefore, to the extent that standardization embodies an ideology, the concept of grammaticality – insofar as it applies to natural languages – is ultimately an ideological construct. In light of this, we can reconsider the avowedly ideological stance of grammarians such as Vaugelas. As we noted, for him the arbiter of admissibility was *le bon usage*, the usage of the best writers and the most respectable part of the King's court. We also observed that modern linguistics dispenses with this value-laden approach in favour of the apparently neutral concept of grammaticality. We have now seen, however, that the modern approach is ideological in its own way. Thus, in crucial respects, the modern approach and the older normative one are not as dissimilar as one might at first suppose. We might, in fact, view them as being comparable to each other in roughly the way a fiat currency is comparable to a gold-standard currency such as the pre-1933 dollar. Modern grammaticality creates its own criterion of validity – just as fiat money defines its own value – whereas the older normative tradition always appeals to an external reference or 'gold standard', be that seventeenth-century usage at the French court or late nineteenth-century usage in the upper echelons of the British Civil Service or some other source of legitimacy.

Below, we present two case studies that illustrate the fiat nature of grammaticality. In each one a productive usage pattern is shown to be arbitrarily excluded from the corpus of legitimate data. In the first case, the exclusion is based on conventional grammatical precepts, which have been uncritically accepted by modern linguistics. In the second case, we see linguists themselves performing the role of normative grammarians (albeit without invoking an overtly ideological discourse).

2.3 Case study 1: impersonal *se/si* in Romance

In Spanish, Italian and other Romance languages the 3rd-person form of the reflexive pronoun, viz. *se* or *si*, can be used in impersonal constructions, as in (1)–(4) below. These patterns have been extensively studied, both in the specifically Spanish and Italian contexts and as a general Romance phenomenon (Belletti 1982; Burzio 1986; Dobrovie-Sorin 1998; Rivero 2002; D'Alessandro 2002; Kelling 2006).

(1a) Aquí se vive muy, muy agitado. (Spanish)
      here *se* lives-3.SING very very agitated
      'Here life is very fast paced.'
      (Habla Culta: Havana: M14; Corpus del Español (Davies 2002–), henceforth CDE)

(1b)   Spesso si arriva in ritardo. (Italian; Cinque 1988: 522)
often *si* arrives-3.SING in delay
'People often arrive late.'

(2a)   [...] se detuvo a trescientos veintiocho campesinos. (Spanish)
se arrested-3.SING ACC[9] 300 28 farmers
'328 farmers were arrested'
(Habla Culta: La Paz: M5; CDE)

(2b)   Si leggerà volentieri alcuni articoli. (Italian; Burzio 1986: 43)
si will-read-3.SING willingly some articles
'People will willingly read some articles.'

(3a)   Las dos casas se vendieron a la vez. (Spanish)
the two houses *se* sold-3.PLU at the time
'The two houses were sold at the same time.'

(3b)   Alcuni articoli si leggeranno volentieri. (Italian, Burzio 1986: 43)
some articles *si* will-read-3.PLU willingly
'Some articles will be read willingly.'

(4a)   Se vendieron las dos casas a la vez.
se sold-3.PLU the two houses at the time
'The two houses were sold at the same time.'

(4b)   Si leggeranno volentieri alcuni articoli. (Italian; Burzio 1986: 43)
si will-read-3.PLU willingly some articles
'Some articles will be read willingly.'

All the sentences above lack a thematic subject, in the sense of a referential subject that denotes the agent in relation to the verb. Sentences (1a) and (1b) also lack a structural subject (unless the clitic *se/si* is analysed as being that). Moreover, they also lack an object, given that the verbs they contain are intransitive. Sentences (2a) and (2b) are like (1a, b) in not having a structural subject, but they do each have an object, which exhibits structural accusative case. This is shown by the fact that in neither sentence does the DP in question (plural) agree with the verb (singular). In addition, *a trescientos veintiocho campesinos* in (2a) is an instance of the Spanish prepositional accusative (again, see note 9). In contrast, in (3a) and (3b) the relevant DPs – *las dos casas* and *alcuni articoli* – are structural subjects, which is reflected in the fact that these items do agree with the verb (which is plural in both cases).[10] Sentences (4a) and (4b) are essentially the same as their counterparts in (3), except that the subjects are postverbal in (4a, b), a possibility that Spanish and Italian generally allow. An additional point to note in regard to (3a, b) and (4a, b) is that the subject is also the thematic object, in the sense that it has the thematic role that the direct object would have in the corresponding active construction. The sentences in (3) and (4) are thus roughly equivalent to copular passives.

The paradigm in (1)–(4) dovetails nicely with certain constructs of modern syntactic theory. In the first place, the possibility illustrated in (3a, b) of the thematic object being the surface subject can be treated as an instance of A-movement; that is, 'movement of an element to what is known as an argument position – roughly, a position in which an element can be base generated and bear a crucial semantic role with respect to the main predicate of a clause' (Baltin 2001: 226). Here the DPs *las dos casas* and *alcuni articoli* would be analysed as originating in object position and then undergoing movement to subject position – both subjects and objects are arguments in the favoured sense. Secondly, the contrast between (2a, b), on the one hand, and (3a, b) and (4a, b), on the other, illustrates verb–subject agreement. In (2a, b) there is no structural subject, so the verb defaults to the 3rd-person singular, whereas in (3) and (4) there is a structural subject, which determines plural agreement on the verb. In current versions of generative theory, agreement – or 'Agree', if we adopt the terminology of Chomsky (2001) – is assumed to be one of a very small number of fundamental syntactic operations. It is further claimed that a by-product of Agree in languages like English is that the structural subject must be in the left edge of the basic clause,[11] but this constraint is assumed not to apply in null subject languages like Spanish and Italian. This construct accounts for the contrast between (3a, b), with preverbal subjects, and (4a, b), with postverbal ones. The case instantiated by (4a, b) would be analogous to an in situ passive (Baltin 2001: 229), a structure available in languages like Spanish and Italian in which the passive subject (thematically the object) remains in what is assumed to be its base position (that of direct object). An example from Spanish is given in (5):

(5) [...] fue localizada una carga de mil 370 ollas con doble fondo [...]
     was found a cargo of thousand 370 pans with double base
     'a cargo of 1370 pans with false bases was found'
     (Guatemala, *Gerencia*, 17 May 1998; CDE)

In one way or another, the basic analysis just described is widely assumed in the literature, although it is not necessarily expressed in the terms just given. For present purposes, the key point to note is that all authors draw a broad distinction between a structure that has a structural subject – examples (3a, b) and (4a, b) – and one that has no such subject – examples (1a, b) and (2a, b) – with plural marking on the finite verb being possible only in the first type of case. For example, Dobrovie-Sorin (1998), who expresses the distinction in terms of nominative *se/si* (= examples (1a, b) and (2a, b)) versus accusative *se/si* (= examples (3a, b) and (4a, b)), states that:

> In modern Romance languages, nominative *si* and accusative *si* thus appear to be two completely distinct linguistic entities, as different from each other as *man* and *sich* in German or *on* and *se* in French. (Dobrovie-Sorin 1998: 404)

However, this neat dichotomy completely ignores a further variant, which appears to partake of both types of construction. This is illustrated in the examples below:

(6) Durante semanas se alimentaron a las gallinas con el doble de ración.
for weeks *se* fed-3.PLU ACC the hens with the double of ration
'For weeks the hens were fed double rations.'
(*Barrio palestina*, Susana Gertopan, 1998; CDE)

(7) ¿Y cómo se elegirían a los candidatos?
and how *se* would-choose-3.PLU ACC the candidates
'And how would they choose the candidates?'
(Habla Culta: La Paz: M21; CDE)

(8) [...] no piden que se investiguen a los medios de comunicación [...]
not they-ask that *se* investigate-3.PLU ACC the media of communication
'they are not asking that the media be investigated'
(Costa Rica, *Prensa Libre*, 5 May 1998; CDE)

In this type of case, the DP associated with the verb (*las gallinas, los candidatos, los medios de comunicación*) is clearly the object, given the presence of the object-marking preposition *a*. Despite this, the verb exhibits plural agreement, implying that the object is conditioning the agreement. Here, then, *se* is like the *se* of (1a, b) and (2a, b), but the associated DP behaves as if we were dealing with the *se* of (3a, b) and (4a, b).

As we shall see in due course, this 'hybrid'[12] pattern is stigmatized in the normative manuals, but it is commonly heard in speech (including that of educated speakers) and can also be found in writing, particularly in settings like the Internet, where self-monitoring is typically less rigorous than in novels, national newspapers and other conventional sources of written data. With this in mind, an idea of the frequency in practice of this pattern can be derived by comparing the volume of Google hits for this variant of the impersonal *se* construction (i.e. '*se* + plural verb + *a*') with the volume for the normatively correct '*se* + singular verb + *a*'. To do this, we identified four verbs that naturally occur with impersonal *se* and the prepositional accusative (agentive transitive verbs that select [+ human] objects) and, for each one, searched for two versions of the string '*se* + verb + *a* + *los*', one in which the verb is 3rd-person plural present tense and one in which it is 3rd-person singular present tense. For example, for the verb *acusar* 'accuse' this returns hits like *Se acusan a los acusadores de Garzón* 'Garzón's accusers are being accused', which exhibits the stigmatized plural verb form, and *¿Por qué se acusa a los Conservadores de reaccionarios?* 'Why are the Conservatives accused of being reactionaries?', which is unimpeachable from the normative perspective. The results of the survey are shown in Table 2.1.

Table 2.1 Spanish impersonal *se* with the prepositional accusative: Google hits for plural and singular verb forms (as at 29 December 2011 – repeated entries are excluded)

	acusar 'accuse'	criticar 'criticize'	escoger 'choose'	matar 'kill'	Totals
Sing.	510	480	470	460	1,920
Plu.	146	246	410	409	1,211 (38.68%)

Clearly, the stigmatized plural variant is less common than the normatively acceptable form. Nevertheless, with a rate of occurrence (based on the figures in the table) of just under 39% in a large corpus (3,131 tokens overall), it is unquestionably a productive option.

Despite this, the hybrid pattern does not figure as legitimate data in most linguistic studies of impersonal *se*, either as a Spanish-specific phenomenon or as a general Romance one. Kelling (2006: ex. 23c) and Tremblay (2005: 256) explicitly discount the structure as ungrammatical, while Dobrovie-Sorin (1998) and Rivero (2002) do not include it in their data and, in addition, assume that agreement between the verb and the overt DP diagnoses that the latter has nominative case (in our terms, is the structural subject), which implicitly rules out agreement when the overt DP has accusative case, as in (6)–(8).[13] For example, Rivero makes the following generalization (where 'impersonal' corresponds to the (1)/(2) pattern and 'passive' to the (3)/(4) type):

> Case/agreement […] are morphological clues to distinguish between impersonal and most notably {passive/middle} constructions. The last show a NOM NP and a tensed predicate that agrees with it in PHI-features […] (Rivero 2002: 174)

The theoretical significance of the pattern in (6)–(8) is potentially quite high, because it calls into question the basic framework in which impersonal *se/si* is analysed. This framework assumes two clearly distinguished structural manifestations, one involving an agreeing, nominative DP (or structural subject) and one involving either no DP at all or a non-agreeing accusative

DP (i.e. a structural object). Moreover, as discussed above, this model dovetails nicely with basic assumptions concerning agreement, A-movement and subject inversion. However, there is no place within this model for the pattern in (6)–(8). There, the DP exhibits the agreement pattern of a postverbal subject but is overtly case marked as an object. It is not clear by any means how, or even whether, this hybrid formulation could be accommodated under existing assumptions.

In terms of the main theme in this chapter, the interesting issue is why the pattern in (6)–(8) has been so studiously ignored by linguists. Here we see a direct effect of the facts: (i) that linguistics tends to focus on well-codified standard language and (ii) that the latter is defined by ostension and not by native speaker intuition. For, despite its robustness at all social levels, the hybrid pattern is excluded from discussion because it is deemed not to belong to the standard language. For example, the Real Academia Española states the following:

> No debe ponerse el verbo en plural cuando la oración impersonal lleva un complemento directo plural, pues la concordancia de número solo se da entre el verbo y el sujeto, y no entre el verbo y el complemento directo; así, hoy no sería correcta una oración como *Se vieron a muchos famosos en la fiesta*, en lugar de *Se vio a muchos famosos en la fiesta*.[14] (Real Academia Española 2005: *Se*, 2.1)

This prescriptive prohibition appears to be of relatively recent origin. There is no mention of it, for example, in the Real Academia Española's *Gramática* of 1771. The earliest statement of it that we could find is in Bello's *Gramática de la lengua castellana*, which was completed in 1847. In a footnote to §793 he makes this observation:

> Aquí notaremos que en algunos países de América se adulteran estas construcciones del modo más absurdo, concertando al verbo con el término de su complemento: «se azotaron a los delincuentes».[15] (Bello 1984/1847: 244)

The first reference to the structure in the grammars of the Real Academia appears to be in their 1931 edition (Real Academia Española 1931). There (pp. 261–2) they censure the *barbarismo* noted by Bello and, like that author, they assume it to be a Latin American phenomenon. In fact, the usage is probably of Peninsular origin and it is as old as the use of impersonal *se* with the prepositional accusative. The examples below are from the sixteenth and seventeenth centuries (only the second is from an author born and bred in the Americas):

(9)   […] se acusaban a sus Ichúris o confesores, aun de los pensamientos.
      se accused-3.PLU ACC their Ichuris or confessors, even of the thoughts.

'their Ichuris or confessors were accused, even of thoughts.'
(José de Acosta, *Historia natural y moral de las Indias*, 1570; CDE)

(10) y para averiguarlo, se llamaron a los indios
and to verify+it *se* called-3.PLU ACC the Indians
'and to verify this, the Indians were summoned'
(Ruy Díaz de Guzmán, *La Argentina*, 1594; CDE)

(11) [...] cuando se engullen a los ricos que devoran a los pobres y mendigos.
when *se* sate-3.PLU ACC the rich who devour ACC the poor and beggars
'when the rich are sated who devour the poor and beggars'
(Francisco de Quevedo, *La Hora de todos y la Fortuna con seso*, 1612; CDE)

We see, then, that the exclusion of the agreeing form of the '*se* + verb + prepositional accusative' from Standard Spanish is empirically arbitrary. The *a priori* assumptions behind the exclusion are clear, however. In the first place, as the quotation above from the Real Academia Española (2005) indicates, the pattern cannot be reconciled with the conventional assumption that (in languages like Spanish) the finite verb agrees with the subject and not the object. Secondly, there is a belief, in both the normative paradigm and in the philological tradition, that the range of impersonal uses of *se* form a binary taxonomy, involving an agreeing construction – with a nominative subject – and one in which the verb is fixed in the 3rd-person singular (and any overt DP then has accusative case).[16] For example, the Real Academia Española (2005: *Se*, 2.3) describes formulations such as *Se elegirán a los cargos del partido* 'The leaders of the party will be chosen' as resulting from a 'mixing' of the two constructions (*Lo que no debe hacerse es mezclar ambas construcciones* 'What one should not do is mix the two constructions'). In a similar vein, the noted philologist Lapesa (2000: 812–13) states, in respect of the fifteenth-century example *se suelen recibir a los reyes* 'the king and queen are often received', that:

Aquí se han cruzado dos construcciones, la de pasiva refleja con concordancia entre el verbo y el sujeto pasivo («se suelen recibir los reyes»), y una nueva en que el elemento *a* indica que *los reyes* ya no es sujeto sino objeto [...][17]

Notice that this normative and philological dichotomy is in essence exactly the one that is assumed in the theoretical literature. In all three traditions, a clearcut distinction is assumed between *se* that co-occurs with a nominative or agreeing DP (i.e. a structural subject) and *se* that occurs with an accusative or non-agreeing DP (i.e. an object). While this accords with received assumptions about the nature of verbal agreement in European languages, it does not actually correspond to the reality of usage, because, in the case of this particular construction, the subject–object distinction is blurred insofar as it relates to agreement on the finite verb. For all its scientific veneer, then, theoretical linguistics in this instance does little more than recapitulate received beliefs.

Arguably, what the *se* construction exemplifies is marginal codification (Matthews 1981), the phenomenon whereby the boundaries between the linguistic categories posited by analysts may not be clearcut in practice. In this particular instance, the categories in question are subject/nominative and object/accusative. A priori assumptions dictate that these should be completely discrete but, in the case at hand, usage cannot be reconciled with this principle. The standardizing process is typically sensitive to salient grammatical distinctions of the kind implicated here. Given that the standard language is ultimately defined by fiat, the recalcitrant data in this particular case have simply been excluded from the domain of the standard, providing a striking example of grammaticality as a cultural epiphenomenon. Note that an exclusion of this type does not necessarily imply that a specific authority is conditioning behaviour across the speech community. For while Vaugelas-type figures certainly play a role in defining the standard – and in this particular case we have evidence that from the nineteenth century onwards the exclusion has been explicitly legitimized by various authorities – it seems likely that self-editing by individual speakers is a factor of equal or greater significance.

Abstracting away from the specificities of the *modus operandi*, standardization can in this particular instance be regarded as imposing a degree of structure that goes beyond what is warranted by the underlying linguistic reality, and theoretical linguistics has accepted the outcome of this process uncritically. Moreover, this convergence between normative grammar and linguistic analysis is not simply a result of negligence on the part of the latter. On the contrary, the analytical frameworks adopted in the two fields converge quite strikingly in the present case, with the result that it suits linguistics to adopt the restriction imposed by normative grammar, and hence treat the hybrid *se* construction as not constituting legitimate data.

2.4 Case study 2: long *wh* extraction

Most languages that allow *wh* movement appear to also allow long *wh* movement (or long *wh* extraction), as in the examples below:

(12) They are the ones who the industry says should be cleaning up or abating any dangers. (*ABA Journal*, July 2002; Corpus of Contemporary American English (Davies 2008–), henceforth COCA)

(13) Greta, remind us, what did this woman claim that she heard and who was she? (Gibson, Fox, 11 August 2007; COCA)

In (12), the relative pronoun *who* corresponds to the subject of the embedded clause *should be cleaning up or abating any dangers*. Analogously, in (13) the interrogative pronoun *what* corresponds to the object in the embedded clause *she heard*. 'Long' dependencies such as these are structurally quite complex and typically are acquired relatively late. Probably as a consequence of this, they may give rise to uncertainties in usage and, more importantly from the present perspective, they may attract unwarranted or arbitrary assumptions concerning what is and what is not grammatical. As we shall see, however, making overall sense of the various pieces of evidence is not a completely straightforward task.

To start with, we can consider the basic structural relations involved in examples like (12) and (13). Modern syntax typically analyses *wh* dependencies in terms of movement from an underlying base position (or extraction site) to a surface position at the beginning of the relevant clause. This can be represented notationally by inserting a copy of the moved *wh* expression at the extraction site. The copy is conventionally shown in strikethrough font, to indicate that it is not actually pronounced. Using these conventions, the *wh* movement in (12) and (13) can be represented as in (14) and (15):

(14)   They are the ones who the industry says ~~who~~ should be cleaning up or abating any dangers.

(15)   Greta, remind us, what did this woman claim that she heard ~~what~~ and who was she?

In each case we can envisage the movement as a chain, linking the clause-initial (overt) copy of *who/what* with its unpronounced copy at the extraction site. Notice that in both (14) and (15), this chain crosses a clausal boundary, viz. the left boundary of the clausal complement of *says* and *claim* respectively. It is because the movement chain crosses such a boundary that the movement is said to be long.

Now in the first of the above examples, the clausal complement of *says* lacks the complementizer *that* (*says should be* rather than *says that should be*). In contrast, in the second example the complementizer is present (*claim that she heard* rather than *claim she heard*). The possibility of deleting (or not realizing) the complementizer *that* is a well-known feature of English, particularly at the spoken level. In fact, Perlmutter (1971) argued that the deletion of *that* is obligatory in the case of long extraction of a subject, which is the type of extraction illustrated by our example (12). We can see what Perlmutter was getting at by inserting *that* into (12), an operation which yields (16), which some might regard as a rather awkward formulation:

(16)   They are the ones who the industry says that should be cleaning up or abating any dangers.

The awkwardness is arguably more pronounced in some of the examples given in the linguistic literature, particularly those that involve interrogative movement rather than relativization:

(17)   Who do you think that saw Bill? (Chomsky and Lasnick 1977: 450)

(18)   the girl that you know that likes John[18] (Burzio 1986: 87)

(19)   Robin met the man Lesley said that was the mayor of the city.[19] (Culicover 1993: 557)

(20)   This is the tree that I said that had resisted my shovel. (Culicover 1993: 558)

(21)   Who do you think that believes John to be innocent? (Rizzi 2001: 107)

In the articles from which we cite them here, all of the above examples are marked with an asterisk, indicating ungrammaticality. Indeed, the general consensus in the theoretical literature is that formulations of this type are ungrammatical – see Chomsky and Lasnick (1977), Rizzi (1982), Burzio (1986), Pesetsky and Torrego (2001), among many others. Crucially, the ungrammaticality (or awkwardness) disappears if the complementizer *that* following the *think/know/say/believe* verb is deleted.

The descriptive generalization that has been derived from data of this kind is that a subject cannot be extracted across an overt complementizer. Within a theory of *wh* extraction that assumes movement, this can be expressed in terms of a prohibition on unpronounced copies occurring immediately to the right of a complementizer. For example, if we show the unpronounced copy in (16), analogously to (14), we end up with the following:

(22)   They are the ones who the industry says that ~~who~~ should be cleaning up or abating any dangers.

As can be seen, the copy ~~who~~ is immediately to the right of the complementizer *that*, infringing the prohibition just alluded to. Compare this state of affairs with the situation in (15), which is unproblematic. There, it can be seen, the unpronounced copy is not next to *that*; hence there is no infringement of the prohibition. Until quite recently, unpronounced copies were called 'traces'. Because of this, the pattern described here is known as the 'Comp-trace effect' or, alternatively, the '*that*-trace effect'.

Intriguingly, French appears to show an analogous effect. Thus while the direct equivalent of *that* as a complementizer is *que*, the latter item must be replaced by the relative pronoun[20] *qui* 'who/which' whenever there is long *wh* movement of a subject:

(23) des idées qu'elle sait qui ne peuvent qu'irriter
      some ideas that+she knows which NEG can only+irritate
      'some ideas she knows will only annoy people'
      (Gabriel Matzneff, *Ivre du vin perdu*, 1981; Base textuelle FRANTEXT, henceforth FRANTEXT)

(24) Que croyez-vous qui restera de tout ce que vous avez fait comme ministre ou comme député?
      what think-you which will-remain of all that which you have done as minister or as deputy
      'What do you think will remain of everything you have done as a minister or member of the Assembly?'
      (Jean L'hôte, *Le Mécréant ou les preuves de l'existence de Dieu*, 1981; FRANTEXT)

For long extraction of non-subjects, *que* is used, analogously to English *that*:

(25) le jeune homme que je savais qu'elle aimait
      the young man that I knew that+she loved
      'the young man that I knew that she loved'
      (André Gide, *L'école des femmes*, 1929; FRANTEXT)

We can regard *that* deletion and the substitution of *qui* for *que* as two strategies that achieve the same goal, namely the avoidance of subject extraction across an overt complementizer. English deletes the complementizer, whereas French replaces it with a relative pronoun. The latter strategy results in formulations that are exactly analogous in the relevant respects to English formulations like (26) (which no doubt would be considered ungrammatical from a normative point of view):[21]

(26) one of the people they say who was killed was actually an elderly Iranian
      (Nic Robertson, CNN, Live Today, 12 January 2003; COCA)

A further point to take into account is that null subject languages like Spanish and Italian are systematically immune to the Comp-trace effect. For example, the direct equivalents of the problematic English sentences in (17) to (21) are all perfectly acceptable in Spanish – indeed they are the normal way of expressing this type of content:

(27) ¿Quién crees que vio a Bill?
      who think-2.SING that saw ACC Bill?
      'Who do you think that saw Bill?' (= example (17))

(28) la chica que sabes que quiere a John
      the girl that know-2.SING that loves[22] ACC John
      'the girl that you know that loves John' (≈ example (18))

(29) Robin conoció al hombre que Lesley dijo que era el alcalde de la ciudad.
      Robin met ACC+the man that Lesley said that was the mayor of the city
      'Robin met the man Lesley said that was the mayor of the city.'
      (= example (19))

(30) Este es el árbol que dije que había resistido a mi pala.
      this is the tree that said-1.SING that had resisted to my shovel
      'This is the tree that I said that had resisted my shovel.' (= example (20))

(31) ¿Quién piensas que cree que John es inocente?
      who think-2.SING that believes that John is innocent
      'Who do you think that believes John to be innocent?' (= example (21))

Given this rather striking discrepancy between null subject languages like Spanish and Italian and non-null subject languages like English and French, the Comp-trace effect was extensively discussed in the 1980s and 1990s in connection with the so-called null subject parameter (see especially Rizzi 1982). In this way, a rather subtle grammatical phenomenon came to enjoy considerable importance in theoretical circles.

On the other hand, findings reported in Sobin (1987) indicate that the categorical ungrammaticality assigned by linguists to Comp-trace structures in English may be misplaced. In a study of 42 American undergraduates at the University of Iowa, Sobin found that such structures enjoyed quite high levels of acceptance.[23] The most significant results are summarized in Table 2.2.

On the basis of these and some secondary findings, Sobin concludes (p. 46) that 'it is quite plausible to question whether [*that*-trace] constructions are in principle excluded from English'.[24]

In fact, Sobin's scepticism appears to be well founded. This is revealed by a search of the COCA corpus (Davies 2008–), which among other material contains 90 million words in transcripts of unscripted conversation from

Table 2.2 Acceptability of *that*-trace structures among American college students (based on Sobin 1987: Appendix A)

Questionnaire item	% passive acceptance	% active acceptance	% rejection
Who did you say that kissed Harriet?	45.2	47.6	7.1
Who did you say that likes Bill?	35.7	54.8	9.5
Who do you think that saw Tom?	16.7	47.6	35.7

over 150 different TV and radio programmes. There we find plenty of *that*-trace examples, a small selection of which is given below:

(32) What are some of those safeguards you say that have been put in place? (Terence Smith, News Hour, 21 April 2004)

(33) And that is a question he says that has never been adequately answered. (Clancy, CNN Your World, 26 August 2005)

(34) BP continues to use the controversial dispersant Corexit, the only thing they say that works. (Teague, CBS Evening News, 28 May 2010)

(35) Bottom line, what is the issue you think that will win it for you? (Cavuto, Fox, 6 September 2006)

(36) If the Democrats want a bill and will give us some things that we think that are substantive in nature [...] (Sen. Shelby, NBC Meet the Press, 25 April 2010)

(37) What do we know that happened on November 24th, 1997, when the first report came in? (Van Susteren, CNN, Burden, 27 September 1999)

(38) Why won't you support these efforts that you know that work? (Matalin, CNN Crossfire, 20 December 2000)

Note that the speakers in these and other similar examples in the corpus – news presenters, politicians and the like – are individuals who would be expected to conform quite closely to the norms of the standard. Thus even if we limit our attention to 'standard' spoken English, it seems wrong to claim that *that*-trace structures are excluded. Accordingly, the claim that such structures are ungrammatical can only be maintained through arbitrary stipulation.

We might then see a parallel with the Spanish *se* construction discussed earlier. There also we encountered the *a priori* exclusion of a type of data, an exclusion which on closer inspection turned out to be empirically unjustified. In that case, however, a normative imperative for excluding the relevant data could be easily identified, viz. the assumption that no construction could blur the subject–object dichotomy. In the present case, no obvious precept of traditional English grammar appears to be implicated. For example, we find no reference to *that*-trace phenomena in Fowler and Fowler (1922), even though formulations such as *men who we know are honest* are discussed in some detail (pp. 93–4) and there is, moreover, a section entitled *Omission of the conjunction 'that'* (pp. 356–7). We thus have a rather puzzling situation, whereby a marked (arguably) but nevertheless productive usage is deemed ungrammatical by linguists but this exclusion – despite its arbitrary nature – cannot be traced to any commonly held assumptions concerning Standard English.

Note, however, that in other standard language cultures long subject extraction *is* considered to be an issue. This is particularly apparent in French. For example, Grevisse (1986: 1615) draws a contrast between long object extraction and long subject extraction, stating that in the former 'L'interpétation est facile' whereas 'L'explication des phrases de ce second type est plus épineuse et a été fort controversée.'[25] This state of affairs goes back at least to Vaugelas's *Remarques sur la langue françoise*. There (1663: 81), while accepting that (39) below is one of the 'façons ordinaires, dont on exprime cela',[26] the celebrated French grammarian states that he himself would never use such formulations:

(39)   Il marcha contre les ennemis qu'il ſçauoit qui auoient paſſé la riuiere
       [...]
       he marched against the enemies that+he knew who had crossed the river
       'He marched against the enemies that he knew had crossed the river.'

Le Flem (1992: 163) sums up the attitude taken by many French speakers when he states that 'En un mot, la structure [*que ... qui*] est paradoxale, sans que l'on sache d'ailleurs s'il faut y voir la marque d'un niveau de langue recherché ou populaire'.[27] In fact, such uncertainty surrounds this structure that, as Posner observes (1996: 307), in modern written French an alternative circumlocution involving *dont* 'about whom/which' is recommended (see also Adli 2005: 13). She gives the example below:

(40)   l'homme dont j'ai dit qu'il est venu
       the+man about-whom I+have said that+he is come
       'the man I said has come'

The French situation demonstrates that long extraction is an area in which normative tinkering is possible. Indeed, given the quasi-logical issues involved – viz. cross-referencing across clausal boundaries and the reconstruction of argument structure – one might expect this to be an area that *attracts* normative attention. Thus the absence of any coverage of this topic in the English normative tradition might be viewed as more of an accident than as an indication that the phenomenon in question is in some sense beyond the reach of the usual sources of authority. Unlike the case of Spanish *se*, then, where linguists followed the lead of the normative authorities, in regard to *that*-trace phenomena in English, linguists have to all intents *been* normative authorities. The possibility for this to occur can again be traced to the fiat nature of the standard. What is grammatical is what is *deemed* to be grammatical and, in the absence of any external normative reference point, linguists are to a certain extent free to impose arbitrary constraints of their own.

In light of these considerations, an important issue that needs to be addressed is why *that*-trace structures actually are associated with less than 100 per cent acceptability in English. In other words, what is it that triggers the sense that there is something problematic about them? As was noted above, the equivalent structures in null subject languages like Spanish and Italian are 100 per cent acceptable. We can ask ourselves, then, what is it that null subject languages have that English does not?[28] An obvious answer is that in such languages the subject need not be overtly realized, whereas in English it must be. This apparently unrelated fact has important ramifications for the issue at hand. To start with, we can note that while Spanish speakers or Italian speakers are attuned to processing subjectless finite clauses such as *ha llegado* '[he/she] has arrived', English speakers are not. Indeed, given that in relatives and interrogatives a subject *wh* expression is in the same linear position as a normal subject, it is arguably the case that English speakers are never confronted with a finite clause that is without an overt subject in the expected linear position.[29] Except, that is, in sequences like *says that has arrived*, i.e. *that*-trace constructions. For Spanish speakers, then, (41) holds no surprises – because subjectless *ha llegado* is familiar from countless other contexts – whereas for English speakers the corresponding construction (42) presents a novel processing challenge:

(41) la chica que Pedro dice que ha llegado.
      the girl that Pedro says that has arrived
      'the girl Pedro says has arrived'

(42) the girl Pedro says that has arrived

Plausibly, then, the problem with sequences like (42) is psycholinguistic rather than grammatical: speakers find such formulations awkward because they require them to process a linear sequence that in other contexts is always ungrammatical.

At first glance, the analysis just outlined is contradicted by (43), the *that*-less counterpart to (42). Here the speaker faces apparently the same novel processing challenge as in (42), but in this case the sentence is not regarded as problematic:

(43)   the girl Pedro says has arrived

In our view, however, the reason why the type of example in (43) does not provoke any adverse reaction is that it involves covert reanalysis, with *has arrived* being treated analogously to infinitival *to have arrived* in the example below:

(44)   the girl Pedro believes to have arrived

Rather striking evidence for this comes from the fact that in the (43) type of case the verb – *say, think, believe* etc. – is commonly analysed by speakers as assigning accusative case to the subject of its clausal complement. This is apparent in the examples below, where accusative *whom* rather than nominative *who* is used as the appropriate relative pronoun:

(45)   a phone call from a Marine whom she said wanted 'to send Congressman Murtha a message [...]' (*Newsweek*, 28 November 2005)

(46)   the charges against one dynamiter whom they thought had been killed in the accident (*Anthropological Quarterly*, April 1996)

(47)   [...] some of them openly and repeatedly discussed euthanizing patients whom they believed would not survive their ordeal. (Freed, CNN Sunday Morning, 16 October 2005)

Under the assumption that the relative pronoun in this type of case is extracted from subject position in a finite clause – a nominative case position – Fowler and Fowler analyse (1922: 93) this type of example as involving a 'gross error'. On the other hand, Quirk *et al.* (1985: 368) describe such formulations as 'common' and Radford (1988: 575) states that they are acceptable in his speech variety. Moreover, examples like (45) to (47) are very frequent in the COCA corpus. Clearly then, such examples are part of English. An obvious way of accounting for this is by assuming that *whom* is actually extracted from an accusative case position position. However, this possibility only arises if there is covert reanalysis, with the apparent finite clausal complement of the *say/think/believe* verb being treated as a non-finite clause with an accusative subject (as in (44)).

Note that the analysis proposed for (43) does not entail that the *say* construction in that sentence is capable of being turned into a passive, as is the case with *believe* in (44) (compare *is believed to have arrived*). The verb *want*, for example, shows that not all accusative subjects of infinitival clauses can be converted into matrix passive subjects:

(48)   We want them to leave.

(49)   *They are wanted to leave.

Nevertheless, as the real examples below illustrate, some speakers will in fact passivize from the finite *that*-less complement of a *say/believe*-type verb:

(50)   [...] just a plain rule which was said would lead to a charge. (Graham Poll, *Daily Mail*, 20 September 2012; retrieved via Google)

(51)   [...] several members of his platoon were wounded in retrieving what was thought would be his corpse. (*American Heritage*, December 1994; COCA)

(52)   [...] one of the things that I think was believed will be standard in POW treatment was abrogated today [...] (ABC, Nightline, 21 January 1991; COCA)

Despite appearances, then, the finite *that*-less and subject-less complement of a *say/believe*-type verb is treated by speakers as being analogous to the infinitival structure in (44). For this reason, the problem embodied in (42), viz. how to resolve a subjectless finite clause, effectively does not arise. In our view, it is this difference that accounts for the diverging acceptability of pairs like (42) and (43).

Thus the *that*-trace effect in English appears to reduce to a case of awkwardness or apparent inelegance that can be attributed to a fairly straightforward cause, namely that the problematic structure requires speakers to treat as grammatical a sequence that is invariably ungrammatical in other contexts. However, in a further illustration of the fiat nature of the standard, this awkwardness has been transformed into full ungrammaticality, leading to the drawing of rather far-reaching theoretical conclusions, for example in connection with the null subject parameter (see Rizzi 1982 and much subsequent work).

The disjunction between analysis and reality actually goes beyond this, because by focusing on the narrow issue of whether *that* is or is not deleted, linguists have unduly restricted the field of enquiry and, in so doing, overlooked a phenomenon that is perhaps more significant. For a pattern that enjoys similar levels of productivity to *that*-trace structures is their avoidance (not necessarily deliberate) by overtly spelling out the *wh* pronoun at the extraction site, as in the examples below:

(53) They want to give taxes to people they say who need it [...] (Novak, CNN, 19 August 2000; COCA)

(54) He did not play to that element of the party that I suppose who had been line [sic] with Pat Buchanan before he left. (Williams, Fox News Sunday 21 November 1999; COCA)

(55) And then the other third who I think who are people -- they're here, as my wife and I are here, for a real spiritual purpose. (Unidentified male, CNN Live From, 18 April 2005; COCA)

(56) [...] and the one we believe who jumped from the roof was agent – was an agent. (Mabrey, CBS Special, 19 April 1993; COCA)

(57) The -- the person the police believe who is the murderer walks scot-free. (Bradley, CBS Sixty Minutes; 13 December 1992; COCA)

(58) Could you just talk to us about who you think who is to blame, sir? (Maureen Maher, CBS 48 Hours, 17 December 2003)

The pattern in (53) to (58) is interesting in the present connection because, as was noted in relation to example (26), it is in all relevant respects analogous to the French *que ... qui* pattern (modulo the deletion of the relativizer next to the antecedent in (53), (56) and (57)). However, despite its *de facto* productivity in English, this 'solution' to the *that*-trace problem is not even on the radar in theoretical analyses of the issue. For example, Radford (2010: 158) gives an analogous example involving *which*, but assumes a 'speech error made by the tongue-tied (or brain-drained) BBC reporter' (p. 159):

(59) It's a world record which many of us thought which wasn't on the books at all. (Athletics commentator, BBC2 TV)

Elsewhere, the same structure but specialized to direct questions (e.g. *Who did he say who is in the box?*) is described as being an 'example of children's non-adult (but UG-compatible) productions' (Crain and Pietroski 2002: 180).

Unlike the exclusion of *that*-trace structures, where we hypothesized that linguists have acted in lieu of normative authorities, the exclusion of the type of data in (53) to (59) from the corpus of Standard English can be attributed fairly directly to the covert influence of the normative tradition. As was indicated above, what characterizes the structure in question is that the *wh* pronoun is overtly spelled out at the extraction site, whereas 'normally' trace copies are unpronounced. For example, the more normatively acceptable versions of (53) and (54) would be as in (60) and (61) below, which exhibit a null spell-out of *who* at the extraction site (coincidentally, the relative pronoun in (60) is also unpronounced in its final position next to the antecedent *people*):

(60)   They want to give taxes to people they say ~~who~~ need it

(61)   He did not play to that element of the party that I suppose ~~who~~ had been line with Pat Buchanan before he left.

Theoretical syntax captures this situation by assuming that the rightmost copy in a movement chain is always unpronounced. For example, according to Radford (2010: 159), the 'error' in (59) is due to the fact that the speaker 'fails to delete the original occurrence of *which*' at the extraction site. However, as is shown by real examples like (53) to (58), speakers do in practice sometimes pronounce the rightmost copy. The view that attributes error to this is not motivated by any scientific principle. Rather, it covertly endorses the normative perspective on *wh* movement, which envisages at most one overt copy of the *wh* expression, placed next to the antecedent (in the case of a relative pronoun) or at the beginning of the clause (in the case of an interrogative expression) – see, for example, the discussion of relatives in Fowler and Fowler (1922: 75–107). This perspective itself no doubt embodies a certain amount of quasi-logic, in the sense that an overt copy left at the extraction site is pre-theoretically 'redundant', particularly when the fronted copy is also given an overt spell-out as in (55), (58) and (59).

Looking at long extraction overall, the findings here indicate that much of the discussion in the theoretical literature is unconsciously affected by *a priori* beliefs that either directly stem from the normative/standardizing tradition or which are legitimized by it. Long movement of a *wh* subject can clearly give rise to awkwardness in non-null subject languages like English and French, but the analysis of this has been distorted both by an overzealous application of the grammatical–ungrammatical dichotomy – itself a by-product of the standardizing perspective – and an undue narrowing of the terms of the debate. The analysis proposed here implies that speakers have at least three mechanisms for resolving long subject extraction, viz. (i) violating the *that*-trace prohibition, (ii) spelling out the *wh* pronoun in its extraction site and (iii) treating the *say/believe*-type verb as an accusative case assigner. However, owing to the covertly normative approach adopted in much of the theoretical literature, (i) is assumed to be ungrammatical, (ii) is regarded as a speech error and (iii) is misanalysed. Somewhat predictably, then, long *wh* extraction provides a telling illustration of how a full picture of the grammar of a standardized language can in practice only be attained by looking at both internal and external factors.

2.5   Conclusion

In this chapter we have argued that grammaticality has an *a priori* basis rather than an empirical one. As regards the standard language, the final say on grammaticality lies not with the judgments of native speakers but in a collective body of received beliefs, or, in some cases, with the professional analyst. As regards non-standard varieties, grammaticality can only be ascribed derivatively, by conceptualizing the relevant speech type as a standardized language. In order to carry through the latter procedure, arbitrary decisions must be taken as regards what is and what is not allowed in the relevant variety – decisions that replicate in their essence the dynamics of the historical process of standardization. Thus grammaticality and standardization are two sides of the same coin.

Despite this, linguists treat grammaticality as an empirical primitive, assuming uncritically that the question whether a given linguistic datum is grammatical or not has essentially the same scientific status as a measurement in physics. We looked at two case studies where this assumption was shown to be wholly inadequate. The first of these concerned a structure in which an accusative DP triggers subject-like agreement on the verb. This 'hybrid' formulation conflicts with the simplistic assumption, built into the prescriptive tradition, according to which the subject rather than the object determines verbal agreement. The structure is thus deemed not to belong to the standard language, despite being productive at all sociolinguistic levels. This arbitrary exclusion of data has been naively accepted by academic linguistic analysis, which in fact adopts a similar framework to that manifested in the normative approach. The second case study concerned long subject extraction, initially in relation to the alleged ungrammaticality of sentences resulting from *wh* movement across the complementizer *that*. Here we showed that speakers do in fact quite commonly produce the putative ungrammatical output, demonstrating again that the exclusion of the relevant data is arbitrary. We could find no trend in the normative literature that could account for this random exclusion and thus concluded that by deeming the relevant structure ungrammatical, linguists had themselves acted as *de facto* normative authorities. We also showed that the scope of the phenomenon has been imperfectly defined, because another structure is implicated but is ignored or discounted as erroneous, again on *a priori* grounds.

What the two case studies highlight is that grammaticality is ultimately defined by fiat. It is this basic property that explains why adverse data can simply be dismissed as ungrammatical. Therefore, given that grammaticality represents the link between theory and data, at least at higher levels of linguistic analysis, reservations can legitimately be held about the scientific validity of much linguistic theorizing.

Notes

1. My purpose in this work is to condemn everything that does not belong to correct and elegant usage.
2. 'It is the mode of speech of the best part of the Court.' See 1.2 in the present book for a refinement of this translation.
3. Some formalized approaches to grammar, notably generative grammar in its most recent incarnations, foreswear the concept of rules and instead posit a finite set of universal operations constrained differently in each language (depending on parameter settings). The effect is the same, however, and we abstract away from the distinction between rules and parametrized principles.
4. Note, for example, the title of Section IV, 3 of the preface to Vaugelas (1663): 'Parquel moyen on peut s'éclaircir de l'Vſage quand il eſt douteux, & inconnu' ['By what means usage can be clarified when it is doubtful and unknown'].
5. In this connection, it is worth considering the debate over whether the loss of variable negative concord in Early Modern English was due to direct prescriptive influence (Cheshire 1982: 63; Labov 1972c: 774), or was 'a natural change triggered by some internal factors' (Kallel 2007: 27). Our position is that these two views are not irreconcilable, because self-editing is simultaneously a by-product of the prescriptive ethos and something which, like 'natural' processes of change, operates at the level of individual speakers. Indeed, given the approach to change articulated in Chapter 4, self-editing simply takes its place as one more ideological driver of change.
6. The asymmetric relationship between the standard grammar and the rules operative in non-standard language is reflected in the fact that the latter are often envisaged as being parasitic on the former. Harris and Halle (2005), for example, discuss various non-standard Spanish patterns that relate to the ordering of object clitics and the plural marker -*n* in imperatives. Thus alongside standard *Véndanlo* 'Sell it', we find non-standard formulations such as the following:

    (i) *Véndanlon*
        sell+PLU+it+PLU

    (ii) *Véndalon*
        sell+it+PLU

    These are analysed by Harris and Halle as being generated by the normal rules of Standard Spanish – which place the plural marker -*n* between the verbal stem and the object clitic – augmented by either of two non-standard morphological operations. These are: reduplication, which yields (i), and metathesis, which yields (ii).
7. Here we abstract away from cases in which a salient normative prohibition (e.g. against split infinitives) influences a native speaker's judgment. We also abstract away from unusual standard patterns of usage, which speakers (including many speakers of the standard language) may characterize as ungrammatical because they are unfamiliar with them. For example, it is not uncommon for someone to not know that the English verb *obtain* can be used intransitively in the sense of

'be in force, be applicable'. Such a speaker might then classify a sentence like *The principle no longer obtains* as ungrammatical.

8. For example, a Google search carried out on 25 December 2011 returns 12 hits for the string *'grammatical in non-standard'* but only one for *'ungrammatical in non-standard'*.

9. We use 'ACC' to indicate the prepositional accusative; that is the use of the preposition *a* in Spanish to mark [+ human] or sometimes [+ animate] direct objects.

10. Alternatively, following D'Alessandro (2002), the DPs in (3) are nominative objects.

11. This is Chomsky's 'subject position', which loomed large in the syntactic theory of the 1980s and 90s.

12. We use this term merely as a label, without any commitment to the view that the structure actually does fuse two distinct constructions.

13. Juarros-Daussà (2000) does not include the structure either. Her theoretical framework also appears to rule out plural agreement on the verb when the associated DP has accusative case. Pedersen (2005) mentions the structure (using the example *Se ven a los niños* 'The children are seen'), but simply states that 'object-agreement will normally be refused as agrammatical' (p. 21).

14. The verb must not be put into the plural when the impersonal clause has a plural direct object, because number agreement is only possible between the verb and the subject, and not between the verb and the direct object; thus today a sentence such as the following would not be correct: *'se* saw-3.PLU ACC many famous people at the party' instead of '*se* saw-3.SING ACC many famous people at the party'.

15. Here we will note that in some Latin American countries these constructions are adulterated in the most absurd way, by making the verb agree with its complement: '*se* thrashed-3.PLU ACC the criminals'.

16. This dichotomy is partly based on diachrony, in that the structure with the associated nominative DP emerged before the one with the accusative DP. The first structure is found in even the earliest Old Spanish texts, as is indicated by the example below, which is from the late twelfth or early thirteenth centuries:

(i) En estas tierras agenas veran las moradas commo se fazen
'in these lands foreign they-will-see the homes how *se* do-3.PLU'
'In these foreign lands they will see how our homes are made'
(*Poema de mi Cid* 1642)

In contrast, the construction with the accusative DP does not appear (unequivocally) until the fourteenth or fifteenth centuries (see Lapesa 2000: 812).

17. Here two constructions have been mixed, that of the reflexive passive with agreement between the verb and the passive subject (*se suelen recibir los reyes*), and a new one in which the element *a* indicates that *los reyes* is no longer the subject but the object.

18. *Know* is to be understood here in its epistemological sense (*know that*) rather than its relation sense (*know a person*).

19. In this example, the relativizer next to the antecedent noun *man* is unpronounced: *the man Lesley said that was* rather than *the man who/that Lesley said that was*. That does not affect the point under discussion here.

20. Kayne (1981: 119) treats *qui* in this type of construction not as a relative pronoun but as a 'conditioned variant' of the complementizer *que*. In light of the comparison we draw with English (26), we prefer to adopt the conventional descriptive

approach (see Grevisse 1986: 1614) according to which *qui* has its usual function, viz. that of relative pronoun.

21. The similarity vis-à-vis the French *que ... qui* construction is partly obscured by the omission of the relativizer (*who* or *that*) after the antecedent *people*. The relativizer is retained in the example below:

    (i)   ... and I say he, because there were none of us female types that I thought who were quite ready to do that. (Govenor Richard, CBS Morning, 19 January 1993; COCA)

22. We replace 'likes' with 'loves' in this example, because Spanish uses a dative construction to express the concept of liking which complicates any structural comparison between (18) and its exact semantic counterpart in Spanish.
23. These findings relate to the case when *that* is the complementizer. Sobin's study also revealed that formulations like *Who do you know whether likes Bill*, where the complementizer is *whether*, have a very high rejection rate (97.6%). This appears to be a different type of case, however, as object extraction is also problematic: *Who do you know whether Bill likes?*
24. Pesetsky (1982: 328) notes that African American speakers of what is otherwise Standard English may also allow *that*-trace structures.
25. The explanation for sentences of this second type is trickier and has been much debated.
26. Usual ways of expressing this.
27. In a word, the *que... qui* structure is paradoxical, and people are not sure whether it is a mark of sophisticated or vulgar speech.
28. An answer to this question that we will not pursue here is the one put forward in Rizzi (1982). According to that author, the relevant difference is that null subject languages allow free inversion of the subject. Burzio (1986: 88) summarizes this view very neatly when he writes: 'The Italian equivalent of **Who do you think that came?* is thus grammatical only because Italian has **Came John.*' Under that hypothesis, in long *wh* movement in Italian (and by extension null subject languages generally) the subject is actually extracted from postverbal position. This would mean that the trace was to the right of the verb and so the illicit sequence consisting of a complementizer immediately followed by a trace did not occur.
29. We assume here that the relativizer *that* is perceived by speakers as a relative pronoun (hence as potentially an overt subject expression), rather than as a complementizer. Speakers must treat the *that* of *knows that*, *regrets that* etc. differently from relativizing *that* because, if not, a reverse *that*-trace effect would have to be countenanced for *The man that got arrested was a friend of mine* versus the less widely accepted *The man got arrested was a friend of mine* (on this point see Sobin 2009: 41).

3
Prestige speech patterns

3.1 Introduction

In the previous chapter we were concerned with arbitrary exclusions from the standard corpus. Here we look at the converse phenomenon. By this we mean phonetic patterns or grammatical structures that appear to have become embedded in linguistic practice as a by-product of standardization. Adapting the phrase 'grammatically deviant prestige constructions' (Emonds 1986), we refer to such phenomena as 'prestige speech patterns'. In this formulation, the term 'prestige' is a recognition of the fact that the relevant patterns occupy a characteristic position in the ideology of the standard: typically they are emblematic of the standard variety and they require a degree of conscious effort (self-editing) on the part of speakers. Such patterns are also normally associated with late acquisition: prestige grammar, in particular, is usually acquired during schooling. Analogously to other pedagogical outcomes, an individual's competence in relation to a prestige speech pattern may be 'imperfect', in the sense that it fails to attain the highest levels of prescriptive adequacy, often due to a tendency to employ the pattern beyond its agreed domain of use. Fowler and Fowler (1922), for example, talk in this connection of 'bad blunders' (p. 61) and 'gross errors' (p. 93). Linguists prefer the term 'hypercorrection', which for expository purposes we retain here, despite its implicitly normative perspective. Accordingly, the next section relates to hypercorrection in pronunciation, and includes the case study of intrusive liaison in French. After that we examine prestige grammar, within the framework of 'virus theory' (Sobin 1997). This concept is explained in more detail at the start of Section 3; however, an initial idea of what is involved can be gleaned from the following remark from Sobin:

> The particular rules that facilitate [...] editing toward prestige constructions are called *grammatical viruses* [...] A grammatical virus is a device that can read grammatical structure and affect it, though it is grammar-external.

A virus is parasitic on a grammar, and [...] it facilitates the construction of prestige forms. (Sobin 1997: 319)

Following a general discussion of this phenomenon, we look at three case studies of possible viruses, viz. preposition pied-piping in English, clefting in Peninsular Spanish and past participle agreement in French.

3.2 Hypercorrection in pronunciation

We shall see below that a good deal of complexity attaches to identifying grammatical viruses. This is unsurprising in view of the intricacy inherent in syntactic relations; by contrast, hypercorrection in pronunciation can be discussed in a fairly straightforward way that refers to the influence of spelling and of social structure. Lyons (1981: 50) defines hypercorrection as: 'the extension of some rule or principle, on the basis of a misunderstanding of its domain of application, to a range of phenomena to which, originally, it did not apply', and this seems to apply fairly adequately to pronunciation, so long as the social input to hypercorrection is taken into account. A well-known example from English pronunciation is that discussed by Lyons (1981: 208), where northern speakers of British English cannot rely on spelling as a guide if they wish to acquire the distinction between the set of words exemplified by the pair *putt* and *put* and differentiated in both southern and Standard English by two distinct back vowels, respectively [ʌ] and [ʊ]. Thus the guidance provided by the spelling of *putt* and *put* contradicts that suggested by *puss* (standard realization: [pʊs]) and *pus* ([pʌs]). The complexity results notoriously in hypercorrect forms like *butcher* pronounced [bʌtʃə]. We can relate this to social structure by pointing out that, as is the case with French variable liaison (discussed below), the rules governing a phonologically complex phonolexical set can only be fully internalized through long association with the relevant speech community.

From a diachronic perspective, it is somewhat of a commonplace that fairly recent socioeconomic trends, of the type that we discuss in Chapter 5, have had the effect of dissolving the cohesive social networks that promote localized norms. One linguistic result is an increasing reliance on spelling forms, seen perhaps most clearly in the changing pronunciation of place names. For instance, the Yorkshire town of Pontefract was until fairly recently called Pomfret (the name of the associated liquorice sweet appears still to alternate between Pontefract cake and Pomfret cake). The earlier form is clearly a phonetic erosion of the type common in place names. Impressionistic observation shows variation between spelling and reduced forms in the pronunciation of names like Harrogate [haɹəʊgeit] ~ [haɹəgət] and Bramhope [bɹamhəʊp] ~ [bɹaməp]. These examples may seem trivial and anecdotal, but they do illustrate one effect on language of counter-urbanization, a widespread process which can in general be assumed to have an input into linguistic variation; these examples are particularly illuminating in showing that the effects of social mutations of this kind do not necessarily tend in a 'downwards' or levelled direction.

These English examples are designed to anticipate the observation, evident enough as we shall see, that while the pressure of standardization as exerted through spelling is similar across languages in promoting linguistic insecurity, the pressure will have different effects across languages having different structures and hence different 'weak points'.

As regards French, Damourette and Pichon (1911–39: 4, 542) assert that the contemporary use of /l/ in pre-consonantal *il*, as in *il va* [ilva], is an 'orthographism', normatively motivated and used hypercorrectly by the linguistically insecure. Tuaillon (cited in Blanche-Benveniste and Jeanjean 1987: 37) asserts similarly that the insertion of /l/ in this context is a 'recent orthographic pronunciation', and further claims that its elision was considered normal and 'even distinguished' before the First World War.

Lodge (2004: 134) discusses the insertion of [l] word-finally in sixteenth-century French in words like *musique* and *boutique* giving [myzikl, butikl], presumably designed to run counter to the deletion of the consonant in the word-set exemplified by *table* [tabl]. A contemporary example from southern varieties that is sometimes mentioned is the pronunciation of orthographic final consonants that are standardly mute, in words like *cerf*, *persil* pronounced [sɛrf, pɛrsil] and even [pɔʀk, tabak] for *porc*, *tabac* among older speakers in Provence, although there are no final plosives in Provençal.

Both of these examples show different aspects of the relation between spelling and pronunciation. Lodge's example can only be rationally interpreted in a context where literacy was uncommon, and indeed he cites Estienne's comment that it is committed only 'par le peuple grossier [...] ou pour le moins par ceux qui n'ont aucunes lettres'.[1] The Provençal example shows hypercorrection arising in the classic case, where the orthography of a language is not especially transparent and so provides no sure guide to the standard pronunciation.

A third type of case is illustrated by intrusive intervocalic /d/ in Spanish, which sees words like *Bilbao* and *Colacao* (a popular brand of hot chocolate powder) articulated as [bilβaðo] and [kolakaðo]. This results from over-extension of the prestige pattern that requires the intervocalic /d/ in the past participle suffix *-ado* to be overtly pronounced giving, for example, [aβlaðo] *hablado* 'spoken' rather than the more colloquial (and arguably more frequent) form [aβlao]. Spanish intrusive /d/ can be encountered among well-educated speakers and hence, unlike the *musique* and *boutique* examples from sixteenth-century French mentioned above, cannot be attributed to unfamiliarity with the relevant spellings. Moreover, Modern Spanish has one of the most transparently phonemic orthographies of any of the familiar standardized languages. Arguably, then, what intrusive /d/ illustrates is the extremely resilient nature of the phenomenon of orthographically induced uncertainty.

Conversely, however, there is a further level of complexity which in a literate society sees the socially and linguistically secure happy to ignore the guidance of spelling. This is seen more vividly in a stress-timed language like English, where upper-class speakers will avoid spelling pronunciations in words like *caramel, magistrate, secretary* etc. by realizing the vowel in the third syllable as schwa, or eliding a syllable such that *temporarily* is homophonous with *temporally*. These are in addition to other non-orthographic pronunciations such as [wɛskɪt] for *waistcoat, forehead* rhyming with *horrid, hideous* having the now archaic form [hɪdʒɪs] and contemporary resistance to the spelling-influenced pronunciation of words like *tissue*, i.e. as [tɪsju] rather than [tɪʃu] or [tɪʃju]. Although these examples are marginal in affecting few speakers, it is worth mentioning that the similar and far from marginal area of h-dropping is also capable of provoking linguistic insecurity as manifested in hypercorrection. The case is similar because it also concerns the relation between spelling and pronunciation, and the conditions for hypercorrections are fulfilled: the variable has sociolinguistic value and there is some complexity. Thus in *Henry has lost his hat*, realization of /h/ in the grammatical words results in the classic effect of failed pedantry that is characteristic of hypercorrection.

The condemnation of the use of pre-consonantal French /l/ as an orthographism is related to this, since the essence of what one might call anti-orthographisms of the type just mentioned is that they take no heed of prescriptivism. It certainly appears that variable use of pre-consonantal /l/ has restricted sociolinguistic value; Armstrong (1996) and Ashby (1984) report high deletion rates in this context, and respectively little stylistic and social variation. It seems, however, much more likely that these high deletion rates shared by all speakers are the result of linguistic factors than that they stem from grammarians' comments.

The difference between the sixteenth century and now is clearly that literacy is much more widespread. In this reasoning, then, resistance to spelling-influenced pronunciation results in the creation of shibboleths that can be employed with confidence only through long immersion in the appropriate social milieu. Thus where guidance from the spelling is available to almost everyone, other means of achieving social distinction must be sought, although as Rickard (1974: 138) remarks of French spelling, '[it] is an inconsistent mixture of etymology and phonetics, a great burden on the memory and further complicated by grammar'. The same remarks can be applied to pronunciation, and it seems just as likely of the standard phonology, as Rickard suggests regarding the spelling (ibid.), that 'the system [is] an almost impossible one to master perfectly'.

Anti-orthographisms like those mentioned above are in any event the property of a small minority. Forms that resist spelling coincide of course with allegro speech processes like deletion and vowel centralization and these, especially deletion, appear to be used by all French speakers, in less guarded styles at least. We can suggest that the relatively levelled or simplified nature of French pronunciation leaves little scope for hypercorrection or indeed its opposite, as against morphosyntax and lexis, if it is accepted that variation in French is mostly to be found at these latter linguistic levels. We discuss below the influence upon pronunciation of morphological input like gender and number, from a theoretical viewpoint that also takes account of standardizing influences. Rare examples of classic hypercorrection in French are words like *sculpter* 'to sculpt' and its related forms, where etymological letters were reintroduced at the time of the intensive codification of spelling. These are regarded as hypercorrect if pronounced following the spelling (the prescriptive forms in this example are [skylte] etc.). Against this, *lorsque* 'when' pronounced [lɔʀsəkə] also attracts criticism; this is due perhaps to the analogy of *parce que* 'because', which is sometimes in slow or hesitant speech pronounced [paʀsəkə]. The difference between the two is that the first schwa in *lorsque* is intrusive. These two examples illustrate quite neatly the forces of normativism pulling in opposite directions.

One important contemporary phenomenon that can be addressed in terms of hypercorrection is intrusive liaison in French, which we discuss in detail below. This seems to be the exception to the general rule that little hypercorrection occurs in French pronunciation. Arguably, however, this is because intrusive liaison is at the crossroads of phonology, morphosyntax and lexis.

Erratic and intrusive liaison in French. It is worth recalling that liaison in French, the pronunciation before a vowel of a word-final consonant elsewhere silent, divides into four types (the traditional terms are in parentheses, and an underscore shows a liaison of the type referred to, except in the intrusive examples where an orthographic letter has been added):

- invariable (*obligatoire*), part of the core grammar and used by all speakers irrespective of social and stylistic influences (*les_ans* 'the years', *vous_avez* 'you have')
- variable (*facultative*), which does respond to social and stylistic factors (*c'est_un immeuble* 'it's a block of flats', *quand_il est là* 'when he's there')
- erratic (*interdite*), where spelling or analogy can induce speakers to make a liaison when standardly none is required (*soldat_américan* 'American soldier', *un homme et_une femme* 'a man and a woman', *les_haricots* 'the beans')
- intrusive (*fausse*), which differs from erratic in not corresponding to a consonant in the spelling (*donne-moi-z-en* 'give me some', *je suis bien-t-aise* 'I'm very glad', *mille-z-élèves* '1000 pupils').

Liaison that can be construed as hypercorrect is capable of occurring in all categories except the invariable, although it seems most common as an erratic or intrusive type. Armstrong (2001: 184) discusses the following example, which intruded into the variable category. It was produced by a 16-year-old girl when speaking to the author in a sociolinguistic interview:

(1) je trouve que les hommes politiques sont trop [z] âgés
     I find that the men political are too [z] old
     'I think politicians are too old'

In this example *trop* [z] *âgés* was pronounced [tʀozaʒe]; formal style would have called for [tʀopaʒe], and informal for [tʀoaʒe]. The speaker produced the utterance three times, so that a one-off 'slip of the tongue' can be ruled out. The insertion of the liaison consonant [z] was perhaps prompted by the desire to mark plurality, whereas of course no marker is in fact required after the invariable adverb *trop* in the standard variety. An additional influencing factor may be the rarity of the liaison consonant /p/. Léon (1984) speculates in this connection that /z/ and /t/, being the liaison consonants that productively provide morphological information (/z/ conveys plurality, /t/ 3rd-person verb form) are capable of spreading as intrusive liaisons by analogy. This is in contrast to /n/, the other frequent liaison consonant. Léon cites examples from the public speech of subjects having presumably a fair level of education:

(2) [ils] se sont rendus [t] aujourd'hui sur les lieux (journalist)
     [they] themselves are taken [t] today on the places
     'they arrived on the scene today'

(3) ils se sont mis [t] à réfléchir ('internationally renowned financier')
     they themselves are put [t] to reflect
     'they started to reflect'

Among examples with /z/ are:

(4) plus de cent [z] étudiants (university professor)
     more of 100 [z] students
     'more than 100 students'

(5) deux vases lui ont été [z] offerts (journalist)
     two vases to-him have been [z] offered
     'two vases were offered to him'

These examples certainly reinforce Léon's suggestion concerning the morphological information conveyed by /z/ and /t/. They seem to be the 'extension of some rule or principle' (to invoke Lyons 1981: 50), though whether 'on the basis of a misunderstanding of its domain of application', we can only speculate. It is however possible to see examples (2) and (3) as resulting from a sort of metathesis that transfers the [t] of *sont* to the right, perhaps prompted by the wish to convey 3rd-person marking where the syntax rules this out. Examples (3) and (4) seem similar to (1), but other intrusive liaisons with [z] show the plurality of factors influencing intrusive liaison. Some examples need to be analysed by invoking analogy, like the very common *donne-moi* [z] *en* and *moi* [z] *aussi*. In these cases, one can argue that intrusive consonants are inserted to avoid vowel hiatus, or possibly, in the first example, on the analogy of *donne-nous-en*. These are in any case not hypercorrect, and consultation of native speakers suggests that *donne-moi* [z] *en* is not generally regarded as incorrect and that the standard form, *donne-m'en*, is little known.

An erratic liaison made before a word in the *h aspiré*² lexical set seems too to be a good candidate for inclusion in the hypercorrect category. Here liaison is prescriptively blocked; for example before *hall, haricot, handicapé*. It may be that speakers wish to mark plurality by pronouncing the [z] in these instances, following Léon's theory. A form like [lezaʀiko] is likely to be regarded prescriptively as a *liaison interdite*, and thus characteristic of lower-class speech. What distinguishes the *h aspiré* set within liaison is its opacity; the 150 or so words in the set are of Germanic origin or are English loan-words, a fact known to scholars of French and presumably few others. The *h aspiré* set is therefore a particularly good example of the opacity, complexity and lack of clear motivation that standardization can impose. The present case also highlights the fundamentally normative import of the concept of hypercorrection.

The results of Smith (1996) and Ashby (2003) show fairly unambiguously that variable liaison is in slow decline. In this context continuing hypercorrection might seem surprising, but clearly language change does not proceed uniformly, and it leaves much litter behind as the pressures of standardization and de-standardization continue in tension. In any case, variable liaison seems to respond to broader social conditions in a fairly unusual way. Smith (1996: 22–7) has argued that the recent history of variable liaison shows it to have ebbed and flowed in response to large-scale social conditions; in particular, to the relationship between the upper-middle and lower-middle classes. Smith points out that in the nineteenth and early twentieth centuries, the *haute bourgeoisie* (the upper-middle class living on inherited income) used liaison more sparingly than the class below in familiar and colloquial speech. The *bourgeoisie*, like the aristocracy before them, showed relaxed attitudes to certain normative tendencies which were more scrupulously observed by the aspiring classes, similarly to what was argued earlier in this section concerning the avoidance of spelling-influenced pronunciation. This was, therefore, perhaps as much a matter of social confidence as the wish to signal social distance; nor can these two motivations be easily untangled.

In the period between about 1900 and the 1960s, the use of variable liaison probably saw an increase, with some liaison forms that had fallen into disuse being reintroduced, e.g. *nous sommes_arrivés* 'we have arrived' and *ils doivent_aller* 'they must go' (Encrevé 1988: 259, citing Martinon 1913). According to Smith, the important change in the early and mid twentieth century was the increasing importance of education as a 'legitimating' element. Those who direct France are still drawn largely from the upper-middle classes, but the possession of inherited wealth is no longer generally accepted as sufficient qualification for accession to the commanding heights of French industry or administration. Social privilege at this time required the sanction of a high degree of educational attainment, typically in a *grande école* (elite university). This is because education, including to the highest level, is commonly perceived as being in principle open to all. There is of course in reality still a very strong correlation between the social-class background of students and their chances of admission to a *grande école*. According to this view, the educational system has two functions: firstly to perpetuate upper-middle class domination, and secondly to conceal the first function. Thus in the pre-1960s period, we can hypothesize that the high levels of variable liaison used by middle-class speakers responded to an association in the public mind between level of education and equitable access to power and wealth.

The decline in the use of variable liaison on public-service radio since the 1960s (Smith 1996) and in unscripted speech (Ashby 2003) can be thought of as an indicator of informalization and of a less deferential attitude to the written norm. The 1960s is commonly accepted as the great turning-point, when populist values prompted widespread reaction against the hierarchical order. In this connection Gadet (2007: 209) has recently evoked 'un lent ébranlement du privilège à la langue écrite'.[3] To cite Rickard again (1974: 138), 'school syllabuses no longer allow as much time for the study of spelling and grammar as they did in the days when children learned little else'. Against the backdrop of the possible fluctuation and certain decline of liaison forms, there persist nevertheless continuing uncertainties over which liaisons should be made, and using what consonant. These certainly bear witness to the continuing, if declining, 'privilège à la langue écrite'. The hypercorrect errors made by speakers seem, as Léon suggests, to be in the direction of the frequent consonants /t/ and /z/, as in *trop* [z] *âgés* discussed above, or *un long* [t] *apprentissage* (Hornsby 2012). This can be understood as hypercorrection in one of its aspects, viz. regularization, which implies imperfect mastery of the irregularities of the standard. Once again, variable liaison fulfils all the conditions discussed above that fall under the concept of hypercorrection.

3.3 Grammatical viruses

3.3.1 Introduction

We now turn to prestige patterns in grammar. As was mentioned in 1.4, Chomsky has implicitly drawn a distinction between natural and unnatural grammatical phenomena, the latter being a side effect of standardization (hence, in our terms, prestige patterns). Chomsky expresses his position eloquently in the extended quotation below:

> I think sensible prescriptivism ought to be part of any education. I would certainly think that students ought to know the standard literary language with all its conventions, its absurdities, its artificial conventions, and so on because that's a real cultural system, and an important cultural system. They should certainly know it and be inside it and be able to use it freely. I don't think people should give them any illusions about what it is. It's not better, or more sensible. Much of it is a violation of natural law. In fact, a good deal of what's taught is taught because it's wrong. You don't have to teach people their native language because it grows in their minds, but if you want people to say, "He and I were here" and not "Him and me were here," then you have to teach them because it's probably wrong. The nature of English probably is the other way, "Him and me were here," because the so-called nominative form is typically used only as the subject of the tense sentence; grammarians who misunderstood this fact then assumed that it ought to be, "He and I were here," but they're wrong. It should be "Him and me were here," by that rule. So they teach it because it's not natural. Or if you want to teach the so-called proper use of shall and will—and I think it's totally wild—you have to teach it because it doesn't make any sense. On the other hand, if you want to teach people how to make passives you just confuse them because they already know, because they already follow these rules. So a good deal of what's taught in the standard language is just a history of artificialities, and they have to be taught because they're artificial. But that doesn't mean that people shouldn't know them. They should know them because they're part of the cultural community in which they play a role and in which they are part of a repository of a very rich cultural heritage. So, of course, you've got to know them. (From Olson and Faigley 1991: 30)

The view we take here is that standardization, together with the prescriptive impetus that grows up around it, is simply one ideology among many that determine linguistic practice. Thus it is arguably the case that the 'natural law' envisaged by Chomsky, evoking as it does some pristine linguistic state that can be accessed through careful science, is something of a fantasy. Nevertheless, as we remarked in 1.4, the influence of standardization does have its own DNA profile, in that grammatical structures that owe their presence to normative influence are typically less regular and more lexically specific than other structures. Conventional grammar typically treats such prestige constructions on a par with others, or simply lists them as exceptions. A more accurate representation of linguistic behaviour ought, however, to embed prestige rules within an overarching model of competence, while nevertheless distinguishing between rules of that type and core grammar. Virus Theory (Sobin 1997, 2009; Lasnik and Sobin 2000) offers perhaps the best articulated framework to date for achieving that purpose, in that it attempts to integrate prestige and non-prestige patterns within a single 'machine'. The key construct of Virus Theory is the grammatical virus, which is envisaged as a surface rule that is acquired relatively late (for example during schooling). The effect of a virus is to trigger (or 'license') a prestige usage that core grammar would not normally be expected to produce. Below we summarize the basic properties of grammatical viruses and then propose three possible candidates for inclusion among the growing list of viral structures.

3.3.2 Anatomy of a virus

With the notable exception of Construction Grammar (Croft 2000, 2001), modern theories of syntax converge in the assumption that grammatical rules are, in principle, maximally general in scope. This view is taken to its logical conclusion in Minimalism, the most codified – and arguably the most widely accepted – of all the formal theories of grammar. Within that framework, there are no constructions as such. Instead, linguistic utterances answer to a relatively limited array of general principles, which take partially different shapes in different language varieties. Whatever one may think of the specifics of the Minimalist Program, the underlying view just outlined is a plausible one, given that basic grammar is acquired without instruction, something that would be difficult were that process to involve the learning of ad hoc rules.

In contrast, prestige usage contains a relative abundance of idiosyncratic operations whose full mastery – in the sense of attaining a normatively defined paradigm – is available only to a well-educated minority. Such rules stem largely from *a priori* conceptions about how grammar ought to be organized, rather than how it actually is. For example, they often reflect the cultural kudos that, among people from a wide range of social backgrounds, can attach to older linguistic patterns or to languages that occupy a privileged position within the collective consciousness (Latin being the prototypical example in European societies). As indicated earlier and discussed in more detail below, prestige usage can be conceptualized in terms of grammatical viruses. These, in light of the remarks just made, can be regarded as a natural and perhaps inevitable by-product of the emergence of a standard language ideology. The latter is a fertile stimulus to prescriptive tinkering that seeks to enhance the clarity or elegance of the standard language or to arrest the forces of change, envisaged as essentially degenerative in their effect. Where such interventions endure, it is usually in the guise of an artificial rule; that is, as a grammatical virus.

In addition to this, the very act of standardization, understood as the 'imposition of uniformity on a class of objects' (J. Milroy 2001: 531), may result in the freezing in place of a particular principle that is either arbitrary to begin with – a grammarian's chance selection of a particular paradigm of usage – or becomes so over time, as the rest of the language evolves naturally. Ayres-Bennett (1993: 38) makes precisely this point in connection with the work of seventeenth-century French grammarians, such as Vaugelas, who sought to standardize the French language in order to eliminate uncertainty over usage: 'The danger is that in fixing a language in mid-evolution without having a clear historical perspective, the result may be arbitrary and complicated rules which have their own illogicalities.' In our view, such 'arbitrary and complicated rules' are nothing other than grammatical viruses.

Thus viruses seem to arise as a consequence of the way of looking at language that standardization encourages. Given their unpredictability – from a linguistic point of view – they require active enforcement (usually, but not exclusively, through schooling) and they are normally associated with delayed acquisition. In addition, they have certain characteristic formal properties. Summarizing some of the observations in Lasnik and Sobin (2000), we can highlight the following:

(a) Lack of generality. Unlike normal grammatical rules, viruses typically make reference to specific lexical items. Consider for example, the *It is/was I* construction that is sometimes found in prestige English usage. The nominative case form of the post-copular pronoun in this construction clearly diverges from the unmarked pattern, according to which post-copular position correlates with accusative case. For example, Lasnik and Sobin (2000: 350) attribute ungrammaticality to the formulation in (6):

(6)   In this picture, the person in the purple shorts is I. (Lasnik and Sobin 2000: 350)

We can thus infer that the rule that allows *It is/was I* in prestige varieties is an addition to the basic usage. But notice how this rule is specific to the circumstance in which the structural subject is expletive *it* and the structural complement is the 1st-person singular pronoun *I*. Thus (6) above illustrates the fact that post-copular nominative case is not normal with subjects other than *it*, while (7) below, again deemed problematic by Lasnik and Sobin (p. 350), shows that even when the subject is *it*, nominative case on post-copular pronouns other than *I* results in reduced acceptability:

(7)   It was we.

This is arguably quite an extreme case, in that the virus is so narrowly constrained that it has very limited productivity. As will become apparent from the case studies considered later in this chapter, it is likely that at least some virus rules can be triggered by specific sets of lexical items rather than just by a specific word, meaning that they can enjoy quite a reasonable level of productivity (at the appropriate register). Nevertheless, the basic principle still holds, namely that viruses lack the full generality associated with normal grammatical rules and thus do not apply to the full range of instances of a given pattern. In short, they under-extend (Lasnik and Sobin 2000: 366–7).

(b) Blindness to the larger structural context. Viruses appear to be relatively simple rules that operate at a superficial level. As a consequence, they appear to be insensitive to deeper structural relations, a phenomenon that is nicely illustrated by English *whom*. Lasnik and Sobin (2000) argue that this accusative case form is licensed by a virus, unlike normal accusative pronouns such as *him* or *me*. If the pronoun *whom* was a true *wh* counterpart to *him, me* etc., we would expect it to be possible when, and only when, it was associated with a position calling for accusative case. In many instances, *whom* does indeed appear to parallel the normal accusative pronouns:

(8)   They saw him.

(9)   They saw whom?

(10)   Whom did they see ~~whom~~?[4]

However, accusative pronouns are also the norm in post-copular position – see the discussion in relation to example (6). While this context may perhaps allow in situ *whom* (e.g. *It was whom?*), fronted *whom* that has been extracted from post-copular position does not appear to be a viable possibility:

(11)   Whom was it ~~was whom~~?[5]

Interestingly, while post-copular position is an accusative case position in English, according to the theory of inverse copular sentences (Moro 1997) the phrase occupying that position may have the grammatical function of subject. This is noticeable in languages like Spanish and Italian, where the post-copular phrase may exhibit the formal attributes of the subject, viz. person and number agreement with the verb and nominative case:

(12)   El culpable soy yo. (Spanish)
       the guilty am I
       'The culprit is me.'

Here the sentence is said to instantiate an inverted copular construction, with the predicate (*el culpable*) in the structural subject position and the underlying subject in predicative position. If sentences with post-copular personal pronouns are inverted copular constructions in English also, then while *whom* is linked to an accusative case position in both (10) and (11), it differs in terms of its grammatical function across the two examples: object in the first but subject in the second. A possible explanation for the contrast in acceptability between (10) and (11) would then be that the rule that allows *whom* is sensitive to grammatical function rather than to case. This would further confirm that *whom* is not like *him, me*, etc., because the latter forms are determined by case alone.

Additionally, however, the *whom* rule must be limited in terms of its analytical reach. Consider (13) below, which represents a common type of example at the relevant socio-stylistic level, but one that fails to achieve the highest standard of prescriptive acceptability – in a somewhat heavy-handed fashion, Fowler and Fowler (1922: 93) describe it as a 'gross error':

(13)   It is only those converted by the Gospel whom we pretend are influenced by it. (*Daily Telegraph*)

From a normative perspective, *whom* in the above sentence is the subject of the finite subordinate clause *are influenced by it* and hence is incorrect (assuming finite subjects should not be in the accusative). In fact, we argued in 2.4 (see examples (45) to (47)) that reanalysis occurs in this type of case, making the finite subordinate clause analogous to an infinitival one. On that view, given that infinitival clauses do take accusative subjects (e.g. *I believe them to have already left*), accusative *whom* in (13) is entirely predictable. Nevertheless, if, as we are assuming, *whom* is licensed by a virus, speakers can be assumed to be pursuing the prescriptive gold standard when they use this pronoun and hence the relevant analytical framework is the normative one that does not recognize the reanalysis just alluded to. Assessed in those terms, the virus can indeed be deemed to have missed its target in an example like (13). The 'malfunction' is due to the fact that the virus lacks the capability to recover the complex subordinating structure which, from the normative perspective at least, resides in cases such as (13). Lasnik and Sobin (2000: 367) express this in the following terms:

> Viruses […] are simple rules which cannot access a larger context. A virus is only able to see a finite sequence of surface elements. On the surface, *wh*-movements are unbounded dependencies. Therefore, an attempt to construct a virus which can consistently see both a moved *whom* and its source position is doomed.

Chomsky (2008: 138) posits a 'no-tampering condition', the import of which is that core grammatical dependencies cannot be interfered with. Without necessarily endorsing the absoluteness of this formulation, we recognize the underlying intuition, viz. that grammatical practice learned in infancy is not easily reversed. In light of that, it is unsurprising that viruses, imparted through education or absorbed through exposure to self-edited speech, have the superficial quality alluded to in the Lasnik and Sobin quotation.

(c) Directionality. Viruses appear to exhibit a strong directional bias. In other words, it is often the case that a virally generated item is constrained to occur in a particular linear order in relation to the other elements that comprise the licensing environment. Typically, the required sequential order is not predictable from any general principle of core grammar. We can illustrate this using the example of nominative pronouns in coordinated subjects.

This usage does not appear to be characteristic of instruction-naïve language, but becomes relatively common once a speaker has been exposed to prescriptive inputs. For example, a formulation such as (14) below would be a very typical juvenile utterance, whereas (15) bears a familiar pedagogical stamp:

(14)   Me and Jack are going on the X-Box.

(15)   Jack and I are going on the X-Box.

The viral nature of examples like (15) is indicated by the fact that nominative case generalizes poorly to other pronouns in coordinated subjects.[6] This can be seen, for example, in some of the results from Quattlebaum's (1994) research into prestige case forms among two classes of university-bound high school pupils (22 in one class and 24 in the other; all native speakers of English). While 100% in both classes identified coordinated subjects of the form 'DP *and I*' as prestige forms, only 42% in one class and 60% in the other selected subjects of the form 'DP *and he*' over 'DP *and him*'. Syntactic rules do not usually exhibit random discrepancies of this type.

For these and other reasons, Sobin (1997: 328–30) posits a virus that, for any instance of the linear sequence *and I*, licenses nominative case on the pronoun *I*.[7] Clearly this virus is lexically very specific. However, it also makes reference to a specific linear ordering. So, for example, it does not license a sentence such as (16):

(16)   I and Jack are going on the X-Box.

This captures the fact that speakers who regularly use 'DP *and I*' typically eschew '*I and* DP'. The latter structure was selected in Quattlebaum's survey by only 17% of one class and 35% of the other. This restriction is again rather arbitrary from the linguistic point of view, in that there is no structural reason why nominative case should be capable of reaching the second conjunct but not the first. Thus the *and I* rule illustrates the way in which viruses tend to be randomly sensitive to surface linear order.

Overall, then, viruses are structurally limited and highly specific rules that apply at the surface. Lasnik and Sobin (2000: 355) suggest that they apply at *spell-out*, the operation that assigns phonetic form to finalized syntactic structures. We make the same assumption, but we diverge from them in one key respect. For technical reasons that go somewhat beyond the scope of this book, we propose that viruses actually *are* phonological spell-out rules. Under that view, viruses work by replacing the normal phonetic output with the prestige form, whenever a given condition is satisfied. For example, rather than there being two separate units *who* and *whom*, the latter is simply the spell-out form of the former that is delivered by the relevant virus. In this conception, grammatical viruses operate in an identical way to prestige-driven pronunciation rules, such as that which causes the word *butcher* to be spelled out as [bʌtʃə] rather than the more normal [bʊtʃə].

We end this introductory section by listing what we take to be the signature characteristics of viruses:

(i) They have as their output prestige constructions, which may be commoner in writing than in unscripted conversation.

(ii) They are associated with delayed acquisition (or, equivalently, are absent from instruction-naïve speech).

(iii) They are typically associated with a programme of normative enforcement.

(iv) They lack the generality normally associated with grammatical rules and hence may be lexically specific or prone to under-extension.

(v) They operate within a limited domain and hence are blind to the larger structural context. This often leads to over-extension.

(vi) They are typically sensitive, in a random way, to surface linear order.

(vii) Their output cannot be replicated using the normal grammatical resources of the language in question.

(viii) They are not part of deep syntax: in our view they are spell-out rules.

3.3.3   Viral case studies

In the foregoing introduction to viruses, the examples all had a relatively limited import. In particular, the consequence of the virus was largely limited to whether a given element was spelled out with an accusative or nominative form. In this section, we would like to suggest that viruses are more widespread and can have apparently deeper effects than has been assumed to date. To demonstrate this, we present three case studies in which virus-based accounts are proposed for certain phenomena that are conventionally regarded as central to the grammars of the languages in question. Our purpose in doing this is to highlight further the extent to which the grammars of familiar natural languages have been shaped by the ideology of standardization.

3.3.3.1 Preposition pied-piping in English wh constructions.

One of the staples of school grammar (now in abeyance in the UK) was the injunction to 'avoid ending a sentence with a preposition'. To the extent that this programme was effective, it enforced the operation of preposition 'pied-piping', primarily in the context of *wh* movement. The operation is illustrated in (17) below:

(17) Northern Desserts is the company in which we've invested most.

Here the entire prepositional phrase (PP) *in which* has been placed at the beginning of the relative clause, an effect which can be analysed in terms of the pronoun *which* being targeted for movement but dragging its containing PP along as well. This contrasts with non-pied piped (18), where the pronoun *which* has been extracted from the PP, leaving the remainder of the latter – in other words the preposition *in* – in its base position. In this type of case, the preposition is said to be *stranded*:

(18) Northern Desserts is the company which we've invested most in.

While it has long been known that preposition pied-piping is associated in English with registers in which self-editing is likely to be an issue, most accounts appear to assume that it is not in any way an abnormal structure – for a robust defence of this position, see Hoffmann (2011). On the other hand, McDaniel, McKee and Bernstein (1998: 328) suggest that the phenomenon results from a virus in the sense of Sobin (1997), although they do not indicate how the virus would actually work. Here we attempt to do precisely that. Before that, we present evidence that supports a viral analysis.

First, preposition pied-piping appears to be rare in unscripted conversation. Gries (2002), for example, reports not being able to find a single instance of it in the spoken parts of the British National Corpus. He did, however find roughly equal quantities of pied-piping and stranding examples in the written parts of the corpus.

Secondly, we can note that English-speaking children do not spontaneously pied-pipe PPs in *wh* constructions; rather, they acquire this option as part of their educational and cultural development. While anyone familiar with child speech will know this intuitively, there is some experimental evidence that can be adduced as well. Specifically, McDaniel, McKee and Bernstein (1998) failed to elicit a single instance of preposition pied-piping in relative clauses among 115 American children aged 3–11 (although 3% of 3–5 year olds, 6% of 6–8 year olds and 54% of 9–11 year olds adjudged the structure grammatical when actually presented with it).[8] We know of no equivalent study for interrogative clauses (i.e. one focusing on pied-piping, or its absence, in child speech). However, it seems unlikely that such a study would have a different outcome from the McDaniel, McKee and Bernstein survey.

Thirdly, preposition pied-piping is associated with a clearly identifiable prescriptive tradition. Initiated apparently by John Dryden in 1672 apropos of Ben Jonson's 'the bodies that those souls were frighted from',[9] the principle that prepositions should not be stranded clause-finally appeared in a number of eighteenth-century grammars and from the nineteenth century was widely taught in schools (Pullum and Huddleston 2002: 627). For example, in his *A Short Introduction to English Grammar* Robert Lowth makes the following remark in relation to stranding:

> This is an Idiom which our language is ſtrongly inclined to; it prevails in common converſation, and ſuits very well with the familiar ſtyle of writing; but the placing of the Prepoſition before the Relative is more graceful, as well as more perſpicuous· and agrees much better with the ſolemn and elevated Style. (Lowth 1763: 141)

In addition to being salient in the scholarly tradition, the anti-stranding view appears to have influenced linguistic behaviour. According to Bergh and Seppänen (2000), the historical trend in English prior to the modern period was towards an ever greater use of stranding (at least in relative clauses). However, these two authors identify (p. 307) a noticeable increase of pied-piping in late modern written English, which they attribute to prescriptive pressure: 'The drop in the incidence of stranding is thus not an expression of a genuine grammatical change but due to notions of correctness derived from the grammar of Latin and affecting written usage' (p. 295).

A fourth argument that points towards a virus is the fact that when the *wh* pronoun is potentially either *who* or *whom*, pied-piping exerts strong pressure towards the latter. Thus while post-prepositional *who* is normal when stranding occurs, as (19) shows, pied-piping prefers *whom*, as is shown by the greater acceptability of (20a) over (20b):[10]

(19)   Who did they speak to?

(20a)   To whom did they speak?

(20b)   To who did they speak?

As discussed earlier, the licensing of *whom* can be attributed to a virus. Therefore a structure that appears to rely on *whom* is, *prima facie* at least, also likely to involve a virus.

A fifth reason for positing a virus is that prepositional pied-piping in English often results in preposition doubling, a phenomenon that meets the criteria for over-extension, in the sense that overt pronunciation of the preposition at the extraction site rules out, under normative assumptions, the possibility that it can also be pronounced in clause-initial position. Radford (2010: 157) gives a number of examples of such doubling (he terms it 'copying'), showing clearly that the phenomenon is common. We reproduce two below:

(21)   In what enormity is Marcius poor in? (Shakespeare, *Coriolanus*, II.i)

(22)   IKEA only actually has 10 stores from which to sell from. (Economics reporter, BBC Radio 5)

As discussed earlier, over-extension is a typical signature of viruses. Moreover, the cause of the over-extension in this particular type of case appears to lie in the fact that the rule licensing the clause-initial copy of the preposition is blind to the existence of the copy at the extraction site. This would be consistent with pied-piping being associated with a rule that has limited structural reach, which again suggests a virus.

Finally, pied-piping in modern English is arguably lexically specific. Bergh and Seppänen (2000: 299) adduce data such as the following which show that pied-piping was possible in *that*-relatives in Middle English:

(23)   we byseche God Almy3ty that he have evremore 3oure roial persone in hys kepynge with encrece [of] all manere of Honours, after that 3oure noble and roial hert desires. (Ellis's Original Letters, 1419)
       'We beseech God Almighty that he holds evermore your royal person in his keeping and increases all manner of honours, for which your noble and royal heart longs.'

In modern English, by contrast, pied-piping is restricted to items in the *wh* lexical class (e.g. *whom* and *which*).

Pied-piping in English thus exhibits a number of viral signatures. On the other hand, a viral analysis is problematic at first glance, given that the phenomenon involves deep syntactic dependencies as opposed simply to surface aspects of the grammar. It is also the case that, cross-linguistically, preposition stranding is rare (van Riemsdijk 1978), being confined primarily to English and some of the Scandinavian languages. In other words, the pied-piping process that we are suggesting might be attributable to a virus is actually the norm overall in those languages that allow *wh* movement. Given this fact,

Chomsky's implicit attribution of pied-piping to a principle 'that sometimes bars preposition stranding' (1995: 264) seems, intuitively at least, to get things the wrong way round. In short, while pied-piping in English has the look of a virus-generated phenomenon, both technical and cross-linguistic factors appear to militate against actually analysing it in that way.

A possible way out of this apparent impasse is suggested by the analysis of preposition doubling in Radford (2010: 158). That author suggests that doubling results from a failure, in a pied-piped construction, to delete the preposition in the trace or unpronounced copy that the fronted PP is hypothesized to leave at its extraction site.[11] So, for example, (21) would result from the movement of the PP *in what enormity* followed by only partial deletion of its rightmost copy:

(24)   [$_{PP}$ In what enormity] is Marcius poor [$_{PP}$ in ~~what enormity~~]?

From this perspective, preposition doubling is essentially a spell-out phenomenon, in that an item normally receiving a null spell-out is actually spelled out overtly.[12] While this basic approach appears to be on the right lines, it needs to be refined somewhat. In particular, it fails to capture the fact that double spell-out of the preposition occurs only in languages that allow preposition stranding: the phenomenon is unknown in purely pied-piping languages like Spanish. This suggests that stranding must somehow be implicated in preposition doubling structures such as (21) and (22).

One way in which this issue might be addressed, while simultaneously tackling the problem of how to account for English pied-piping in terms of Virus Theory, would be to assume that preposition stranding itself is a spell-out phenomenon. Under that view, a sentence such as *Which house do they live in?* would in principle involve fronting of the full PP, just like its pied-piped counterpart *In which house do they live?* The difference between the two would arise at spell-out, with the preposition being spelled out at the extraction site in the stranded case and in clause-initial position in the pied-piped case:

(25)   ~~in~~ which house do they live in ~~which house~~

(26)   in which house do they live ~~in which house~~

Under this account, the difference between languages like English and purely pied-piping languages like Spanish reduces to a spell-out convention in the latter disallowing pronunciation of the preposition at the extraction site.

Preposition doubling falls out straightforwardly from the foregoing model: it is what happens when the preposition is spelled out at both the extraction site and in clause-initial position:

(27)   in which house do they live in ~~which house~~

Moreover, given the above assumption that purely pied-piping languages have a convention disallowing overt spell-out of the preposition at the extraction site, the absence of preposition doubling in such languages is immediately accounted for.[13]

We will tentatively assume that the foregoing model captures the range of options available to speakers in relation to *wh* PPs. This puts us in a position to see how a virus might be responsible for pied-piping in English. As noted above, the problem facing a viral account is that pied-piping appears to involve deep syntax, whereas viruses are assumed to be surface rules. Under the account proposed here, the pied-piping versus stranding distinction *is* a surface phenomenon, in the sense that it is determined by phonological spell-out rules. Therefore, it could in principle be subject to manipulation by a virus.

More specifically, to account for stranding within the proposed framework, we assume a generalized spell-out rule as follows:

(28) Stranding rule:
      For any fronted *wh* PP: pronounce P at the extraction site but not at its surface position.

We can then posit a pied-piping virus that replaces (28) with what is in effect its converse. For reasons that will become apparent in a moment, we can assume this virus has the form of two separate rules:

(29) Pied-piping viral rule A:
      For any fronted *wh* PP: delete P at the extraction site.

(30) Pied-piping viral rule B:
      For any fronted *wh* PP: pronounce P at its surface position.

For example, a sentence such as *To which author are you referring?* would be derived as in (31), where italic font indicates the operation of rule A and bold font the operation of rule B:

(31) **to** which author are you referring *to which*

In a case like (31) the virus successfully mimics the effect of Spanish or Italian-style pied-piping. However, in cases of prepositional doubling the similarity breaks down. We can attribute this to the fact that the two virus rules responsible for *wh* pied-piping in English operate independently of each other: preposition doubling occurs when rule B is applied but rule A is not. Note that the independence of rules A and B is not an ad hoc stipulation, but follows directly from the fact that virus rules have limited structural reach: the respective domains of application of A and B are too remote from each other for either rule to take the other into account.

It might seem that A and B are not completely independent of each other, in view of the fact that formulations such as (32), where A but not B has been applied, do not seem to occur:

(32)   Whom did you speak?

At first glance, this suggests that rule B cannot fail to apply if rule A has been applied, and hence B must be capable of detecting A's effect. In fact, however, the (32) type of case is ruled out without the need to assume a linkage between B and A. In the first place, the issue of the application of A and B only arises if the speaker is consciously editing their speech towards the prestige pattern. If there is no targeting of the prestige pattern, then neither A nor B can apply and an output such as that in (32) cannot be produced. So (32) could only even *potentially* occur in self-edited speech. However, here too it is ruled out. This follows from the fact that the essence of the target structure is that a preposition must introduce the fronted *wh* expression: this is what defines the presumed prestige model. So if the speaker is aiming for a prestige effect – in other words if the pied-piping virus is invoked – then rule B must necessarily apply and so a sentence like (32) cannot occur.

To summarize: Preposition pied-piping in English exhibits a number of properties that are typically associated with viruses, viz. rarity in unscripted speech, delayed acquisition, association with normative enforcement, over-extension and (arguably) lexical specificity. In addition, it typically prefers *whom*, plausibly also the product of a virus, to *who*. In order to bring pied-piping within the scope of Virus Theory, we analysed it as a spell-out phenomenon, given the ancillary assumption that preposition stranding itself can be treated as resulting from a spell-out convention.

3.3.3.2   Cleft sentences in Spanish

This case study concerns sentences such as (33) and (34) below, which are the Peninsular Spanish equivalents of English cleft sentences:

(33)   Fue con Pedro con quien hablamos.
       was with Pedro with whom we-spoke
       'It was Pedro who we spoke to.'

(34)   Es en Pedro en el que confío.[14]
       is in Pedro in whom I-trust
       'It's Pedro who I trust.'

The surprising feature of these is the way the preposition and relative pronoun introducing the subordinate clause 'resumes' the fronted prepositional phrase. While this is normal in Peninsular Spanish, at least in educated speech, it has a controversial status in much of Latin America.[15]

In Argentina and Uruguay, for example, this pattern is commonly replaced by a structure that has more in common with clefting in English, in that there is no repetition of the preposition and the subordinating word is a bare complementizer, viz. *que*:

(35) Precisamente fue con él[16] que hablamos primero [...].
precisely was with him that we-spoke first
'In fact it was to him that we spoke first [...].'
(Uruguayan Senate, 11 July 2001; retrieved via Google.)

(36) [...] es de esto que trata la astrología.
is about this that deals the astrology
'It's this that astrology deals with.'
(Eugenio Carutti, *Casa XI (Ciudad de Buenos Aires)*, 2001; Corpus de referencia del español actual (Real Academia Española, undated (b)), henceforth CREA.)

The Latin American variant turns out to be more faithful to the clefting pattern that is discernible in Medieval Spanish, whereas the construction illustrated in (33) and (34) does not appear until the Golden Age, a time when a number of prestige innovations made their presence felt. Moreover, Dufter (2010) has adduced considerable evidence of strong normative pressure against the pattern with bare *que*, which appears to have been regarded as a Gallicism (a characterization which is in practice unlikely to be correct – see also Lapesa 1981: 593).

Before looking in more detail at a possible viral source for the modern Peninsular Spanish pattern, we need to examine more closely the syntactic structure of clefts in general. English often employs a relative clause construction:

(37) It was Starghill who Tavon confided in, [...] (*Jet,* October 1995; COCA)

(38) It was Hugo to whom the family turned when Anna lapsed into one of her phases. (*Southwest Review,* 2003; COCA)

An alternative involves the complementizer *that*, with movement of a prepositional phrase or some other adverbial from the subordinate clause to the main clause (often, though not exclusively, with a prestige effect):

(39) It is to Federico that the Trattati are dedicated. (*Geographical Review,* October 2005; COCA)

(40) It was last week that questions swirled about why the alert level was raised for financial sectors of New York, New Jersey and Washington. (CNN, Sunday Live, 8 August 2004)

The structure below is ambiguous between the relative clause-based cleft and the complementizer version (if the latter, then it is also a *that*-trace construction – see 2.4):

(41)   And it was Bobby that got her to move there, right? (King, CNN, 27 March 2001; COCA)

The complementizer cleft appears to represent the normal way of clefting in Italian and French, although the latter language uses a relative clause (introduced by *qui* 'who/which') when the clefted element is the subject (example (44)):

(42)   È a quell'amico che ho consegnato il pacco. (Sornicola 1988: 347)
       is to that+friend that I-have given the parcel
       'It is to that friend that I gave the parcel.'

(43)   C'est à elle que Negresco s'en prend avec humeur.
       it+is to her that Negresco goes-on-at with humour
       'It's to her that Negresco jokingly grumbles.'
       (Dominique Perrut, *Patria o muerte*, 2010; FRANTEXT)

(44)   C'est le typhus qui l'a tuée, mais tout en elle était épuisé.
       it+is the typhus which her+has killed, but all in her was exhausted
       'It's the typhus that killed her, but she had lost her will to live.'
       (Simone Veil, *Une vie*, 2007; FRANTEXT)

As regards Spanish, the Latin American type of cleft in (35) and (36) appears rather clearly to be a complementizer cleft, like English (39) and (40), Italian (42) and French (43), whereas the Peninsular pattern in (33) and (34) appears to be a relative clause-based cleft, given that the subordinate clause is introduced by what is obviously a relative pronoun, *quien* or *el que* (both meaning 'who' or 'whom'). However, as was mentioned earlier, the pattern in (33) and (34) also exhibits fronting of a PP to post-copular position in the main clause. To that extent, it also resembles a complementizer cleft. From one point of view, then, the Peninsular cleft is a hybrid structure, manifesting properties of both main types of cleft construction.

In principle, this could simply be a case of marginal codification (Matthews 1981), the phenomenon whereby linguistic practice does not map perfectly onto the discrete categories put forward by the analyst. In 2.3, we suggested that marginal codification is apparent in relation to the Spanish impersonal *se* construction, because the boundary between the two constructions that are identified in the prescriptive and the theoretical traditions becomes blurred in the stigmatized formulation involving a verb that agrees with its accusative object. We noted there that the exclusion of this 'hybrid' structure from the standard corpus is arbitrary. Matters are somewhat different, however, in relation to the Peninsular cleft. For one thing, the latter is very much a part of the standard language. Indeed, it is the Latin American type of cleft that, in the Peninsula at least, is often regarded as ungrammatical. In fact, the Peninsular cleft has certain properties that are arguably viral signatures, implying that it has been shaped, in part at least, by forces stemming from the standardization process.

In the first place, this construction appears to under-extend, in two rather subtle ways. It is well known that the word order in Spanish is relatively free, at least from the purely syntactic point of view. One consequence of this is that, for any array comprising a form of the copular verb *ser* 'be' together with a relative clause and a PP, any ordering of these three elements is possible. Thus (45) could perfectly well be reordered as in (46) or (47):

(45) [...] de lo que se trata es de su reinserción y de su redención.
      of what *se* treats is of his reinsertion and of his redemption
      'It's about his reintegration and his rehabilitation.'
      (España Oral: CCON012A; CDE)

(46) de su reinserción y de su redención es de lo que se trata

(47) es de su reinserción y de su redención de lo que se trata

However, although the constituents are in principle identical – viz. a form of *ser*, a PP and a relative clause – a cleft such as (48) below does not enjoy the flexibility illustrated by (45) to (47):

(48) [...] fue con su riqueza con la que se consiguieron los mercenarios para derrotar a Maxtla [...]
      was with their wealth with which *se* obtained the mercenaries to defeat ACC Maxtla
      'it was with their wealth that the mercenaries were hired to defeat Maxtla'
      (*Revista española de antropología americana*, vols. 34–35, p. 137, January 2004)

As it stands, (48) has the same order as (47), viz. 'copula – PP – relative clause'. It can perhaps be reordered on the model of (46) – an operation which yields (49) – but not on the model of (45), which would give (50), a structure that does not occur in Spanish:

(49) con su riqueza fue con la que se consiguieron los mercenarios para derrotar a Maxtla

(50) con la que se consiguieron los mercenarios para derrotar a Maxtla fue con su riqueza

In order to express the intended content of (50), it would be necessary to replace the agreeing relative pronoun *la que* with its neuter counterpart, as in (51) below:

(51) con lo que se consiguieron los mercenarios para derrotar a Maxtla fue con su riqueza

The foregoing somewhat random restriction applies whenever the relative pronoun introducing the subordinate clause agrees in number or gender with the noun in the clefted PP.[17] This is not the case in (45) to (47) but it is the case in (48) to (50). Thus the Peninsular cleft is associated with a narrowing of the normal word order options that are available for constructions of its type. This implies that the rule associated with this construction cannot generalize in the usual way.

The construction also appears to under-extend in terms of the syntactic composition of the clefted PP. Empirical research involving Peninsular speakers revealed a clear preference for the Latin American strategy (with bare *que*) when the clefted phrase involves an infinitival clause. The survey involved 37 students from various Spanish universities attending Newcastle University in the academic session 2010–2011 as part of the Erasmus exchange programme. Each student was given four sentence pairs of the type shown in (52) and (53) below and asked to decide in each case whether one sentence was more acceptable than the other and if so, which. A preference for the (52) type of pattern was registered on 120 occasions (out of a possible total of 148), giving a preference rate for that pattern of 81.08 per cent.

(52) Es para bajar la inflación que hemos hecho recortes.
      is for reduce the inflation that we-have made cuts
      'It's in order to reduce inflation that we have made cuts.'

(53) Es para bajar la inflación para lo que hemos hecho recortes
      is for reduce the inflation for which we-have made cuts

Here again we see that the Peninsular cleft does not generalize very well beyond its core domain.

The construction also appears to be subject to random lexical restrictions. In relative clauses generally, the post-prepositional context allows any item from the *quien* and *el que* series and also bare *que*:

(54) la mujer de quien habla tu canción
      the woman of whom talks your song
      'the woman your song speaks of'
      (Osvaldo González Real, *Anticipación y reflexión*; CDE)

(55) [l]a tradición de la que habla mi compañero
      the tradition of which talks my friend
      'that tradition that my friend talks about'
      (Carlos Sariñana, *Del Papa y otros Atentados*; CDE)

(56) esa historia de que habla Fukuyama
      that history of which talks Fukuyama
      'that history that Fukuyama talks about'
      (Eugenio Trias, *ABC*; CDE)

However, post-prepositional relative pronouns in the Peninsular cleft construction are restricted to *quien* and *el que*, and hence exclude bare *que*. For example, while *quien* in (57) below can be replaced by *la que* (from the *el que* series), it cannot be replaced by bare *que*:

(57) Pero sobre todo es a Europa a quien debe abrirse la logosfera.
      but above all is to Europe to whom must be-opened the airwaves
      'But above all it is Europe whose airwaves must be opened up.'
      (Javier Marías, *ABC*; CDE)

Restrictions also apply to the preposition that can be used. Butt and Benjamin (2000: 511), for example, report that PPs headed by *bajo* 'under' may be problematic for clefting. They state that the Peninsular equivalent to the Latin American-style cleft in (58) would typically be avoided in favour of the circumlocution in (59):

(58) Fue bajo esta impresión que continuamos con el programa.
      'It was under this impression that we continued with the programme.'

(59) Fue así, bajo esta impresión, como continuamos con el programa.
      was thus under this impression how we-continued with the programme

We have been unable to find a single naturally occurring example of a Peninsular cleft that exhibits *bajo* as the head of the clefted PP.

Thus the Peninsular cleft both under-extends structurally and is lexically specific, facts that represent *prima facie* evidence of a grammatical virus. The way the structure is embedded in relevant ideologies appears to confirm this diagnosis.

In the first place, taking the Spanish-speaking world as a whole, the Peninsular cleft is a prestige pattern. Thus, according to Butt and Benjamin (2000: 509, note 2), despite the fact that the structure is not common in informal speech in Latin America, it is quite often used in formal contexts. They give the example that appears as (60) below:

(60) [...] es por lo anterior por lo que nos gusta la idea de Ecopetrol [...]
    is for the previous for which us pleases the idea of Ecopetrol
    'it is because of the previous point that we like the idea of Ecopetrol'
    (*El Tiempo*, Colombia)

Moreover, as discussed extensively in Dufter (2010), there is a long tradition of condemning the Latin American-style clefting pattern with bare *que* as a Gallicism (an assumption that in fact is likely to be incorrect). Indeed, following Cuervo (1907: 338), this usage is often referred to as the '*que galicado*' – see, in particular, Real Academia Española 2005 (*Que*, 1.5). Dufter offers a revealing quotation from the eighteenth-century Spanish author José Cadalso, who parodies the supposedly French style of his contemporaries' letters by concocting the following piece of incorrect Spanish:

(61) Esto es con el más gran placer que yo prendo la pluma para aprender de las nuevas de vra. salud [...]
    this is with the most great pleasure that I take the pen to learn of the news of your health
    'It is with the greatest pleasure that I take up my pen to learn news of your health'
    (J. Cadalso, *Al marqués de Peñafiel* 1778; from Dufter 2010)

The satirical device here is the direct calquing of a typically French style of beginning a letter, viz. *C'est avec le plus grand plaisir que ...* 'It is with the greatest pleasure that ...'. In the Spanish version, the sentence-initial neuter pronoun *esto* is intended to mimic expletive French *c(e)*, which corresponds to English *it* in the cleft construction. Overt expletives are in fact not possible in Spanish, so this use of *esto* is a deliberate 'error'. Apart from that, however, the structure ridiculed is exactly that of the cleft with bare *que*. As Dufter himself makes clear in his paper, criticism of this supposedly French construction was as much stylistic as syntactic, with Spanish-speaking writers professing a liking for more direct mono-clausal structures. Nevertheless, it does appear that the cleft with bare *que* somehow came to be viewed as a foreign incursion into the native grammar of Spanish, something that was incompatible with *un español castizo* 'pure Spanish'. It is also significant that this supposedly foreign structure was thought to be specifically of French origin, given the long history of Spanish cultural insecurity vis-à-vis France.

The likely effect of normative censure of the cleft with bare *que* would be to encourage the use of alternative strategies, including what we have characterized above as the Peninsular clefting pattern, where *el que* or *quien* is used in place of *que* and the fronted preposition is repeated. The latter structure appears to have originated at least a century before the normative testimonies cited by Dufter. Those are from the eighteenth century, whereas the Corpus del Español (Davies 2002–) yields examples of the cleft structure with *quien/el que* and the doubled preposition from at least the seventeenth century, the example below being the earliest that we could find:

(62)   [...] solamente es a Leonor a quien temo [...]
       only is ACC Leonor ACC whom I-fear
       'it's only Leonor that I fear'
       (Juana Inés de la Cruz, *Los empeños de una casa*, 1673; CDE)

This time lag may simply be due to a gap in the cultural historiography. In other words normative pressure against the *que* cleft – and hence implicitly in favour of alternative strategies – may predate the eighteenth century, but we simply lack the relevant evidence. Alternatively, criticism of the *que* cleft may indeed postdate the emergence of the variant with *quien/el que* and preposition doubling. In either case, it seems clear that intellectual and cultural pressures have consistently tended towards enforcing use of the latter structure at the expense of the *que* cleft. An excellent illustration of this normative programme can be found in Cuervo (1907: 335–57), where various strategies are presented for 'castilianizing' sentences involving *que galicado*. This kind of sociolinguistic context appears to us to be ideal for the genesis or spread of a syntactic virus, as well as providing an interesting case study in how linguistic behaviour can act as a proxy for national ideology.

To sum up so far: The Peninsular-style cleft is a prestige construction that has long benefited from normative protection and it is subject to apparently random limitations. In key respects, then, it bears the hallmark of a virus-generated structure. Assuming that a virus is indeed responsible, the question to resolve is what the nature is of the mechanism involved.

We can start by positing that the Latin American pattern is the unmarked one. It has the widest geographical distribution and is structurally simpler than its Peninsular counterpart. Moreover, it can be seen as a 'reserve' pattern, in that that even Peninsular usage defaults to it at times. In addition to cases like (52), for example, Peninsular speakers typically use the Latin American pattern to express 'that's why':

(63)   [...] es por eso que van en bicicleta en Turpan [...]
       and is for that that they-go in bicycle in Turpan
       'and that's why they cycle in Turpan'
       (Barcelona, *La Vanguardia*, August 1994; CREA)

In a search specialized to just Peninsular sources, the CREA corpus returns 24 hits for the above structure but only nine for the 'Peninsular' equivalent, viz. *es por eso por lo que* ...

Following È Kiss (1998: 258), we analyse complementizer clefts (i.e. the Latin American pattern) as involving movement of the clefted phrase from the subordinate clause to post-copular position in the main clause, as in (64) below (which refers to the Argentinian example (36)):

(64)   es de esto [que trata la astrología ~~de esto~~]

Now Chomsky (2004, 2008) assumes that phrases that are moved out of subordinate clauses are linked not just to their extraction site (the position corresponding to their grammatical function) but also to the beginning of the subordinate clause. On that basis we could explain the third *who* in the Oprah Winfrey example below:

(65)   But everybody who's watching is – has their own favorite, who they know who they would pick. (Oprah Winfrey, 20 July 2006; COCA)

The second *who*, following the antecedent noun *favorite*, occupies the normal position at the beginning of its relative clause. Syntactically speaking, it is the object of the verb *pick* and so can be analysed as having been extracted from immediately to the right of *pick* (the direct object position). In addition, however, *who* appears at the beginning of the clause *who they would pick* which is embedded under the verb *know*. The relevant portion of (65) can thus be represented as follows:

(66)   who they know [who they would pick ~~who~~]

Here we can see that the relative pronoun *who* is linked not just (implicitly) to its extraction site (object position in relation to *pick*) but also (overtly) to the beginning of the bracketed subordinate clause. Chomsky's argument is that this pattern arises whenever a phrase is extracted from a subordinate clause, even if the copy of the phrase is not actually spelled out phonetically, as it is in the Winfrey example. From that perspective, the analysis in (64) omits a silent copy of the moved PP *de esto* at the beginning of the subordinate clause (analogous to the middle *who* in (66), but not spelled out overtly). Thus a fuller representation would be as in (67):

(67)   es de esto [~~de esto~~ que trata la astrología ~~de esto~~]

Given (67), in order to derive the viral Peninsular equivalent, we can posit a rule that deletes *que* and then spells out the middle (unpronounced) copy of the PP *de esto*, but with a relative pronoun in place of the DP *esto*. This is shown below in (68), where the bold font indicates the output of the viral rule:

(68)   es de esto [**de lo que** ~~que~~ trata la astrología ~~de esto~~]

Here the complementizer *que* has been deleted and ~~de esto~~ at the beginning of the subordinate clause has been spelled out as *de lo que* (with the neuter relative pronoun corresponding to neuter *esto*).

The above analysis presupposes the availability of *que* deletion in Spanish. While this is less common than *that* deletion in English, it is clearly possible, as example (69) below shows:

(69) Señoría, ruego guarden silencio.
      ladies-and-gentlemen, I-ask keep-SUBJUNC.3.PLU silence
      'Ladies and gentlemen, please be silent.'
      (España Oral: BPOL047A; CDE)

As regards why the DP – *esto* in (68) – is not spelled out as itself, this can be attributed to the fact the target output of the virus is a string of words that looks in every sense grammatical. With the complementizer *que* deleted, the subordinate clause would lack an overt subordinator, and hence lack the appearance of grammaticality, if the DP were spelled out as itself. Relative pronouns, in contrast, are legitimate subordinators, as well as being DP level constituents and hence suitable proxies for the DP. The fact that only relative pronouns from the *quien* and *el que* series can be used, and not bare *que* (in its function as a relative pronoun rather than as a complementizer), follows naturally from the assumption that the relative pronoun in the cleft is really a proxy for an ordinary DP and as such is required to express as much of the latter's semantic and grammatical content as possible. While items in the *el que* series are formally marked for gender and number and *quien* is both marked for number and semantically specified as [+ human], *que* is maximally unmarked. The latter is thus unsuitable as a DP proxy.

To sum up this section: We propose that the Peninsular-style cleft construction is a prestige structure generated with the help of a virus. The purpose of the virus is to fend off 'Gallic' bare *que*, which has long been the object of normative criticism. The input to the virus is a standard cleft with the bare complementizer *que*. The virus deletes the latter and spells out the intermediate trace copy of the clefted PP as 'P + *quien/el que*'.[18] In this way the final output has a look that is both non-Gallic and overtly grammatical (in that the subordinate clause is introduced by a legitimate subordinator).

3.3.3.3 *Participle–object agreement in French*

As will be familiar to anyone who has learned French, transitive perfective participles in that language exhibit gender and number agreement with a preceding accusative clitic or *wh* phrase if the latter can be identified as the object of the participle:

(70) Ces conséquences, je les avais prévues. (Grevisse 1986: 1368)
      those consequences$_{FEM}$, I them had foreseen-FEM.PLU
      'Those consequences, I had foreseen them.'

(71)   les efforts que nous avons faits (Grevisse 1986: 1368)
the efforts$_{MASC}$ that we have made-MASC.PLU
'the efforts that we have made'

In (70), agreement on the past participle *prévues*[19] is triggered by the clitic pronoun *les*, which is plural in form and feminine in virtue of the fact it is bound by the feminine DP *ces consequences*. In (71), the agreement on the past participle *faits* is determined by the *wh* pronoun, which has been fronted from the direct object position and can be surmised to be masculine plural, in view of the antecedent *les efforts*.[20]

The foregoing principle, a so-called *règle de position* (Smith 1993: 87), is a highly curious phenomenon. On the one hand, it bears almost every possible hallmark of normative intervention: it was introduced into French by a specific individual, viz. the sixteenth-century poet Clément Marot, it is confined largely to writing, and is regarded as artificial by even such prescriptive luminaries as Maurice Grevisse (see Grevisse 1986: 1369 [Remarque]). On the other hand, it has been adduced by linguists as evidence to support major theoretical claims about the basic architecture of language. In particular, Kayne's (1989) analysis of it in terms of movement to the edge of a so-called 'agreement projection' was a major impetus to the development of the concept of the 'checking domain', which held sway in syntax throughout much of the 1990s and the early 2000s – see Chapters 3 and 4 of Chomsky 1995 for a good snapshot of what was then cutting-edge thinking. And more recently, in a partial reworking of Kayne's original idea, Radford (2010) cites the contrast between the two sentences below as evidence for Chomsky's theory of phases (Chomsky 2001, 2008):

(72)   Il a commis quelle bêtise?
he has committed-MASC.SING what blunder$_{FEM}$
'He has committed what blunder?'

(73)   Quelle bêtise il a commise?
what blunder$_{FEM}$ he has committed-FEM.SING
'What blunder has he committed?'

In (72) the *wh* phrase *quelle bêtise* has remained in situ, whereas in (73) it has been fronted. Radford analyses the fronting operation as involving two stages, with *quelle bêtise* moving initially to the left periphery of the verb phrase. This would explain the agreement manifested by the participle, assuming that agreement somehow requires the *wh* phrase to move through the participle's periphery. In that hypothesis, participle agreement provides evidence for the claim that the left periphery of the verb phrase is an intermediate landing site for *wh* movement, as is claimed in Chomsky's theory of phases.[21]

Despite the rather far-reaching claims that have been made on the basis of French participle–object agreement, we will argue that it is licensed by a virus and hence is primarily an epiphenomenon of standardization. If we are correct in this, then much of the apparently scientific analysis of this grammatical phenomenon by professional linguists (as opposed to prescriptivists) can be regarded as illustrating a classic analytic pitfall alluded to by J. Milroy (2001: 545). That author notes that 'when the standard variety is selected, it is difficult to avoid smuggling into an internal linguistic account a set of unanalyzed assumptions that are conditioned by the standard ideology'. Milroy is in fact concerned with general assumptions pertaining to such matters as correctness, prestige, uniformity and stability. However, if the foregoing *règle de position* is indeed a child of the standardizing enterprise and its attendant ideology, essentially the same principle would be at work, namely an unwitting acceptance – due to a narrow preoccupation with the standard language – of a construct driven by external rather than internal factors.

Turning then to that very question, we can start with the sociolinguistic evidence. Here the indications of a viral source are plentiful. As was mentioned above, the normative rule for participle–object agreement has a long and illustrious history within the French literary and intellectual tradition. This really begins in 1538, with Marot's famous epigram 'À ses disciples'. There Marot states that 'Nostre Langue à ceste facon, Que le terme, qui va deuant, Voulentiers regist le suiuant.'[22] He then illustrates this point with three examples of good practice, each involving a past participle that agrees with a direct object to its left. The first one, *m'Amour vous ay donnée* 'my love to you [I] have given', is deliberately archaic and reflects the fact that participle–object agreement was a productive option in Old French. The other two, *Dieu en ce monde nous a faictz* 'God has made us in this world' and *Dieu en ce monde les a faictes* 'God has made them in this world' appear to be inspired by the Italian model *Dio noi a fatti*, which appears a few lines below. Despite Marot's claim that the rule he is proposing is somehow an integral part of French, it is clear that his purpose is to create a mini-ideology. In particular, by alluding to Italian, to whose speakers he overtly attributes the greatest eloquence in the world ('L'italien, dont la faconde Passe les vulgaires du Monde'), he is attempting to attach a positive social index to the agreeing structure. The testimony from Marot's approximate contemporaries Sylvius, Palsgrave, Meigret and Ramus (cited in Smith 1993: 90–2) suggests that the picture was nothing like as neat as that painted in Marot's epigram, with variation prevailing both in regard to whether agreement was actually made and in regard to whether agreement (if made) was limited to preceding direct objects.

Notwithstanding its somewhat shaky empirical foundation, Marot's precept was debated in detail and discussed at length in the subsequent century, with the grammarian Vaugelas (see Vaugelas 1663: 140–5) playing a pivotal role in its eventual widespread acceptance (Grevisse 1986: 1369). Note, for example, Vaugelas's statement that 'En toute la Grammaire Françoife, il n'y rien de plus important, ny de plus ignoré' – a revealing comment in a number of ways.[23] According to Ayres-Bennett (1993: 35–7), Vaugelas exercised considerable and lasting authority due to a convergence of propitious circumstances. On the one hand, his explicit adoption of court usage coincided with the centralizing tendencies of the age and specifically the consolidation of an absolute monarchy. Secondly, his avowed objective of promoting clarity and purity dovetailed perfectly with the ideology embedded in the newly founded Académie Française. Third, he found a ready audience among the newly created nobility, who were anxious to assimilate themselves to the mores of the traditional nobility, in language as in behaviour and dress. And finally, his work satisfied what was felt to be genuine linguistic need. Demands for a codification and standardization of usage had been made from the early sixteenth century and, by promoting unambiguously a particular model of usage (that of the royal court), Vaugelas effectively addressed this issue. As Ayres-Bennett (p. 37) puts it, 'it was Vaugelas's definition of good usage, focussed on the court and the best authors, which resolved the dispute for some time and established an elitist norm for good usage which still finds its echoes today'.

In the seventeenth to the nineteenth centuries, while the basic *règle de position* came to be adopted as a cornerstone of prestige grammar, there was considerable debate over various categories of exception (see Smith 1993: 95–103). The actual details of these are not strictly relevant to present concerns – suffice it to say that the debate was largely based on stylistic and pseudo-logical considerations rather than empirical facts of usage. What is significant, however, is that by the end of the nineteenth century the rule for participle–object agreement was deemed to have become both overcomplicated, in the sense of having too many random exceptions, and to be falling into obsolescence. This prompted the Ministry of Public Instruction, in a ministerial decree of 31 July 1900 (Smith, p. 105), to describe the rule as 'une cause d'embarras dans l'enseignement'[24] and to recommend its effective abolition (by tolerating complete invariability of the past participle when conjugated with *avoir*). The normative instinct runs deep, however, and the proposal was quickly withdrawn (under pressure from the Académie Française).

In the French language today, the rule has the ideal sociolinguistic profile of a prestige construct. Though an integral component of received literacy, its observance is entirely optional in speech and appears to be absent or marginal in instruction-naïve language (Müller 1999; Pirvulescu and Belzil 2008). The latter state of affairs is no doubt compounded by the fact that in Modern French the relevant agreement features can only be marked orthographically except in a small minority of verbs (1.24% according to the survey in Tanase 1976). Furthermore, basic schooling appears to be only partially successful as a means of inserting the rule into speaker competence. According to Campbell (2008: 2), '[g]rammar books, and hundreds of websites, are devoted to this sole cause, with the *méthode Wilmet* a favoured recipe for simplicity and clarity'.

The foregoing picture inevitably calls to mind some of the words from Chomsky cited earlier in this chapter: 'You don't have to teach people their native language because it grows in their minds, but if you want people to say, "He and I were here" and not "Him and me were here," then you have to teach them because it's probably wrong.' Participle–object agreement in French is a strikingly similar case, in that it relies on the educational system for its survival. Moreover, as we have seen, it belongs precisely to that corpus of received artificialities that Chomsky in the same quotation characterizes as a 'repository of a very rich cultural heritage'.

A comparison with verb–subject agreement is instructive at this point. The latter is acquired without instruction, is devoid of prestige value and, once acquired, is not optional. Even before the strictly linguistic facts are considered, then, participle–object agreement looks considerably less natural than more familiar paradigms of verbal agreement.

Turning in fact to structural questions, two superficial aspects of the *règle de position* stand out immediately as possible viral signatures. Firstly, there is the rule's obvious directionality: the output of the rule (participle–object agreement) is sensitive to whether the linear order 'object ... participle' obtains or not. As discussed earlier, sensitivity to surface linear order is characteristic of viruses. Secondly, the rule operates in a lexically restricted environment, namely in relation to verbs selected by the auxiliary verb *avoir*. As was also discussed earlier, viruses differ from normal grammatical rules in being highly specific from the lexical point of view.[25]

More importantly, however, the rule of participle–object agreement in Modern French appears to under-extend in a number of ways. To see this, we first need to define the basic nature of the rule. One point on which most theories concur is that agreement on the participle is related to movement, in the sense that the agreement-triggering item – an object clitic or *wh* expression – must be analysed as originating in object position (immediately to the right of the participle) and then moving to its surface pre-auxiliary position (see Kayne 1989; Belletti 2001; Radford and Vincent 2007). This is illustrated in (74) and (75) below, which refer back to examples (70) and (71):

(74)   Ces conséquences, je les avais prévues ~~les~~.

(75)   les efforts que nous avons faits ~~que~~[26]

On the other hand, as Chomsky (1995: 325) notes, long object extraction – that is, from a finite subordinate clause – does not trigger agreement (on the matrix verb). He gives the example below, where agreement on the matrix participle *dit* would be regarded as incorrect, despite the fact that the relative pronoun – extracted from *dit*'s clausal complement – now precedes *dit*:

(76)   la lettre qu'il a dit que Pierre lui a envoyé
       the letter$_{FEM}$ that+he has said-MASC.SING that Pierre to-him has sent
       'the letter that he said Pierre sent to him'

The discrepancy between the case in (74) and (75), on the one hand, and (76) on the other has a rather technical explanation in the theoretical literature, based on the so-called Improper Movement constraint (Belletti 2001) or, more recently, the Inaccessibility Condition of Radford and Vincent (2007: 146). In essence, however, those accounts amount to the following generalization:

(77)   Generalization on participle–object agreement in French:
       A perfective participle optionally agrees with a moved object (clitic or *wh* expression) to its left unless the latter has been long extracted.

This captures the agreement in (74) and (75) and the non-agreement in (76), which appear to represent the limiting cases. We can now consider how the *règle de position*, as enshrined in the normative canon, under-extends.

Under-extension is primarily apparent in relation to infinitival clauses. Consider, for example, the apparently mysterious contrast below (cited in Belletti 2001, but ultimately stemming from Ruwet 1982: 150):

(78)   une femme qu'on aurait dite belle
       a woman that+one would-have said-FEM.SING beautiful
       'a woman that one would have called beautiful'

(79)   une femme qu'on aurait dit ne pas être belle[27]
       a woman that+one would have said-MASC.SING NEG not be beautiful
       'a woman that one would have said wasn't beautiful'

In much of the theoretical literature, the above contrast is actually regarded as confirming the generalization in (77). Abstracting away, again, from complex theoretical phraseology, the usual claim is that (78) involves only one full clause whereas (79) involves two. This is based on Kayne's (1981: 356–62) analysis of French sentences such as (80) below, which he classifies as ungrammatical (unlike their English equivalents):

(80)   Je crois Jean être le plus intelligent de tous.
       'I believe Jean to be the cleverest of all.'

According to Kayne, the infinitival complement in (80) is a full clause (making it structurally equivalent to a finite subordinate clause). The ungrammaticality of the overall sentence would then be due to the fact that the French verb *croire* 'believe' cannot govern across a full clausal boundary, meaning that the infinitival subject *Jean* is ungoverned and hence unlicensed. This analysis generalizes to all verbs in this class, including *dire* 'say'. From that perspective, (79) is analogous to (76), in that the relative pronoun has been long extracted (moved from a full subordinate clause to the matrix clause). Participle–object agreement is thus ruled out. In contrast, the relative pronoun in (78) has not been long extracted, because the participle's complement is a 'defective' verbless clause, so agreement is possible (see Belletti 2001, who expresses this in terms of Improper Movement).

However, it is by no means clear that infinitival complements of 'believe'-type verbs are full clauses in French. A well-established diagnostic test for determining whether a subordinate complement is a full clause or not involves seeing whether the subject of the complement can be made into the passive subject of the matrix clause. For example, this can be done to the subject *Gore* in the infinitival complement in (81) below – as we see from (82) – which confirms that (in English at least) the infinitival complement of a 'believe'-type verb is not a full clause.

(81)   [...] they believe Gore to have been sincere in opposing the CAFE rider [...] (*E: the Environmental Magazine*, January/February 2000; COCA)

(82)   Gore is believed to have been sincere in opposing the CAFE rider.

On the other hand if, instead of an infinitival complement, we have a finite subordinate complement, as in (83), the subordinate subject cannot be made into the passive subject of the main clause, given that (84) does not seem to be a structure that occurs in English usage:[28]

(83)   They believe that Gore was sincere in opposing the CAFE rider.

(84)   Gore is believed that was sincere in opposing the CAFE rider.

Now if we apply the foregoing diagnostic to French verbs in the 'believe' class, we see that in fact the majority of them allow the subject of their infinitival complements to be passivized. The two examples (85) and (86) below illustrate this for the verbs *découvrir* 'discover' and *dire* 'say' (in each case the relevant text is underlined):

(85)   À quelle époque n'y a-t-il pas eu d'homme public, cru un saint par ses amis, et qui est découvert avoir fait des faux, volé l'État, trahi sa patrie?

'In what period has there not been a public figure, thought a saint by his friends, and who is discovered to have made mistakes, stolen from the state, betrayed his fatherland?' (Marcel Proust, *À la recherche du temps perdu*; FRANTEXT)

(86) <u>Qu'un clan soit dit être tel ou tel animal</u>, il n'y a rien à tirer de là; mais que deux clans compris dans une même tribu doivent nécessairement être deux animaux différents, c'est beaucoup plus instructif.
'That a clan should be said to be such or such an animal, there's nothing that can be concluded from that; but that two clans comprised in the same tribe must necessarily be two different animals, that is much more instructive.' (Henri Bergson, *Les Deux Sources de la morale et de la religion*; FRANTEXT)

Given examples such as the above (see also Veland 1998), it seems wrong to say that infinitival complements selected by French verbs in the 'believe' class are full clauses. Accordingly, past participle agreement in cases like (79) should in fact be possible. Interestingly, at earlier periods such agreement was in fact possible, as we see from the example below:

(87) cette méthode de distillation que nous avons dite être si propre à isoler les essences
that method$_{FEM}$ of distillation that we have said-FEM.SING be so appropriate to isolate the essences
'that distillation method that we have said is so appropriate to isolating essences'
(Marcellin Berthelot, *La Synthèse chimique*, 1876; FRANTEX)

The absence, then, of agreement in the (79) type of case (in Modern French) represents an instance in which the rule does not generalize to the full range of cases that can be expected to fall under it.[29]

A further instance of under-extension – again involving infinitival complements – relates to the causative/permissive verbs *faire* 'make' and *laisser* 'let', as well as to perception verbs such as *voir* 'see', *entendre* 'hear' etc. All of these can be used in a construction in which the subordinate infinitive has a passive interpretation, as in (88) below:

(88) J'ai fait acheter un grand nombre d'exemplaires de ce journal [...]
I+have made buy-INF a large number of+copies of this newspaper
'I had a large number of copies of this newspaper bought'
(Christian Boltanski and Catherine Grenier, *La vie possible de Christian Boltanski*, 2007; FRANTEXT)

For the verb *faire* at least, it has been proposed that the infinitive in this type of case adjoins to the matrix verb, thus creating a complex predicate (see e.g. Guasti 1996, Kayne 1977, Aissen 1974). This implies syntactic restructuring, such that the overall structure is treated as a single clause. We cannot apply the passivization diagnostic to confirm this, however, because the infinitival clause lacks an overt subject (compare (88) with (81)). An alternative test is to see whether the object can be cliticized. Sentence (89), for example, is a perfectly normal French structure, derived by extracting the partitive clitic *en* 'of it/them' from the object of the subordinate infinitive *acheter*:

(89)   J'en ai fait acheter un grand nombre d'exemplaires.
       I+of-it have made buy-INF a large number of+copies
       'I had a large number of copies of it bought.'

We can make the hypothetical extraction process more transparent, using the conventional strikethrough notation:

(90)   J'en ai fait acheter un grand nombre d'exemplaires ~~en~~.

The operation in (89)/(90) is not possible, however, if the relevant object is contained in a full subordinate clause. Thus (91), for example, is a structure that never occurs in French (although we can attach a viable meaning to it):

(91)   J'en crois que quelqu'un a acheté un grand nombre d'exemplaires ~~en~~.
       'I think that someone has bought a large number of copies of it.'

By the cliticization test, then, the *faire* construction in (88) is indeed monoclausal (in the sense of having only one full clause). The same test shows that analogous constructions involving perception verbs like *voir* 'see' also involve just one full clause:

(92)   ce vieux homme qui peut tout et qui en a vu tuer d'autres
       that old man who can everything and who of-them has seen kill-INF
       others
       'that old man who can do anything and has seen others be killed'
       (Jean Anouilh, *Antigone*, 1955; FRANTEXT)

Given the status of the relevant constructions as involving just a single clause, we should expect participle–object agreement to be possible in relation to restructuring occurrences of *faire, laisser, voir* etc. However, the normative convention governing these constructions is that the past participle is always invariable, a situation that for *laisser* was actually instituted by the Conseil Supérieur de la Langue Française with the following statement (1990: 13): 'le participe passé de **laisser** *suivi d'un infinitif* est rendu invariable'.[30] Illustrative examples are given below (the second is from the Conseil's 1990 report):

(93)   Je les ai fait chercher partout. (Grevisse 1986: 1376)
       I them have made-MASC.SING look-for-INF everywhere
       'I had them searched for everywhere.'

(94)   la maison qu'elle a laissé saccager
       the house_FEM that+she has let-MASC.SING wreck-INF
       'the house that she allowed to be wrecked'

(95)   les airs que j'ai entendu jouer (Grevisse 1986: 1375)
       the tunes that I+have heard-MASC.SING play-INF
       'the tunes that I heard being played'

Interestingly, Radford and Vincent (2007: 155–7) argue that the absence of participle agreement in the case of *faire* and *laiser* is due to a virus, given that it is not predicted by general theory and also because it is so clearly traceable to prescriptive sources: secondary school inculcation in the case of *faire* and the 1990 normative decree alluded to above in the case of *laisser*.[31] In fact, as we have just seen, the problem affects the whole class of restructuring verbs and not just these two lexical items.[32] Here again, then, we have a range of cases to which the past participle agreement rule could be expected to apply but to which (by normative convention) it does not. This in fact produces the slightly paradoxical situation whereby agreement is allowed in formulations like (96) but not in those like (95):

(96)   les violonistes que j'ai entendus jouer (Grevisse 1986: 1375)
       the violinists that I+have heard-MASC.PLU play-INF
       'the violinists that I heard play'

In this type of case, the relative pronoun corresponds to the subject of the infinitival complement (rather than the object, as in the previous examples). As was mentioned in 2.3, normative grammar is typically more sharply attuned to the subject–object distinction than speakers are in their everyday practice. Thus the convention whereby agreement is possible in the pattern in (96) but not in that illustrated in (95) appears to owe more to the ruminations of grammarians than to the pressure of usage.

A final type of under-extension is apparent in relation to impersonal structures involving the expletive subject *il* 'it/there'. Here past participle agreement is systematically ruled out, both for relative pronouns and object clitics:

(97)   les chaleurs qu'il a fait (Grevisse 1986: 1373)
       the heats_FEM that+il has made-MASC.SING
       'the heat wave there has been'

(98)   Pour avoir une Phèdre parfaite, il l'aurait fallu écrite par Racine sur le
       plan de Pradon. (Grevisse 1986: 1373)
       to have a Phèdre~FEM~ perfect, *il* it+would-have needed-MASC.SING written
       by Racine on the model of Pradon
       'To have a perfect version of Phèdre, it would need to be written by
       Racine in the manner of Pradon.'

According to Radford and Vincent (2007: 149), agreement fails to be manifested in this type of structure because the past participle does not assign
accusative case to its apparent object. However, past participle agreement
in the perfect is not in general subject to the condition that the agreeing
phrase be accusative. In the case of unaccusative verbs, for example, which
take the auxiliary *être* 'be' in the perfect, the participle agrees with its surface
subject, which presumably has nominative case. An example is given below,
in which the participle agrees with the nominative pronoun *elle*:

(99)   Elle est entrée sans frapper. (Grevisse 1986: 1376)
       she is entered-FEM.SING without knocking
       'She entered without knocking.'

Thus agreement on the past participle is not in principle conditional upon
the participle's ability to assign accusative case. There is no general reason,
then, why agreement should be prohibited in examples like (97) and (98)
and so the exclusion appears to be another instance of under-extension.

   Overall, then, the *règle de position* for participial agreement under-extends
in several ways, with the result that a significant minority of cases where
agreement should be possible in principle are randomly excluded. This fact,
together with the superficial viral signatures noted earlier (viz. directionality
and lexical specificity) and the rather clear evidence of normative intervention, suggests strongly that we are dealing with a grammatical virus. This
would also be consistent with the fact that the past participle agreement rule
is fundamentally a spell-out phenomenon, in that its effects are limited to
the phonetic form of the participle.[33]

   Assuming then that French past participle agreement (with auxiliary *avoir*
at least) is indeed viral in nature, the question to be addressed is what the
likely form is of the virus. In fact, the actual *règle de position* can itself be
regarded as the basis for a formulation of the virus. The *règle* states that the
past participle conjugated with *avoir* agrees in gender and number with its
direct object whenever this object precedes it (Grevisse 1986: 1368). This
covers the basic pattern enshrined in Generalization (77). In particular,
the fact that the direct object is specifically identified as the object of the
participle rules out the possibility of agreement with a relative pronoun or
interrogative expression that has been extracted from a finite subordinate
clause commanded by the participle (so-called long extraction). Problems

arise, however, in cases of what Matthews (1981: 187) calls 'marginal subordination', where a syntactic dependency exists between the matrix verb (i.e. the participle) and a phrase inside an infinitival subordinate structure. Here there is no clearcut procedure for deciding whether the phrase in question is the participle's object or not. An analogous situation exists in relation to object-like elements in certain impersonal constructions. Here again, the precepts of conventional grammar provide no clear guidance as to how the elements in question should be analysed. As a consequence of these uncertainties, a series of ad hoc stipulations have arisen within the normative tradition, making full mastery of the normative paradigm an almost impossible task. Thus some degree of 'listing' is inevitable:

(100)   Viral rule for participle–object agreement in French:
        For any transitive participle with a moved (but non-long extracted) direct object to its left: spell out the participle with an agreement form corresponding to the object, except:[34]
        (i)   if the object has been extracted from the infinitival complement of a 'believe'-type verb or of a restructuring verb;
        (ii) or if the object is the complement of an impersonal verb.

To summarize the main points of this third case study: Participle–object agreement with auxiliary *avoir* is a phenomenon that is largely confined to the written language and is associated with an illustrious tradition of normative tinkering and pedagogical enforcement. Moreover, it under-extends in a significant minority of cases, resulting in a very fine-grained normative paradigm that speakers find very difficult to replicate. Accordingly, we have posited a virus, which causes participles to be spelled out in an agreeing form when they have a moved direct object to their left. However, given the very subtle character of the target paradigm, a number of exceptions have to be explicitly listed.

3.4   Conclusion: viruses and ideology

In this closing section, we consider the motives that appear to lie behind the adoption of the grammatical viruses identified in the course of this chapter. As regards preposition pied-piping, one possibility would be that this device signals structural relations more clearly than preposition stranding, by keeping the preposition and its *wh* complement in their canonical order. The pied-piping virus would thus reflect an attempt to inject greater clarity into the system. Such an account would in fact be consistent with the views of the eighteenth-century archbishop Robert Lowth, cited earlier. That commentator, it will be recalled, characterized the pied-piping construction as not just 'more graceful' but also 'more perspicuous' than the stranded alternative. However, it could equally well be claimed that pied-piping obscures structural relations – and hence undermines clarity – by removing all overt traces of the PP from its source position as complement to the verb. In other words, just as stranding separates P and its complement, so pied-piping separates V and its complement. Thus any 'gain' in clarity due to the selection of the pied-piping operation is matched by a corresponding loss at a different point in the clause structure.

An arguably more likely explanation lies in a phenomenon mentioned by Bergh and Seppänen (2000: 295) in their study of pied-piping, namely 'notions of correctness derived from the grammar of Latin' (see also Hoffmann 2011: 76). At first glance, this might appear unlikely, given that one of the effects of pied-piping is to prevent the prepositional head from appearing to the right of its complement and much of Latin syntax is actually head-final (i.e. with the head to the right of the complement). In particular, Latin allowed complement–head order in both the verb phrase (the verb in relation to is object) and in the basic clause overall (the auxiliary in relation to the verb phrase). This gives the characteristic Object-Verb-Aux order that is often regarded as the basic pattern in Latin:

(101) ipse [...] hostium copias conspicatus est (Caes. *Gal.* 5.9)
       himself enemy's troops spotted AUX(PERF)-3.SING
       'he himself spotted the enemy's troops'

However, somewhat surprisingly, Latin exhibits a rigorous head-initial order within the prepositional phrase and there are no attested examples of preposition stranding. Thus preposition pied-piping was obligatory if the *wh* complement of a preposition was fronted. This is illustrated in the example below:

(102) Primum in filio, de quo commemoravi supra, suam vim exercuit.
       first in son, of whom I-made-mention earlier, her power exercised
       'First, she exercised her power over [his] son, of whom I made mention earlier.' (Nep. *Dion* 6, 2)

The equivalent formulation with preposition stranding – *quo commemoravi de* – is completely unattested in Latin.

Latin provides, then, a rather clear anti-stranding model. Moreover, as noted by Aitchison (2001: 9), Latin was widely admired in Britain in the eighteenth century, the period at which the anti-stranding principle began to acquire momentum. This was a legacy of its use as the language of the Church in the Middle Ages and as the language of scholarship from the Renaissance onwards and reflects a situation that was general in western Europe. So, although it is impossible to know for certain what was in the minds of the various prescriptive authorities that advocated preposition pied-piping, there is no obvious reason to disagree with Fowler (1926: 458) when he characterizes the anti-stranding principle as an unconscious attempt to 'deprive the English language of a valuable idiomatic resource, which has been used freely by all our greatest writers except those whose instinct for English idioms has been overpowered by notions of correctness derived from Latin standards'. The preposition pied-piping virus can thus be viewed as stemming from the belief that the English standard must approximate as far as possible to an admired linguistic model, viz. Latin. This in turn reflects a common component of the ideology of the standard, namely the belief that the standard language is or should be endowed with properties that are indicative of quality or excellence or which attract prestige.

Turning now to the Peninsular Spanish cleft structure, the evidence here suggests the associated virus reflects an assumption that the cleft with bare *que* is a Gallicism that somehow undermines the purity of Spanish. Note, for example, the characterization provided by the Colombian linguistic authority Rufino José Cuervo:

> Vamos à tratar del grande escollo no solo de los bogotanos sino de la mayor parte de los americanos, del *que* galicado por excelencia, del *que* contrapuesto mediante el verbo *ser* à adverbios y complementos.[35]
> (Cuervo 1907: 338)

While accepting that the prestige of the French language may have reinforced the use of the *que* cleft at a certain historical juncture, Dufter (2010) calls into question the idea that it is simply a syntactic calque of the corresponding French structure. As he rightly observes, the cleft with bare *que* was already present in Medieval Spanish, whereas the assumption that is implicit in the Gallic hypothesis is that post-Renaissance French supplied the model. In a sense, however, the veracity of the hypothesis is less relevant than the attitude it betrays, viz. a fear or rejection of French influence on the Spanish language. As noted earlier, that attitude runs deep in the fabric of Spanish intellectual discourse throughout the eighteenth and nineteenth centuries. Revealingly, in his defence of Latin American patterns of usage, the nineteenth-century Venezuelan grammarian Andrés Bello makes the following point:

> En ellas se peca mucho menos contra la pureza y corrección del lenguaje que en las locuciones afrancesadas, de que no dejan de estar salpicadas hoy día aun las obras más estimadas de los escritores peninsulares.[36]
> (Bello 1984/1847: 34)

Here, as in so many other places, we encounter the almost instinctive assumption not just that Gallic calques are invading the language but that they are detrimental to it. Thus while grammarians are happy to remodel linguistic behaviour on the basis of remote yet culturally sanctioned languages such as Latin, the opposite appears to be true when it comes to languages that are merely foreign. Influence from the latter simply dilutes the purity of the national language. Nevertheless, we can still detect the influence of the standard ideology insofar as the notion of purity is not ideologically neutral but rather implies a positive evaluation of the entity to which purity is attributed and a corresponding negative one of potential sources of contamination.

As regards French transitive past participle agreement, the initial motivation for the prescriptive rule appears to have been standardization in the strict sense, viz. the promotion of invariance in language structure (J. Milroy 2001: 531). The French perfect with *avoir* is the continuation of a Latin construction in which the participle always agreed in number and gender with the object. In the example below, *tua ...consilia* (the object) and *cognita* (the participle) are both neuter plural:

(103)   haberem a Furnio nostro tua penitus consilia cognita (Cic. *Fam.* 10.12.1)
        I-had from Furnius our your thoroughly plans found-out
        'I had learned of your plans in detail from our Furnius'

In French in the late medieval period, participle–object agreement had become variable. The effect of the *règle de position* discussed in 3.3.3.3 was to identify one pattern within this variability and to embed it within the standard grammar. However, by preserving participle–object agreement, albeit in a narrow range of circumstances, the rule also put an artificial brake on what appears to have been a process of long-term decline. The result appears to have been the classic freezing in place of an archaism, rendered all the more anomalous in this particular instance by the general loss of French gender and number morphophonology.

So much for the genesis of this particular virus. In contemporary French, its original motivation is long forgotten and its continued existence is arguably due to little more than linguistic inertia. Campbell (2008: 3), for example, poses the following question: 'Would it [...] be fair to conclude that the rule is being maintained on an Academy ventilator, not because it is useful, but because it is there?' Certainly, the docile absorption of the rule by the well-educated, together with its high profile in televised rituals such as Bernard Pivot's *Grande Dictée*, give the impression that its observance is ceremonial rather than spontaneous, suggesting that Campbell is basically right. This picture in fact reflects an important property of viruses, viz. that once they are embedded in the standard they become to a certain extent immovable. Moreover, this staying power is only to be expected. Languages that have been standardized are by nature more resistant to the causes of language change than those that have not been. Viruses, which are pure artefacts of standardization, can be predicted to offer rather extreme illustrations of this tendency.

Our three case studies thus show that both standardization proper and the existence of a concomitant standard language ideology can have the genesis of a virus as a by-product. Moreover, as just observed, viruses acquire a life of their own, leaving behind the reason for their genesis and merging seamlessly into the fabric of received usage. They thus give substance to a certain view of the standard language, according to which it is 'a precious inheritance that has been built up over the generations, not by the millions of native speakers, but by a select few who have lavished loving care upon it' (J. Milroy 2001: 537).

Notes

1. By the vulgar masses or at least by those who have no education.
2. Letter *h* that is unpronounced but which acts like a consonant for sandhi purposes.
3. The slow destruction of deference to the written language.
4. As in 2.4, we adopt the normal convention of using strikethrough font to indicate 'trace copies' of fronted *wh* expressions. These mark the so-called extraction site of the *wh* expression, the position that determines its grammatical function.
5. The strikethrough font on *was* has an analogous function to the strikethrough font on *whom* (see note 4). The intuition here is that the order of the subject *it* and the copula form *was* has been reversed in the formation of the question, given that direct questions in English exhibit subject–verb inversion.
6. By highlighting the viral nature of this construction, we are not in any way implying that it is ungrammatical or defective, merely that it represents a prestige addition to the core practice learned during infancy.
7. Obviously enough, it is the structural simplicity of this rule that leads to 'hypercorrections' such as *He went with Maria and I*. In Sobin's formulation, the rule is unable to discriminate between coordinate structures that are subjects and those that are objects. It thus over-extends.
8. Hoffman (2011: 80) argues that the fact that some children regarded the pied-piped relative clauses as grammatical indicates that 'the grammar of this small group of children (e.g. 3% of the 3–5 year olds) already includes this structure'. While this is true, it does not rule out that the structure is present in these children as a grammatical virus. The fact that *no* children spontaneously produce the structure while only a small minority of younger children accept it as grammatical should suffice to indicate it has a highly marginal status in this age group.
9. From *Catiline his conspiracy: A Tragoedie* (c. 1616).
10. A total of 57 British undergraduates at Newcastle University were asked in November 2011 to indicate which of (20a) and (20b) was more acceptable. All 57 choose (20a).
11. For an explanation of unpronounced copies, see the discussion at the beginning of 2.4.
12. In a subsequent paper (Radford and Felser 2011), Radford appears to reject this proposal. Radford and Felser state (p. 9) that the low frequency of preposition doubling in their corpus in comparison to preposition pruning (where the preposition is completely deleted) 'suggests that preposition copying is more likely to be a sporadic processing error than a productive spellout phenomenon'. The frequencies in question are 15 for copying and 67 for pruning. In our view, the adverse frequency ratio is not overwhelming. Moreover, an approach that treats

doubling as an error runs the risk of simply replicating the normative stance according to which preposition doubling is 'illogical', 'inelegant' or 'redundant'.

13. The proposal in the text implies that the preposition stranding resulting from *wh* movement and the stranding that arises in pseudo-passive sentences (e.g. *John was laughed at*) are separate phenomena. This would be consistent with the fact that some languages (e.g. Icelandic and Danish) allow *wh*-related stranding but not pseudo-passives. On this latter point see Maling and Zaenen 1985.

14. The form *el que* in this example is one of a series of compound relative pronouns consisting of a form of the definite article followed by *que*. It thus corresponds grammatically to English *who/whom*, as the morpheme by morpheme translation indicates.

15. Our remarks concerning the Peninsular cleft are not intended to apply when the clefted phrase is a subject or an object not introduced by the prepositional accusative (see Chapter 2, note 9). In that type of case – i.e. when the clefted item is a DP rather than a PP or some other adverbial – the divergence between Peninsular and Latin American usage is much less clearcut, in that the structure with bare *que* is stigmatized in both varieties (see e.g. Butt and Benjamin 2000: 509; Bentivoglio, De Stefano and Sedano 1999: 108).

16. The pronoun *él* 'him', with an accent on the *e*, should not be confused with the definite article *el* which forms part of the relative pronoun *el que*.

17. An apparent exception to this is when the reference is to a person, as in the example below:

(i) Con la que hablé fue con María.
    with whom I-spoke was with María
    'It was María that I spoke to.'

Here, however, *la que* does not agree directly with *María*. Analogously to Latin, Spanish often uses overtly masculine or feminine pronouns to refer implicitly to either male or female persons. For example, the feminine demonstrative *esta* in principle simply means 'this one', but it is often used to mean 'this woman' or 'this girl'. Similarly, the feminine relative pronoun *la que* 'which/who' can implicitly mean 'the woman/girl who'. This is how *la que* should be understood in the above example.

18. We assume that a variant of this virus is responsible for structures such as the following:

(i) Es allí donde viven.
    is there where they-live
    'It's there that they live.'

Here the clefted item is the adverb *allí*. We posit a virus that spells out the intermediate trace as the corresponding relative adverb, viz. *donde*.

19. In this and in fact the majority of cases, the agreement can only be manifested in the orthography. Thus feminine plural *prévues* is pronounced identically to masculine singular *prévu*. For the moment, we can regard the unpronounced *-e* and *-s* affixes as orthographic markers of abstract feature values (feminine and plural respectively).

20. French has two perfect auxiliaries, *avoir* 'have' and *être* 'be', the latter being reserved for unaccusative and reflexive verbs. Whereas the participle agrees with the object in the case of *avoir*, it agrees with the surface subject when the auxiliary

is *être*. While the two patterns have been argued to fall under the same generalization (Burzio 1986; Belletti 2001), we limit the discussion here to the case in which *avoir* is the auxiliary.

21. Other theoretical works that touch on this topic to varying degrees include Sportiche (1988), Ura (1993), Bošković (1997), Richards (1997), Déprez (1998) and Radford and Vincent (2007). We mention the latter later on in this section.
22. Our language has this principle, that the term that comes first willingly governs the following one.
23. In the whole of French grammar there is nothing that is more important or less well known.
24. An impediment to education.
25. It might be objected that the lexical specificity of the *règle de position* is in some sense accidental, a reflex of the fact that *avoir* is the only auxiliary for transitive past participles (excluding so-called transitive reflexives, which may or may not actually be transitive – see Reinhart and Siloni 2004). While this is certainly true, it does not alter the fact that the operation of the rule is lexically highly restricted. That this restrictiveness stems from considerations external to the rule itself is in our view incidental.
26. For ease of exposition we show *que* as having moved. More commonly it is claimed that *que* is actually a complementizer and that what moves is a null relative pronoun.
27. The normative principle that disallows agreement in this type of case (i.e. when the *wh* expression has been extracted from the infinitival complement of a verb like *dire* 'say', *croire* 'believe' etc.) is stated in Grevisse (1986: 1377).
28. Note, however, that when the complementizer *that* is deleted from the finite complement of a 'believe'-type verb in English, speakers may treat this finite complement as if it were non-finite. In that case, passivization of the subordinate subject does occur – see examples (50) to (52) in Chapter 2.
29. Kayne (1981: 361) proposes that infinitival complements of 'believe'-type verbs in French sometimes are and sometimes are not full clauses. Even if we accept that, the argument given in the main text here still applies, because for every case in which the infinitival complement was a full clause there would be a superficially identical one in which the infinitival complement was *not* a full clause. In the latter case, the impossibility (from a normative perspective) of participle–object agreement would be an instance of under-extension.
30. The past participle of *laisser* followed by an infinitive is henceforth invariable.
31. Like so much of modern Standard French, the prohibition on past participle agreement in relation to *faire* goes back to Vaugelas (1663: 143).
32. Depending on the precise analysis adopted, the problem also appears to affect verbs like *envoyer* 'send' and *mener* 'lead'. In the examples below (from Grevisse 1986: 1375–6), these verbs appear to have restructuring occurrences and yet the participle is invariable:

(i) Je les ai envoyé chercher.
   I them have sent-MASC.SING search-for-INF
   'I had them searched for.'

(ii) les brebis qu'on a mené égorger
   the ewes_FEM that+one has led-MASC.SING slaughter-INF
   'the ewes that one has led to be slaughtered'

33. As was mentioned at note 19, the majority of verbs in Modern French have phonologically invariant past participles. In those cases, there can be no phonetic manifestation of agreement. However, we can take the corresponding orthographic agreement to indicate a capability for such a phonetic manifestation in the given environment (i.e. it would occur if the participle had a rich enough morphology). From the production point of view, speakers in such cases presumably infer the agreement by analogy with cases in which agreement is manifested phonetically.

34. In a more technical account, this could be expressed in terms of Chomsky's Phase Impenetrability Condition (see D'Alessandro and Roberts 2008).

35. We are going to investigate the great threat faced not just by the inhabitants of Bogotá but by the majority of Latin Americans, namely the *que* that is prototypically Gallic, the *que* that is linked to adverbs and complements by means of the copular verb *ser*.

36. These constitute a much lesser violation of the purity and proper use of language than those French-style expressions that appear even in the best works of contemporary Peninsular writers. (Translation from Moré 2000: 62).

4
Language change

4.1 Introduction

In Chapter 2 we re-examined the notion of grammaticality, arguing that it was ultimately a projection or epiphenomenon of standardization. From that perspective, the grammar constructed by a professional linguist is simply an alternative codification to that provided by a normative grammarian, superior perhaps in terms of the quality of the analysis, but not fundamentally different in nature. The corollary of this view is that grammars themselves have no reality other than as analytical tools – an obvious point to many people, but one that is obscured in at least some approaches to language. In this chapter we examine the implications of this for diachronic linguistics. We start by considering the view that language change is intrinsically paradoxical. This perception, we argue, results from a false *a priori* assumption about the nature of language, an assumption stemming ultimately from the ideology of standardization. After that, in Section 4.3, we show how conceptualizing language change in terms of systemic change is problematic in a number of ways. As part of this, we examine the difficulties involved in reconciling the abruptness that is implicit in the notion of parameter resetting with the normally long timescales associated with diachronic change. In Section 4.4, we elaborate the notion that variation – and hence change too – is due primarily to the indexical nature of language; that is, the fact that it encodes social meaning for individual speakers. From that perspective, the notion of language change to a certain extent dissolves and what we are left with is simply innovative linguistic behaviour which sometimes does and sometimes does not converge across the speech community. In Section 4.5, we present three case studies (one phonological and two grammatical) from French which illustrate some of the ideas expressed earlier in the chapter. We conclude in Section 4.6 with a brief summary of our model of language change.

4.2 Two dogmas of standardization

In a recent volume, Detges and Waltereit refer to an apparent paradox:

> [I]f synchronically, languages can be viewed as perfectly running systems, then there is no reason why they should change in the first place. And yet, as everyone knows, languages are constantly changing. (Detges and Waltereit 2008: 1)

The above authors are alluding here to Coseriu's paradox of language change (Coseriu 1958: 7), but the basic question they invoke is arguably much older. Within formal theories of language, the commonest solution involves treating change as a by-product of acquisition (Andersen 1973; Lightfoot 1979, 1991, 1999, 2006). According to that approach, innovations arise when new speakers in infancy analyse the speech they hear around them – the Primary Linguistic Data (PLD) – in such a way that they adopt a linguistic system that differs marginally from the existing system. This difference between the system the learner acquires and the system of the speakers supplying the PLD could arise in effect through erroneous learning, under the assumption (due to Andersen 1973) that language acquisition is abductive (probabilistic) rather that deductive (strictly logical). What is envisaged is that acquirers use abduction to explain the observed PLD in terms of the fundamental laws of language (for example, Chomsky's Universal Grammar), the result being the linguistic system they adopt to govern their own linguistic behaviour. The probabilistic nature of abductive reasoning would open up the possibility of new acquirers (unwittingly) introducing innovations. Alternatively, the introduction of an innovation by learners during the acquisition phase might be due to a subtle change in the PLD, itself the result of a shift in the frequencies of certain types of sentence or to linguistic changes elsewhere in the system. Under either view, change results from a deficiency in transmission rather than a defect in the original system that somehow requires fixing, and thus the paradox of change dissolves.[1]

One issue that immediately arises in connection with the above solution to the paradox is the plausibility of the underlying assumption that language change – insofar as it relates to higher levels of linguistic structure – is generally confined to the acquisition phase. The empirical reliability of this claim is potentially less clearcut than is typically supposed,[2] but a revised perspective on the matter presupposes a conceptual shift in terms of what change actually is – a shift, in fact, of the sort we explore below. Thus we refrain from addressing this particular issue. Instead, we adopt a different approach, by questioning the validity of the conceptual framework within which the paradox is actually formulated. This framework, we want to suggest, does not reflect a purely neutral stance, but is (in part at least) an artefact of the standard ideology.

Notice that the paradox rests on the assumption that 'languages can be viewed as perfectly running systems'.[3] Change, then, is envisaged as a transition from one system to another (the paradox being, why should this happen if the system works to begin with?). Thus the basic conception is analogous to that of a finite state machine, that is, a machine that can be in one of a finite number of states, but is only in one state at a time.[4] This view of language as manifesting itself in a series of fixed states is widely held not just in historical linguistics but in theoretical linguistics generally. However, there is arguably nothing intrinsic to language that justifies it. The well-known fact of linguistic variation – the resolution of which often constitutes a change – means that at any given moment a language can embody multiple states. Moreover, this unstable quality becomes more apparent the more one looks beyond the confines of well-standardized modern languages. Early Medieval Spanish, for example, exhibits a degree of variation in morphophonology and syntax that would be unthinkable in a modern standardized language.[5] And it seems likely that this type of pattern is replicated throughout Old Romance, as well as in earlier Germanic varieties such as Old English. Indeed Pintzuk (1999) and others have argued that word order in Old English as observed in texts reflects the operation of multiple grammars.[6] Thus the conception of change as a transition from one fixed state to another tacitly assumes a degree of uniformity in language that may in reality be illusory.

In an insightful article, J. Milroy traces the idealized 'static' conception of languages to standardization:

> Apart from ideas of prestige and correctness, the most general assumptions that are conditioned by the [standard] ideology are that languages are uniform in structure, that they are stable and that they are finite-state entities. However, these are arguably not properties of real *languages* either – they are properties of idealized states of language, and they are, especially, properties of standard languages. (J. Milroy 2001: 545)

Why should this be the case? Here we can see the outcome as being inherent in the exercise of standardization itself. As noted by J. Milroy (2001: 531), 'standardization consists in the imposition of uniformity upon a class of objects'. Where the class of objects to be rendered uniform consists of different modes of linguistic usage, the task of standardization necessarily involves a process whereby the speech mode that is to serve as the standard model is demarcated and decisions are taken – sometimes arbitrarily – over what belongs to it and what does not. Moreover the latter process is continually renewed in various guises, ranging from school-level discussions about whether some instance of language use is 'grammatically correct' – i.e.

whether it falls within or outside the domain of the standard – to academic linguistic research whose terms of reference are overtly or covertly defined by the boundaries of the standard language. Thus the conception according to which a given language is a fixed and clearly delineated entity is a direct consequence of standardization, indeed it is the output that the standardization process was put in motion to achieve. The associated belief that such a conception captures a property that is replicated in languages or language generally – regardless of whether they have been standardized – can therefore be regarded as being part of that complex of beliefs that comprise the ideology of the standard. Hence it is ultimately the latter that lends significance to the question of how one static linguistic system can become transformed into another.

In addition to lacking the static character of an idealized standard language, linguistic practice that has not itself been standardized is much less rigidly segmented or compartmentalized than we in standard language cultures are used to thinking. J. Milroy (2001: 539–43) describes linguistic reality in a non-standardized universe, based in part on findings reported by Grace (1990, 1991, 1993) in connection with certain (non-standardized) Austronesian languages. A striking feature of this non-standardized universe is the fact that the boundaries implicit in the notion of *a* language are not realized in any clearcut fashion, because speakers conceive of their immediate linguistic reality in terms of 'pools of linguistic resources' (Grace 1981: 263–4) rather than as a discrete system. The contrast between this and the type of landscape we have become accustomed to in the more familiar setting of the standard language culture brings out a further component of the standard ideology, namely linguistic reification, the belief that language as a phenomenon is necessarily realized in the form of discrete languages. As with the (closely related) conception of languages as uniform and stable, this belief does not seem to reflect an intrinsic property of language. Mülhäusler (1996: 328), for example, echoes Grace when he states that the belief in the existence of separate languages is not helpful in the study of the traditional languages of the Pacific area. A similar claim could be made in respect of the linguistic situation that prevailed in Europe before linguistic standardization became the norm. For example, throughout much of the Middle Ages the vernacular speech varieties that descended from Latin (and which would eventually become the modern Romance languages) had neither distinct names nor distinct spelling systems.[7] Instead, such speech varieties were typically referred to using a nominalized reflex of the Latin adverb *romanice* 'in the Roman manner' and written communication was effected using a single code, viz. Latin, which speakers do not seem to have thought of as a distinct language from their own local variety of Romance. Apropos of the Iberian varieties of Romance, for example, Wright (1999: 29) argues that a conceptual distinction vis-à-vis Latin was not generally made by speakers until at least the eleventh century, after which Church-related reforms gave rise to the somewhat artificial pronunciation of written Latin known as Church Latin. Whereas the tendency before these reforms was to read out Latin using contemporary local pronunciation, which eventually came to conflict with the conservative Latin spelling (much as the modern pronunciation of a word like English *knee* is now somewhat divorced from the archaic spelling), practice after the reforms strove for a clearer sound–letter correspondence, which inevitably highlighted the disjunction between Latin and spoken Romance. In what is now France, the conceptual distinction appears to have arisen somewhat earlier, due to the ninth-century Carolingian reforms. Prior to this, however, we find a similar pattern whereby local speech, though no doubt different in many ways from other varieties of Romance, was for centuries capable of sharing an orthography with those other varieties and does not seem, in the minds of speakers, to have been regarded as a firmly separate entity.[8]

Thus the tendency to reify usage in the form of particular languages, or even dialects envisaged as quasi-languages, has its roots in standardization. We believe that reification is an additional cause of the widespread belief that linguistic change is paradoxical. This is because it fosters a conviction that the abstract models devised to account for observable usage in a particular language are as real – and arguably more basic – than the usage itself.[9] It seems to us that linguistic change *per se* is not empirically problematic, at least not in the terms in which the issue is expressed in the paradox of change. After all, changes in usage are simply changes in social behaviour and changes of the latter kind are not generally viewed as being somehow paradoxical. Language change only becomes conceptually problematic when viewed in terms of the abandonment of one system and the adoption of another. But such a process only makes sense if the model used to describe the relevant linguistic reality before the change and that used to represent it afterwards are viewed as real entities rather than simply analytical constructs.

Where language is not reified, the only rational approach to linguistic change is to regard it as a change in practice, and hence as fundamentally a social issue. However, perhaps because most linguists work in standard language cultures and thus allow assumptions stemming from the standard ideology to colour their research programmes, rather few scholars have considered in much detail the ways in which language change tracks social change. Even among sociolinguists, the emphasis has mostly been on how changes work through certain linguistic contexts, and by the agency of certain social groups. Any discussion of the relation between language variation or change and the social processes that can be presumed to be propelling it tends to be found appended, often in a rather perfunctory way, towards the end of the account of the linguistic phenomenon. Here, we explore theories of language variation and change that are relevant to the view that language change above all reflects social dynamics, in particular the speaker-based approach. In Chapter 5, we present a fine-grained analysis of how recent social changes have been reflected in language change. First, however, we consider in more detail how much academic research into language change suffers from what we term the standard language fallacy, a powerful doctrine that fuses the belief that languages are intrinsically uniform and stable with a tendency towards linguistic reification.

4.3   The illusion of systemic change

The effect of the approach just described is felt most keenly in treatments of syntactic change, perhaps because syntax itself is the linguistic discipline in which the vision of language as a self-sustaining system is most deeply entrenched – note for example Longobardi's (2001: 277–8) ponderous claim that '*syntax*, by itself, is diachronically completely inert'. Most significantly, the idealized conception of grammars based on notions of uniformity and stability leads to the view that syntactic change involves an abrupt jump from one discrete system to another. This way of looking at matters is in direct conflict with the normally long transitional periods that characterize syntactic change – at least in its observable manifestations – and hence results in the apparent problem of how to account for gradualness in language change.

Kroch (2001: 719) observes that '[s]tudies of syntactic change which trace the temporal evolution of the forms in flux universally report that change is gradual'. In a sense, this hardly needs stating, given that it would be difficult to envisage a syntactic change whose observable effects could somehow be realized within a sudden time frame. Nevertheless, it is worth considering a few individual case studies, just to get an idea of the generally very large time frames that are involved.

A particularly instructive case is that of the shift from head-final to head-initial word order that occurred in both the verb phrase and the tense/auxiliary phrase in English. Early Old English is assumed to have had a basic word order in which the object preceded the verb and the latter preceded the auxiliary (if present). This is illustrated in the examples below (the referencing of the source texts follows Healey *et al.* 2011):

(1)   Ac he sceal þa sacfullan gesibbian
      but he must the quarrelsome reconcile
      'but he must reconcile the quarrelsome'
      (ÆLet 2 (Wulfstan) B1.8.2 [0194 (188)]; cited in Pintzuk and Taylor 2006: 249)

(2)   ða se Wisdom ða ðis leoð [...] asungen hæfde
      when the wisdom then this song sung had
      'when Wisdom had sung this song'
      (Bo B9.3.2 [1322 (36.103.23)])

Both examples show a word order in relation to the verb and the object that is the mirror image of that which obtains in modern English. This is particularly striking in (2), where the object (*ðis leoð*), the verb (*asungen*) and the auxiliary (*hæfde*) are sequentially arranged in the order O-V-Aux, whereas modern English would have Aux-V-O. From this we can see that a major shift in word order has occurred.

However, if this shift is reflected in variation between the older and the newer word orders, then it seems to have been many centuries in the making. For example, using the figures provided by Pintzuk and Taylor (2006: 259, Table 11.9), we can derive an overall rate of preverbal placement for (non-pronominal) objects in early Old English (i.e. prior to 950 AD) of 58.5%.[10] This implies that objects were postverbal at a rate of 41.5%, which in turn suggests that the change to the newer VO system was already well under-way. Looking at the other end of the timescale, we know that the postverbal placement of objects did not become categorical until at least the mid 1400s (see van der Wurff 1999). Thus, on the basis of these facts, the process of displacement of OV order by VO order in English appears to have lasted for at least 600 years. Similarly detailed quantitative studies for the V-Aux to Aux-V word order shift do not appear to be available. However, a rather long period during which the two orders were both available can again be assumed. The newer Aux-V pattern is well-attested, for example, in Ælfric's *Lives of Saints*, which dates from the late tenth century. An example is given below:

(3)   þurh þa heo sceal hyre scippend understandan
      through which it must its creator understand
      'through which it must understand its creator'
      (ÆLS (Christmas) B1.3.2 [0068 (157)])

On the other hand, the older V-Aux pattern still appears to have been available (and not just as a marked stylistic operation) in early Middle English. In their study of five Middle English texts from the early thirteenth century, Kroch and Taylor (2000a) find 212 'surface INFL-final' (i.e. Aux-final) sub-ordinate clauses out of a total of 2198 (= 9.65%). Despite the label used by Kroch and Taylor, the clauses in question include both those in which the auxiliary is in absolute final position and those in which it merely follows the main verb. An example of the latter is given below in (4):

(4)   for ði ðat god isæd hadde to Adame: Morte morieris!
      because that God said had to Adam Morte morieris
      'because God had said to Adam "Morte morieris" '
      (Holthausen 1888: 105; cited Kroch and Taylor 2000a: 141)

In later Middle English, the frequency of V-Aux order declines but it clearly remains a possible option. Ohkado (2010) searched the entire Penn-Helsinki

Parsed Corpus of Middle English (Kroch and Taylor 2000b) for subordinate clauses with V-Aux order and reports the continued occurrence of (small numbers of) examples even towards the end of the ME period (fifteenth century). Taken together, these facts point towards a time frame of at least five centuries for the V-Aux to Aux-V transition.

Another rather striking example of gradual change relates to the placement of clitic object pronouns in Romance languages. The specific diachronic processes vary from one language to another, so we limit our discussion here to Spanish. The medieval language exhibits a basic system whereby, in main clauses, object pronouns are enclitic on the finite verb unless the latter is preceded by another (tonic) constituent, in which case they are proclitic (Penny 2002: 137). This is illustrated in the two thirteenth-century examples (5) and (6) below (in each case the clitic pronoun and its host verb are shown in bold):

(5) & **leuaron lo** a oña & **enterraron lo** çerca de su padre
& they-carried him to Oña & they-buried him near of his father
'and they carried him to Oña and buried him near his father'
(*Castigos e documentos de Sancho IV*; CDE)

(6) [...] e no mas esto **les otorgamos** ffasta los seys annos sobredichos.
and no more this to-them we-grant until the seven years aforesaid
'and we grant this only for the seven aforesaid years'
(*Documentos castellanos de Alfonso X - Murcia*; CDE)

Peripheral elements, such as preverbal locative or temporal adverbials, are effectively invisible to the operation that chooses between enclisis and proclisis. This means that the object clitic follows the verb in examples such as the following (also from the thirteenth century), even though the verb is not sequentially the first constituent:

(7) sobre esto **dixeron les** que [...]
upon this they-said to-them that
'after this they said to them that ...'
(*Gran conquista de Ultramar*; CDE)

Adapting some of the ideas in the literature (see in particular Rivero 1991, 1993), the pattern just outlined can be analysed in terms of the clitic being in Chomsky's Infl position, now referred to as T (for 'Tense'). This is the position reserved in languages like English for finite auxiliaries as well as the infinitive marker *to*. In examples like (6) above, i.e. when the object pronoun is proclitic, the finite verb can also be analysed as being in T, implying that the clitic is syntactically incorporated to it. In examples like (5) and (7), the verb can be regarded as moving out of T and across the clitic into the clausal edge, as shown schematically below:

(8) levaron lo ~~levaron~~ a oña

The movement operation shown in (8) is a reflex of the Tobler-Mussafia law, according to which clitics in Old Romance could not occupy first position in main clauses. Cases like (7) fall under the same generalization if, as proposed above, peripheral items such as preverbal temporal adjuncts are understood as being in some sense clause-external. Rephrasing the generalization somewhat, we can say that Old Spanish clitics require a phonological host to their left.

In Modern Spanish, enclisis on an inflected form of the verb is only possible with imperatives. This implies that the verb movement operation illustrated in (8) is no longer possible in declarative clauses. Conversely, clitics in Modern Spanish no longer require a phonological host to their left and hence occur freely in sentence-initial position, as is illustrated in the example below:

(9) **Lo iban** a mandar a Portugal [...]
      him they-were-going to send to Portugal
      'They were going to send him to Portugal ...'
      (Salvador Garmendia, *Los pies de barro*, 1973; CDE)

Thus the syntax of Spanish object clitics has undergone a fundamental transformation. While the availability of a clitic position that is adjacent to the finite verb has remained constant,[11] the need for the clitic to have a phonological host to its left, with the associated possibility for the verb to be placed in front of the clitic, has completely disappeared from declarative clauses.

As with word order in English, however, the transformation process was accompanied by a long period of overlap between the older and newer systems. As early as the thirteenth century, for example, while we do not find clitics in absolute first position, it is not uncommon for them to occur in main clauses preceded only by the atonic coordinating conjunction *e/y* or *&* which in theory should not be a viable phonological host. In the extract below, for example, we have three consecutive independent clauses joined by *y* or *&*, but in each case the object pronoun is proclitic in relation to the finite verb:

(10) **yle mandara** el padre matar por ello. & **le colgaron** los escuderos en
       el mont & **lo leuo** ell Rey Polibio
       and+him ordered the father kill for this & him left the servants on the
       hill & him carried-away the king Polybus

'and the father ordered him to be killed because of this and the serv-
ants left him on a hillside and King Polybus took him away'
(*General estoria* II; CDE)

Conversely, as late as the nineteenth century, it is still possible for object
pronouns to be enclitic on a declarative verb (although this is by now a
minority option). In the example below, there are three conjoined clauses,
of which the first two exhibit pronominal enclisis and the third proclisis:

(11) **Fuele** a ver sin embargo a su encierro, **diole** todavía el nombre de hijo,
      y **le consoló** [...]
      he-went+him to see nevertheless in his prison, gave+him still the
      name of son, and him consoled
      'He nevertheless went to see him in prison, continued to call him his
      son and consoled him ...'
      (Manuel José Quintana, *Vidas de los españoles célebres*, 1814; CDE)

Thus while the newer system is already partially visible in the thirteenth
century, remnants of the older system can be found as late as the nineteenth
century. Examples such as the above imply a period of about 600 years for
the change to run its full course. Moreover, the change across this period
appears to have been gradual from a quantitative point of view. We can get
an idea of this by tracking the frequency across the centuries of enclisis of
the 3rd-person singular dative/accusative pronoun *le* on preterite forms of
the verb (other than *di*, which is ambiguous between 'I said' and imperative
'say!'). This obviously does not give an exhaustive picture but we can expect
it to be fairly representative of Spanish object clitics in general. The results
are shown in Table 4.1, which shows quite a steep early decline into the
fifteenth century followed by a more gradual decline after the sixteenth century. In fact, if we interpret the decline of enclisis as implying a corresponding increase in linguistic behaviour that conforms to the modern system,
the pattern of change reflected in the table is essentially that of the classic
S-curve, which is familiar from variationist studies of language change.

Table 4.1 Enclisis of Spanish *le* on preterite forms of the verb (data from Corpus del
Español)

Century	13th	14th	15th	16th	17th	18th	19th
Tokens per million words	716.83	717.34	217.61	92.93	28.11	6.72	5.44

To summarize, then, both the English O-V-(Aux) to (Aux)-V-O change and
the Spanish change in the placement of object clitics are manifested indis-
putably as gradual changes, illustrating the more general point made by
Kroch cited at the beginning of this section. However, despite the apparent

gradualness of syntactic change, there is in the field of diachronic syntax a deeply held conviction that syntactic change is in fact sudden or, to use Lightfoot's (1979, 1991) term, 'catastrophic'. Roberts (2007) expresses this view very persuasively in the following quotation:

> [...] gradual change from one value of a parameter to another is simply impossible: a parameter must be in one state or the other; it cannot be in between [...] This is really a matter of logic, not linguistics: the Law of the Excluded Middle ($p \vee \neg p$) is the relevant concept. Any system which appears to be 'semi-null subject' or 'tendentially VO' [...] must be analyzed as being one thing or the other; strictly speaking, no system can be in a state intermediate between two parameter values. This conclusion holds for any approach to linguistics which makes use of discrete categories, for example, grammatical categories such as verb, noun etc., or phonemes of the usual type. (Roberts 2007: 295–6).

Here Roberts is assuming the model of Principles and Parameters, which developed from Chomsky (1981). The basic assumption in that framework is that what is actually possible in language is limited to a finite set of principles (fundamental operations), with differences between languages being attributable to different settings on parameters (axes of possible variation across languages). Both the principles and the parameters are claimed to be somehow built into the fabric of the human brain, and from early infancy children abduce the specific parameter settings of their native tongues from the speech they hear around them. From that perspective, individual languages are essentially aggregates of parameter settings operating in conjunction with a common core of fundamental principles. Importantly, parameters are viewed as being binary, in that a given language has either a positive or a negative setting for each parameter. Thus if syntactic change represents change from one parameter setting to another, it must by definition be accomplished in one punctual step, with no intermediate transitional stage. In support of this approach, Roberts goes on to cite a remark from Hockett that appears to make the same claim in relation to phonological change:

> Sound change itself is constant and slow. A phonemic restructuring, on the other hand, must in a sense be absolutely sudden. (Hockett 1958: 456–7)

In order not to give the impression that we are concerned with individual theorists rather than approaches to change, we refer to the view articulated by Roberts (but deeply embedded in diachronic syntax generally) as the Abruptness Assumption. As was just noted, this stems from the belief that grammars are largely aggregates of discrete objects (parameters set in one way or the other). There is in reality no fact of nature that forces or even justifies this way of looking at matters. Rather, its widespread adoption is covertly ideological. For, in spite of its apparently atomistic character, the parameters-based approach is ultimately a modern implementation of the idealized conception of languages as stable and uniform. Stable in the sense that parameter settings are not subject to variation, and uniform in the sense that such settings apply uniformly to all associated surface grammatical phenomena. In approaches that are more overtly ideological, the project of distilling a fixed entity from fluid linguistic practice is carried out by specifying a body of rules, some prescriptive, some descriptive. Though more sophisticated in terms of its analytical capability, the parameters approach achieves the same fundamental effect through the notion of 'either–or' settings. Moreover, most parametric analyses of standardized languages largely take for granted the basic descriptive data embodied in the normative canon, with the result that parametric analysis consists largely in replacing the ad hoc rules of received grammar with a more refined conceptual apparatus. Thus while the exponents of modern diachronic syntax would no doubt deny that they are in hock to any unmotivated postulate, the central proposition that syntactic change is necessarily abrupt is no more than a theorem derived from ideological axioms.

Given this, it is legitimate to ask whether the Abruptness Assumption can be reconciled with the abundant evidence that syntactic change is actually gradual. Roberts himself (2007: 376) proposes the following as factors that 'cushion' the effects of abrupt syntactic change, thus giving the illusion of gradualness:

(i) sociolinguistic factors relating to diffusion
(ii) microparametric change and variation
(iii) the possibility of competing grammars
(iv) true formal optionality.

We examine each of these below, though not in the order in which they are listed above.

Taking (iv) first, the basic idea behind this notion is that some syntactic operations are genuinely optional, giving rise to variation in usage. If the balance of frequencies between the variants changes over time, this gives the impression of gradual syntactic change, but in reality there is no change in the actual syntax. However, the concept of formal optionality appears to be limited to a very specific case, viz. that in which syntactic variation arises from the joint availability of pied-piping and stranding (see Roberts 2007: 308). Formal optionality thus lacks general applicability and could not, on its own, bridge the gap between the Abruptness Assumption and the fact that syntactic change is always overtly manifested as a gradual process.

As regards **(ii)** this would account for staggered diachronic changes, for example in relation to auxiliary selection in Romance, where apparently gradual variation and/or change could be seen as being finely segmented into discrete patterns or stages – each one corresponding to a microparameter – and thus would not, strictly speaking, be gradual (see Roberts 2007: 300–5). This again would have limited application, given that the parametric approach tends in the opposite direction, in that it seeks to map multiple change phenomena to single underlying parameters rather than vice versa. Indeed, in practice, the majority of the long-term changes highlighted in the literature assume that a single parameter is involved. For example, the spread of auxiliary *do* in English to a range of interrogative and negative contexts, as well as the loss of certain types of verb-adverb order (e.g. *Quene Ester looked never with swich an eye*), is attributed by Kroch (2001: 719–21) to the resetting of a single parameter (viz. the one that determines whether the finite verb moves to the T position, as it is typically assumed to do in modern Romance languages, for example).

Therefore, as general mechanisms for reconciling the Abruptness Assumption with the fact that overt change is invariably gradual, we are left with **(i)** and **(iii)**. As regards **(i)**, this implies that syntactic variation and change can be reduced to variation and change of the sort studied within the Labovian paradigm. This is because parameters are conventionally envisaged as features of abstract or 'functional' syntactic heads which, like more familiar lexical heads can be regarded as being located in the lexicon. From that perspective, having a particular setting for a given parameter would be analogous to having a particular pronunciation for a given vocabulary item (although the parameter setting would have a vastly more 'leveraged' effect on the speaker's output). For example, let us assume that the parameter responsible for determining whether a language has OV or VO word order resides in v^*, which is the abstract head of v^*P, the transitive verb phrase taken together with its left periphery.[12] Furthermore if, following Chomsky and many others, we use the acronym 'EPP' to designate a movement-triggering feature (see Landau 2007),[13] then OV languages are those in which v^* is [+EPP] and VO languages are those in which v^* is [–EPP]. Thus a linguistic community that exhibited OV ~ VO variation would be one in which some speakers had the [+EPP] variant of v^* while others had the [–EPP] variant. In order for such a community to drift definitively towards VO order, the [–EPP] variant of v^* would have to become diffused among all speakers, at the expense of the [+EPP] variant. As has been demonstrated repeatedly in quantitative studies of linguistic change, the complete diffusion of a variant across speech communities is a gradual process, typically conforming to the logistic or 'S-curve' function. On the other hand, for any individual speaker the transition from OV to VO order, i.e. the resetting of the EPP parameter on v^* from [+] to [–], would be abrupt (presumably a function of imperfect acquisition in infancy). In this way, the sociolinguistics of diffusion would mask the abruptness of the syntactic change itself.

However, as Kroch (2001: 722) observes, the variation associated with diachronic syntactic change is found not just across different texts but also *within* individual texts. This implies that the relevant variation is located in individual speakers and not merely the population as a whole. On the other hand, as we saw earlier in the Roberts quotation, the Abruptness Assumption is part of a wider theoretical approach that explicitly denies system-internal syntactic variation, at least to the extent that the opposing variants represent alternative settings for the same parameter (e.g. v^* that is both [+EPP] and [–EPP]).[14] Thus if each speaker operates with a single system – a single grammar of the language in question – then mechanism (i) cannot be used to reconcile assumed abruptness with observed gradualness.

Therefore, in order to save mechanism (i), we are forced to also adopt mechanism (iii), viz. the possibility of competing grammars. This idea is proposed in Kroch 1989 and Kroch 1994 and can be found in much subsequent work stemming from those papers (see in particular Pintzuk 1999, 2005, Pintzuk and Taylor 2006). The competing grammars approach imputes observable syntactic variation (at least that which reflects alternative parameter settings) to the co-existence of minimally distinct but nevertheless mutually incompatible grammars. The relevant grammars compete not just at the level of the speech community but also within individual speakers or authors. Note, for example, Kroch's (2001: 722) remark: 'it is necessary to allow for syntactic diglossia within individual authors as the normal situation during a period of change'. From this perspective, the apparent gradualness of change results from the slow shift in the relative frequencies of use attaching to each of the grammars that comprise the diglossia, as one drives out the other.

It is possible then, provided we accept Kroch's notion of grammar competition, to have one's diachronic cake and eat it, to simultaneously recognize that syntactic change is typically gradual in its observable manifestations and yet to insist that syntactic change is necessarily abrupt (a sudden jump from one system to another). Arguably, however, Kroch's postulation of multiple grammars is too high a price to pay. For here we see the conception of grammars as stable and uniform coming into direct conflict with the brute empirical fact of grammatical variation. But instead of seeing this as evidence that grammars under this conception are no more than an idealization – and hence are not actually *real* – the proposed solution consists in multiplying the idealizations and thus arguably compounding the initial mistake. In any case, given that languages may show variation in respect of more than one parameter, the competing grammars approach would have to allow potentially for speakers of a particular language to be using, in Harris and Campbell's (1995: 86) words, 'a plethora of grammars'.

More importantly, perhaps, the notion that gradual quantitative shifts are epiphenomenal upon abrupt systemic changes forces strange conclusions in cases where the direction of the quantitative shift does not directly match the direction of the apparent underlying syntactic change. Such patterns are commoner than is typically assumed, but they receive less attention than unidirectional changes because it is the latter rather than the former which supply the basic narrative of the history of any particular language (this bias is also driven by ideology, but we refrain from commenting on that issue in detail here). To illustrate the phenomenon we have in mind, we can again turn to the system of clitic placement in Spanish. However, this time the point of interest is clitic placement in infinitival clauses (headed by a preposition), as opposed to finite declarative clauses. In the infinitival clause, in both Old and Modern Spanish the linguistic constraints are rather different from those that apply to finite clauses and, as a consequence, the historical developments are also different.

In infinitival clauses (i.e. those headed by a prepositional complementizer), Modern Spanish categorically requires enclisis (e.g. *para decirle* 'in order to tell him/her'), whereas Medieval and Renaissance Spanish exhibited variation between enclisis and proclisis (*para le decir*). We can again track the behaviour of the system overall by considering the 3rd-person singular dative/accusative clitic *le*. Quantitative data for the thirteenth to the eighteenth centuries are given in Table 4.2.

Table 4.2 Placement of *le* in infinitival clauses headed by a preposition (data from Corpus del Español)

Century	13th	14th	15th	16th	17th	18th
Enclisis (%)	67.45	17.59	16.54	83.36	99.43	99.21
Proclisis (%)	32.55	82.41	83.46	16.64	0.57	0.79
N (total tokens)	553	381	937	6828	6510	3683

Table 4.2 shows that at the earliest stage for which we have reliable data, the thirteenth century, enclisis was significantly commoner than proclisis. Given that enclisis (in the relevant context) is categorical in Modern Spanish, we would be inclined to expect on the basis of just the thirteenth-century data that the direction of change overall was towards the elimination of proclisis. But that narrative is completely belied by what happens in the fourteenth and fifteenth centuries, during which proclisis is very significantly in the ascendancy. From a purely quantitative perspective, this pattern is interesting but not problematic. A social trend – a fashion, in effect – went in one direction for a while and then in the opposite direction. Why this happened is a social rather than a linguistic question. However, if we are committed to the view that underneath gradual quantitative movements in the frequencies of competing variants lie abrupt systemic changes, an obvious question here is what is the pattern of change in this particular case?

It is not clear which of the two variants, enclisis or proclisis, represents conservative usage in the thirteenth century. Let us entertain first the assumption that proclisis represents the newer parameter setting, which we will designate schematically as a positive value for feature [β] on functional head H, i.e. H that is [+β]. Accordingly, at some unspecified moment during or before the thirteenth century, H in Spanish changed from being [−β] to being [+β]. The picture of variation we see in the thirteenth and subsequent centuries would then reflect the 'cushioning' effect of the sociolinguistic diffusion of this change. However, given the subsequent loss of proclisis, it has to be inferred that the Spanish syntax subsequently underwent exactly the opposite change, i.e. H became [−β] again. But in what sense did this latter change actually take place? The data clearly indicate that in the thirteenth century and for a long time afterwards both parameter settings were available – in the sense that both enclisis and proclisis were available – so we would in effect be claiming that a parameter was reset to an already existing value.

Let us now entertain the alternative assumption, viz. that enclisis represents the newer parameter setting in the thirteenth century. This implies that at some point during or before the thirteenth century, H went from being [+β] to being [−β]. Moreover, given that enclisis is categorical in Modern Spanish, the natural assumption would be that H remained [−β] throughout the Middle Ages and into the modern period. This avoids the problem of having to posit a return to a parameter setting that never actually went away, but now we are faced with a situation in which the putative underlying change – i.e. H [+β] > H [−β] – is associated for two centuries (fourteenth and fifteenth) with a pattern of diffusion that is indicative of the very opposite change (i.e. H [−β] > H [+β]).

Under either assumption, then, the type of pattern exhibited by the data in Table 4.2, which is not in practice uncommon, does not seem to be elucidated by the idea that observable long-term quantitative shifts mask abrupt underlying systemic changes. In fact, were one not wedded to the idea that grammatical practice always maps on to a static and uniform system, the most natural way of interpreting the data would be in terms of loss of variation, rather than in terms of change from one discrete parameter setting to another. And indeed, given that the accusative and dative Latin pronouns from which the Spanish object clitics descend did not have a fixed position in relation to the infinitive, it is quite likely that both the proclitic and enclitic options were always available in infinitival clauses. In other words, variation was built into linguistic usage from the outset. From that perspective, subsequent developments would not directly reflect any systemic change at all. They would merely be drifts in the balance of frequencies, reflecting sociolinguistic trends that cannot be reconstructed at this distance. The final loss of proclisis would then in a sense be accidental, the end state to a negative quantitative drift but not one triggered by any systemic reorganization.

It is instructive at this point to reconsider the quotation from Hockett given earlier:

> Sound change itself is constant and slow. A phonemic restructuring, on the other hand, must in a sense be absolutely sudden. (Hockett 1958: 456–7)

As was mentioned earlier, this is cited by Roberts in support of his claim that change from one discrete system to another is necessarily abrupt. However, another way of interpreting Hockett's remark is as a comment on the relationship between reality and the analyst's construal of reality. The reality in question would be the constant and slow stream of sound change. A phonemic restructuring would then be no more than an analyst's waypoint, a position in the constant stream of change at which it ceases to be plausible to analyse the synchronic data in terms of phonemic system *a* and a new system *b* has to be put forward. The final outcome of the competition between pronominal enclisis and proclisis in Spanish infinitival clauses should be seen as being entirely analogous to this. In other words, in a reversal of the normal assumption, any discrete systemic changes that may be said to have occurred are epiphenomenal and it is the observable quantitative drifts that constitute the basic diachronic reality (or at least a first approximation to it). Put another way, the primary locus of linguistic change is the relevant community of speakers and it is only in a secondary sense, essentially metonymic or symbolic, that change can be said to have occurred in a particular language. The general conclusion, then, is that abruptness is located in the passage from one analytical model to another and not in anything that is actually part of the linguistic landscape. Led astray, however, by a prevailing ideology that requires languages and their component grammars to be viewed as discrete objects, linguists working in the field of diachronic syntax have tended to reify their analytical models and hence confuse them with linguistic reality.

In the non-standardized universe alluded to at the beginning of this chapter, there arises neither the problem of gradualness nor the potentially problematic solution just discussed. As indicated, the gradualness problem (such as it is) stems from the belief that grammatical systems are discrete and finite entities and thus transitional stages are logically impossible. However, where conceptual boundaries between language varieties are not clearly delineated (as is the case among non-standardized languages) this 'either–or' approach to grammatical systems is not a natural one. Indeed, variation at all levels, including syntax, is the normal state of affairs rather than something that requires explanation. In such a context, the concept of syntactic change reduces to change in the balance of frequencies between competing variants and thus there is no *a priori* exclusion of gradualness. Rather, as with all quantitative social change, gradualness is what is expected. In reality, as the case studies presented above demonstrate, syntactic change is exactly like this even in well-studied languages like English and Spanish. But here we see the covert influence of the standard ideology, in that for these and similar languages, analysts insist on positing an underlying catastrophic event, a moment when one fixed system became transformed into another.

In the discussion below, we attempt to break out of the conventional standard language mindset. Our approach thus implies that language change cannot be analysed in terms of sudden changes from one stable and discrete system to another. What is required, instead, is an unpacking of the quantitative drifts alluded to above. In theory, these could result from purely random factors. As we discuss below, however, it is more plausible to assume that what underlies upswings (or downswings) in the popularity of a given variant is the way it is socially indexed. From that point of view, language change is the expression of a language ideology. This view contrasts with the broadly structural approach discussed above, in which change is analysed in terms of ideologically neutral transitions from one fixed system to another. Somewhat paradoxically, then, the latter approach, which we have characterized as being covertly ideological in its initial assumptions, sees change as non-ideological, whereas the (hopefully) non-ideological approach adopted here takes the converse view. In a sense, this outcome is not unexpected, given that both language and its analysis are ultimately social behaviours and also that ideology – in one form or another – is a pervasive driver of social comportment.

4.4 Motivations of linguistic change

4.4.1 Introduction

As was mentioned in the previous section, long-term patterns of quantitative variation, though more real than systemic transformations, are no more than a first approximation to the underlying etiology of change. For in order for quantitative shifts to be observable at the macro level of the community overall, it must be the case that many individual speakers are converging in their behaviour. This leads inevitably to a recognition that variation (and hence change) is a speaker-based process. This view is in fact more or less axiomatic in sociolinguistics (although it is not always followed through to its logical conclusion). Trudgill, for example, makes the point in the following way:

> Obviously, languages without speakers do not change. Linguists, however, have not always drawn the correct conclusion from this truism, namely that it is speakers who change languages. A language changes as a result of what its speakers do to it as they use it to speak to one another in everyday face-to-face interactions. (Trudgill 1992: iv)

We can question the (abductive) logic implicit in this ('Languages without speakers do not change, therefore speakers change languages having speakers') but the underlying idea is certainly correct.

Speaker-based change often figures as one term in an apparent dichotomy between change that has a source that is 'external' to language and change that is 'endogenous' or internally motivated. As we saw in 4.3, however, internal changes that are purely structural – parameter resettings, phonemic restructurings and the like – are merely analytical constructs and hence cannot be adduced in any explanatory capacity. Thus endogenous change, to the extent that it plays a causal role, must ultimately be propelled by speaker-based factors, but of types that are less overtly external than factors that reflect speakers' tacit sensitivity to the social indexing of linguistic variants. Examples might include pragmatic factors such as expressivity or the resolution of ambiguity, together with processing considerations, in the case of syntax for example, or acoustic and articulatory constraints in the case of sound change. Even these, however, might also on closer scrutiny turn out to be largely irrelevant to the etiology of change.

J. Milroy points out (2003: 219) that a distinction between innovation and change can usefully be invoked where the difference between internal (endogenous) and external (or exogenous, or speaker-based) explanations is in question. Whereas innovations may be endogenous or exogenous, change itself implies borrowing – from speaker to speaker or group to group – making it a necessarily exogenous process. Milroy has the example of (th)-fronting in contemporary English, a process – currently on an upward quantitative trajectory – whereby the interdental fricatives [θ] and [ð], as in the initial sounds of *thin* and *then*, are replaced by the labiodentals [f] and [v]. He points out that an endogenous 'explanation' is possible, based on factors like the following: the rarity of [θ] and [ð] across languages generally; their late acquisition in children's speech; their lack of perceptual salience and hence their tendency to be confused with [f] and [v] (the latter 'explanation' is incidentally puzzling in view of the apparent social salience of the variables in question). However, these endogenous factors do not in themselves explain the adoption of (th)-fronting in a given speech community at a given moment, since [θ] and [ð] are also found in competition with the stops [t] and [d] in some communities, with zero in others (some Belfast speech communities), and have no competing variants in yet others. In Milroy's formulation (2003: 217), 'for the variationist [...] *a sound change does not get initiated in a 'language'; it takes place in a community of speakers*' [emphasis in original]. In this perspective, it is the exogenous process of borrowing that realizes the change in the community of speakers. Moreover, this propagation through borrowing need not be unidirectional: the innovation may or may not be adopted by other speakers, it may be adopted for a time but may then recede, and so forth.

Note that our insistence on the central role of individual speakers does not imply any intentionality behind language change. Keller's (1994) analysis is useful in this connection, as it provides illuminating parallels between language change and other phenomena 'of the third kind'. The latter are situated in a tripartition that distinguishes between, firstly 'natural' phenomena like flowers, rivers, bee language, etc., while 'artificial' phenomena, the result of human agency, subdivide further into the second category of 'artificial-artificial' (Esperanto, paper flowers, the Morse alphabet) and the third, 'artificial-natural' (the English language, the French Franc, the Latin alphabet). These are some of Keller's examples (1994: 60). Phenomena of the third kind are accordingly neither accidental nor planned, but are those which 'resemble natural phenomena in that they are unintended' but 'resemble artificial phenomena in that they are the result of human action' (Haakonssen 1981: 24, cited in Keller 1994: 59). In this analysis, language, and language change, are 'artificial-natural' in arising through unintended human agency. It is fairly obvious that no language change is intended (leaving aside language planning), but arises from other causes. Other, dysfunctional, examples of phenomena of the third kind discussed by Keller are traffic jams and monetary inflation. In these examples too, outcomes are produced by actions having quite other intentions; it is immediately clear that motorists would avoid causing a traffic jam if they could, and that they perform no action with the intention of causing one. A further parallel is that many language users view language change as undesirable or in some sense problematic (note the discussion of the 'paradox of change' in 4.1 above).

Keller's view of language change as a phenomenon of the third kind is useful because it enables a clear distinction to be drawn between cause, intention and mechanism. From that perspective, we can dispense with any discussion of human intentions that cause language change by concentrating rather on the motivations propelling language variation, since we assume that change arises without volition from socially driven variation, as J. Milroy's discussion, laid out above, makes clear. We examine therefore in this section the social aspects of changes driven by speaker-based factors, defining these more narrowly as 'social' or 'sociolinguistic', where both of these terms imply a pattern of indexing that is oriented in respect of a determinate 'language ideology' (Silverstein 1979). We understand the latter concept in a broad sense, so that the relevant frame of reference may be localized to a particular community (as in the case of the 'local ideologies' discussed in L. Milroy 2003), or it may be more general, as with the range of beliefs and attitudes that swirl around the notion of the standard language. Overall, then, language variation (which may or may not lead to change) is envisaged as a by-product of the fact that speakers use language to construct their social identity.

4.4.2 Mechanisms governing the construction of social identity

One question that the foregoing approach raises is what the mechanisms might be that enable language to be used in this way. This is an issue that tends not to have been extensively addressed within the main sociolinguistic research paradigm, the Labovian or quantitative approach. This point was highlighted by Cameron (1990), who argues that nothing is explained by simply correlating social facts and linguistic facts, an analytical procedure she refers to as the 'correlational fallacy'. However, since the publication of Cameron's paper, more recent sociolinguistic research has taken a more fine-grained approach to the construction of identity through variable language. Much of this research has concentrated on gender identity (one overview of the literature on gender identity is Hall and Bucholtz 1995); for instance, Holmes (1997) has pointed out the advantages inherent in a multi-layered approach to the study of the sociolinguistic gender pattern (SGP: the different orientation of men and women towards the standard language) which integrates the micro (quantitative) level, macro (discourse) and style dimensions of linguistic analysis.[15] She discusses data from New Zealand English that show speakers aligning their linguistic behaviour, both on the micro level of variable phonology and on the macro level of language use that is the province of qualitative analysis.

One of the examples Holmes discusses is that of a middle-aged, middle-class New Zealand woman relating a narrative about her father and daughter to a friend: Holmes argues that the tone of the conversation was 'conservative' because the speaker was engaged in what Holmes terms an 'act of gender identity' that consisted in the speaker's presentation of herself as a conscientious mother and daughter. By 'tone' is meant here the attitude adopted by the speaker to the topic under discussion; clearly, any topic can in principle be discussed using a tone that is solemn, facetious, sarcastic, etc., although in practice speakers are constrained in their choice of tone, perhaps principally by the relationship they have with their addressee. In Holmes's data this conservative orientation was observable on the discourse level through the structure of the narrative as well as the use of various discourse particles. The speaker's linguistic behaviour on the phonological level was also consistent with this act of self-presentation; she showed a probabilistic use of some salient New Zealand phonological variables that aligned very closely with the figures, derived from independent studies, typical of her social group. Given the very generally shared assumptions in her milieu concerning the range of acceptable attitudes towards the social roles of mother and daughter, this aspect of the speaker's persona was almost necessarily situated toward the conservative end of what might be termed a 'conservative–subversive' continuum of conversational tone. This is true even though the conversation was 'informal' in the sense of taking place between two intimates. Holmes points out at the same time the need to bear in mind that this analysis of a stretch of gender-conditioned linguistic behaviour is a snapshot, and that speakers are continually engaged in a process of 'construction' of their gender identity (in this example) that leads them to present different aspects of this identity in response to various motivating factors: 'gender identity is constantly being constructed and people may reinforce norms at one point, but challenge and contest them at others' (1997: 209). This view, emphasizing the dynamic nature of gender differentiation language, presents the SGP as a process of continual accommodation and adjustment, rather than a stasis responding to a binary opposition (male–female) and remaining constant across all speech communities and situations.

An approach of this kind is clearly very different from the broad-brush perspective characteristic of much of the earlier sociolinguistic work that is concerned with inferring change from variation. It is innovative in studying an individual speaker, in integrating 'micro-variation' at the level of individual sounds and 'macro-variation' at the sentence level and beyond, and in focusing on the continuing construction of identity in a dynamic way. Implicit in this approach moreover is an acknowledgment that the various aspects of a speaker's identity can interact in complex ways; one's 'gender identity' is clearly not a uniplex construct, and when, as in the above example, it is in process of construction within what we called a 'conservative–subversive' continuum of conversational tone, this implies other aspects of identity like 'mother' and 'adult'.

We emphasized above some of the positive aspects of the approach exemplified by Holmes's analysis, but it does take as given a correlation between the use of phonological variables and the presentation of a certain social identity. As Cameron points out (1990: 85), this correlation is itself in need of explanation; or we can add that it may be, depending on the nature of the research programme being pursued. Taking the example of variable /r/ in New York City, Cameron remarks:

> [...] it could be claimed that my score for the variant [r] is explained by the fact that I belong to a particular social category – say, working-class women of Italian descent aged 50+ and living in New York City – and am speaking in a particular context, say a formal interview with a linguistic researcher.

Cameron presents this 'explanation' as an example of the 'correlational fallacy' and argues that in fact nothing is explained thereby. The main burden of Cameron's criticism seems to be that it is difficult to see how abstract social attributes like class, situated at the 'macro', ascribed, impersonal, institutional level of society and perhaps not an immediate reality for many speakers, affect a speaker's linguistic behaviour. Regarding the correlation of variable linguistic features and social characteristics, J. Milroy (1992: 169) suggests that 'what the graphs [...] of the quantitative paradigm model is not the behaviour of speakers [...]: what they model is the *linguistic system'* (emphasis in original). This is true in the sense that no speaker employs (say) post-vocalic /r/ 50% of the time in a mechanistic way, as a function of their social identity and the speech situation in which they find themselves. However, it must also be true that a speaker's social identity does determine their linguistic behaviour. If this were not so, we would not expect to see the regularities that do in fact result from the correlational method. Rather, linguistic variation would be predicted to be entirely random when assessed in terms of social categories (or other measures of an individual's social identity). It must therefore be the case that speakers are attuned to the social meaning of language and that the proclivity to deploy a particular variant – or to adopt an innovation – is a direct function of this capability.

A fundamental question, then, is what personal significance the use of variable language has in the construction of social identity, from the individual speaker's point of view. In this connection, Cameron (1990: 88) cites Romaine's (1984a: 37) view, which has the advantage of less abstraction:

> It is legitimate to recognise that an agent's [i.e. speaker's] social position and his relations with others may constrain his behavior on a particular occasion in specific ways [...] People are constrained by the expressive resources available in the language(s) to which they have access and by the conventions which apply to their use.

This formulation goes some way towards reconciling the 'macro' societal level referred to above and the micro level of face-to-face interaction. To it we may add that the 'expressive resources available' to a speaker are coded in such a way as to allow speakers to use their language in ways that they feel express their social identity most meaningfully for them. As Romaine points out, speakers are constrained in their choices, both socially (use of post-vocalic /r/ would be without significance in, say, London, since it forms no central part of the variable pronunciation of that city's native inhabitants) and linguistically (again, use of variable /r/ occurs only after a vowel, so that no variation is possible between *rat* pronounced [ɹat] and [at]). So much is straightforward, but it is important to add that linguistic variants that are socially coded in terms of what we called above the impersonal, institutional level of society, have meaning for speakers in ways that concern their social and personal identity.

The concept of 'social identity' is difficult to describe and theorize, perhaps most obviously because it is experienced subjectively, is multi-faceted and dynamic, is perhaps rarely the object of conscious reflection, and is composed of many elements, which are in any event recalcitrant to precise measurement or even definition.

Region or locality is perhaps one of the least abstract of these, although even the 'construction' of one's regional identity is influenced by a process that is complex and dynamic, because it is subject to continuing socio-geographical developments as well as to personal trajectory. As Trudgill points out (1990: 1), a positive sense of regional identity is nevertheless likely to be imprinted in an individual at an early and hence impressionable age, and so continue to make its force felt. This is simply because many if not most people have happy memories of childhood and youth, and these are likely to be associated with a locality or region that is distinctive, at least to them, because experienced at an impressionable age. Thus, to take the example of the broad north–south linguistic split in the UK (the following remarks are applicable to France and Spain *mutatis mutandis*), northern speakers may feel quite strongly that their social identity is bound up in an intimate way with their pronunciation of the (a) vowel in the lexical set that comprises words like *glass* and *bath*. To pronounce *bath* as [bɑθ], with a southern low back /a/, would be to show disloyalty to that element of one's social identity which might be labelled 'Northerner'. Conversely, so to reconstruct that component of one's accent as to abandon northern front /a/ may be to acknowledge diminished allegiance to one's Northerner status.

To provide a mere hint of the complexity attaching to the element of social identity that derives from regional origin, it is perhaps apposite to cite George Orwell, who in his social document *The road to Wigan Pier*, first published in 1937, has an extended discussion of the UK north–south split. Speaking of the unfamiliarity that can strike the Southerner when visiting the North, Orwell remarks (1959: 110–11):

> This is partly because of certain real differences which do exist, but still more because of the North–South antithesis which has been rubbed into us for a long time past. There exists in England a curious cult of Northernness, a sort of Northern snobbishness. A Yorkshireman in the South will always take care to let you know that he regards you as an inferior. If you ask him why, he will explain that it is only in the North that life is 'real' life, that the industrial work done in the North is the only 'real' work, that the North is inhabited by 'real' people, the South merely by rentiers and parasites.

Orwell goes on to discuss at some length some of the manifestations and implications of this 'Northern snobbishness' – perhaps more accurately, inverted snobbery. A north–south split is of course common to many countries, with one half of the country more prosperous than the other; this is true of the UK, France, Spain and Italy, to name but four. The UK example shows one stereotypical reflex of northernness – industrial, hard-working, unprosperous – while the French reflex, referring of course to the Midi, is quite different: perhaps concerned with lack of prosperity also, but carrying connotations of what Orwell calls 'olive, vines and vices'. He quotes this caricature in a discussion whose tenor is that the inhabitants of northern latitudes are hard-working and self-denying, a theory designed to justify the gains of the British Empire which, if taken to its logical conclusion, as Orwell points out (1959: 113), 'would have meant assuming that the finest people in the world were the Eskimos'. For our present purposes the aspect of social identity exemplified in geographical dichotomies like north and south illustrates in a clear way (because it is over-simplified) a binary pair that is often discussed in terms of stereotypes and indeed caricatures, of the type shown above. There is a reality behind the stereotype, since stereotypes do not arise from the void, although the stereotype inevitably lags behind the reality. The stereotype is perpetuated through an array of informal channels. Their relative weight is impossible to quantify, as is their effect on an individual.

From the listeners' perspective, data that correspond to speakers' perceptions of social identity expressed in variable language are available through the results of perceptual dialectology, the sub-discipline that elicits the perceptions by linguistically naïve informants of the social, regional or other characteristics of varieties of their language. Perhaps the best-known study is the 'matched-guise' experiment reported in Giles (1970), who presented a recording purportedly of 13 speakers of different British English and foreign accents to a panel of schoolchildren for evaluation according to three characteristics: pleasantness, prestige and 'comfort', i.e. 'how comfortable they [the informants] would feel if interacting with the accented-speaker concerned' (1970: 215). The latter attribute related to clarity of communication rather than social ease. The 13 speakers were in fact one; this speaker produced the different accents or 'guises', and the guises were 'matched' in the sense that the idiolectal variable of voice quality was held constant. The panel of listeners consistently rated the RP accent more highly on pleasantness, prestige and communicability. These attributes relate approximately to one side of the duality summed up in Orwell's informal terms, between 'real people' and 'rentiers and parasites'. Kuiper (2005) in a recent article on Parisian and Provençal speakers' perceptions of regional varieties of French provides results that are a 'linguistic' correlate to those of Giles. Parisian French was viewed by most informants as the most 'correct' variety while Provençal was reported as most 'pleasant'. Attributes like these have no basis in linguistic reality, but reflect social judgments; the interest of Kuiper's study is to show that speakers of a language variety will have the same perception of that variety as those who hear it, as demonstrated by the finding that Parisian speakers judged their own variety to be the most correct.

We said above that the stereotype, whether social or regional, inevitably lags behind the reality. This is shown very clearly by the Orwell passage, which presents an account of the UK north–south split which is now outmoded, at least in detail. Kuiper's study throws light on this issue also; he states (2005: 46) that younger Provençal speakers (aged 18–25) imitating Parisian French:

> had already lost all but the most remote traces of Provençal French phonetic features in their speech. Since these speakers already spoke almost entirely in the supralocal norm, it [was] difficult to hear when they broke into the imitation.

Kuiper remarks further of these younger Provençal speakers (ibid.):

> they are unaware that their own speech is nearly indistinguishable from the norm they identify. Clearly, linguistic perception – in this case respondent perceptions of their own relationship to the norm – can affect a speaker's mastery of normative language.

A further aspect not emphasized by Kuiper but germane to our argument here is the diachronic: the perception or stereotype persists even when the linguistic substance scarcely reflects it. The full title of Kuiper's article is 'Perception is reality: Parisian and Provençal speakers' perceptions of regional varieties of French', and as Kuiper puts it (2005: 28), 'respondent perceptions about normative language have little basis in empirical reality [...] but still may have a strong effect on speaker self-image.' As we argue in a slightly different connection in Chapter 5, the stereotype or perception and the reality are indissociable; Kuiper's argument can be applied to 'self-image' as it derives from social as much as linguistic reality.

To return to the example of northern front /a/, although this variable does not fit neatly into the present argument, as most Northerners in the UK have little or no variation in their use of /a/ in this set of words, in the Labovian sense of the term employed here, it does illustrate very vividly how social identity maps on to linguistic structure. At the same time it is unclear why /a/ has this totemic and near-invariable character for speakers of northern English, although Trudgill (1986: 11–21) suggests that in general speakers may have a particular resistance to the importation into their speech of variables that are salient or already have phonemic status in their native variety.

The foregoing description differs from Cameron's example of 'working-class women of Italian descent aged 50+ and living in New York City' speaking formally principally in the addition of a certain amount of sociological flesh added to the skeletal elements of abstractions like region, social class, and social trajectory or mobility. It remains a description, with the addition of an account of what a phonological variable might mean in social terms. Beyond correlation and the fact of language reflecting society, a complete explanation of variation needs also to take into account the social stereotypes or equivalent realities that lie behind linguistic variants. As discussed above, the relevant stereotype here contrasts the 'gritty' North of the UK with the 'effete' South. Like all stereotypes, this is a caricature but, as previously stated, there must inevitably be an element of social reality behind stereotypes, since they are based on reality, however inaccurately and anachronistically. A theoretically motivated account of social factors underlying the north–south divide in the UK and France might refer to the tighter social networks generally held to be typical of the working-class or rural communities that are more widely distributed in the less prosperous region. These social networks are associated in the popular mind with values like warmth and solidarity, and descriptions are not lacking in the sociological literature of how the break-up of tight working-class social networks promotes status-based values like social ambition and the exchange of 'personal' for 'impersonal' respect (cf. L. Milroy 1987b: 82).

These arguments recall Hudson's suggestions (1996: 43–5) that 'it could be that we use pronunciation in order to identify our origins', and that 'pronunciation reflects the permanent social group with which the speaker identifies'. The sketch outlined above adds a dynamic element in describing how pronunciation can show social mobility, and an individual element in showing how speakers can retain, reject or compromise with their social-regional accent. The key issues are, firstly that sociolinguistic variables are socially coded, in the sense of carrying connotations or images of the speakers who use them, or the communities in which they are used. This is reflected in the quite common statements of the type already referred to: 'I think the Yorkshire accent is sloppy' and perceptual judgments relating to correctness and pleasantness discussed above in relation to Kuiper's study. Speaker-hearers identify with or reject these social connotations, if we accept here a broad two-way typology. Secondly, speakers employ these identifications or rejections through their linguistic behaviour in a probabilistic way, seemingly through use of a feedback process that relies on self-monitoring of some kind; for our present purposes we need not go deeper than this, but it seems unlikely that the process can be wholly unconscious. It is from this process that the percentages seen in the literature result. Holmes's study discussed above gives an insight into how a speaker uses items of pronunciation in a variable way as a result of a continuing process of 'construction of identity'. This phenomenon was identified prior to Holmes's unified study, and has been referred to as 'micro-style' variation. Clearly, no speech event is uniform in respect of its tone, and several variationist researchers (Ashby 1981, Romaine 1984a) have commented on this aspect of stylistic variation, albeit anecdotally. Ashby compared realization rates of variable French liaison in the first and second halves of the interviews he conducted, finding slightly lower rates in the second half, when informants were no doubt more relaxed and felt less need to employ a formal speech style. An aggregated percentage rate for an individual speaker or speaker group conceals micro-style variation, and can lead to caricatures of the kind suggested by Cameron. A rate of (say) 50% use of a linguistic variable means a total concealing sporadic (but not random) use that responds to the factors just outlined.

To summarize so far: our concern is with variation caused by 'variable language as construction of identity'. This refers essentially to ideologized linguistic practice, the deployment of particular linguistic items by individual speakers to signal, to themselves and others, their identification with the social values these items represent. However, it is also necessary to consider broad societal tendencies, because the two levels intersect: the percentages seen in the literature for individual speakers or speaker groups, while concealing micro-style variation, at the same time show the expression of speakers' intuitive awareness of what is going on at the societal level – whether this is manifested in the adoption or rejection of an innovation, or in some other way. To that extent, we can agree with Kroch's observation (2001: 722) that 'human beings, like other animals, track the frequencies of events in their environment, including the frequency of linguistic events.'

4.4.3 Acts of identity, prestige

The position of Labov (2001: 24) on the relation between language and society as it affects linguistic change resembles what has been formulated above:

> The orientation to the relations of language and society that is closest to my own point of view is that of Sturtevant (1947). He viewed the process of linguistic change as the association of particular forms of speaking with the social traits of opposing social groups. Those who adopt a particular group as a reference group, and wish to acquire the social attributes of that group, adopt the form of speaking characteristic of that group. The opposition between the two forms of speaking continues as long as the social opposition endures, and terminates in one way or another when the social distinction is no longer relevant.

Labov uses the term 'reference group' in the sense defined by Merton (1968: 287): 'any of the groups of which one is a member, and these are comparatively few, as well as groups of which one is not a member, and these are, of course, legion, [which] can become reference points for shaping one's attitudes, evaluations and behavior.' The position, then, is essentially that speakers may adopt new linguistic forms, the property of a given reference group, because they seek thereby to gain social advantage. As Labov points out (2001: 191), this view is similar to that articulated by Le Page and Tabouret-Keller (1985), who expressed their perspective on the adoption of linguistic forms for this purpose in the well-known phrase 'acts of identity'.

A notion that is relevant here, and commonly employed in sociolinguistics, is that of 'prestige'. 'Overt prestige' is commonly used to denote prestige as thought of in the everyday sense, which derives from access to power and financial resources and which is the attribute of upper-class speakers (in a simple distinction between upper and lower). This notion contrasts with 'covert prestige', the property of lower-class speakers and so called because it has associations with non-standard social values like 'roughness and toughness' and tends therefore not to be the object of overt or explicit admission or comment. We can of course envisage prestige, whether overt or covert, as being linked to other social attributes such as youth and ethnicity.

Labov points out (2001: 191), however, that discussions of language change that start from the position just sketched run the risk of circularity, i.e. of assuming what they set out to demonstrate. In other words, they suffer from the shortcoming that 'the fact that a linguistic form has prestige would be shown by the fact that it was adopted by others' (Labov 2001: 24). From that perspective, prestige-based explanations are post hoc and therefore lack the power of prediction. This perhaps overstates the case, because analyses that invoke the concept of prestige can be reinforced by reference to language-external phenomena, such as informal attitudes expressed in statements like the one cited above concerning the Yorkshire accent. More rigorous evidence, or at least evidence elicited in a systematic rather than anecdotal way, is also available in the perceptual dialectology literature, several studies having shown speaker groups matching personal or social qualities to social accents. The findings of Strongman and Woosley (1967), discussed in Giles and Powesland (1975: 67), reported judgments that were less abstract than those elicited by Giles (1970), who, as was mentioned above, invited informants to rate accents according to their pleasantness, prestige and suitability for clear communication, elements that are often invoked in discussions of standard languages. Strongman and Woosley reported judgments such as the attribution of self-confidence to London speakers by both northern and southern UK informants, and honesty, reliability and generosity attributed to Yorkshire-accented speakers, again by northern and southern UK informants. This again evokes the perception of the north–south divide discussed in Orwell's terms previously.

Analogous results are produced by the self-report test most generally associated with Trudgill (1974), which shows speakers' linguistic production to be closer to a norm than they perceive it to be, when perception is measured against behaviour. Thus when speakers are asked to estimate their own speech, they articulate judgments that refer to a norm that seemingly governs how they wish they spoke, whether this norm is overtly or covertly prestigious. Self-reporting of this type is therefore a normative judgment of one's own rather than another's speech, but is motivated by the same response to the social values that lie behind the speech.

In addition to charging prestige-based accounts with the potential for circularity, Labov suggests a further explanation for the adoption of a variant in the process of diffusion, namely frequency of contact between an innovating and adopting speaker or speaker group. However, as he points out, this frequency could itself be explicable by the motive just referred to. It is also the case that frequency of contact alone seems not to be sufficient to propel many of the changes described in the literature. The essence of the problem is perhaps that it is impossible to establish a chain of cause and effect, of the type that prevails in scientific explanations, between social processes and changes and language variation and change. Arguably, however, in a psycho-social discipline such as linguistics, that level of explanatory adequacy represents an ideal that is wholly unattainable.

To illustrate this, we examine the best-known study that explicitly correlates social and linguistic change (perhaps the best-known study of all), considering the implications that can be drawn from it for the present study.

The Martha's Vineyard study

The first piece of variationist research properly so called was carried out by Labov in 1961 (first reported in Labov 1963, 1972b: 1–42), and was in fact entitled 'The social motivation of a sound change'. The study was carried out in Martha's Vineyard, an island off the Massachusetts coast that had formerly depended on fishing but was at the time of Labov's study (and continues to be) largely a fashionable tourist location. The theoretical interest of this study is multiple: for example, contrary to previous assumptions, it showed that linguistic changes promoted by younger speakers are not always in the direction of innovation; and it showed, for the first time in an accountable way, that language change does not always proceed towards the standard. The assumptions falsified by Labov's study derived from the dialectological tradition that preceded the methods initiated by him; these later methods were of course made possible by the use of portable recording equipment and systematic social sampling. We discuss other relevant issues after describing the results.

From our present point of view, the interest of the Martha's Vineyard study is that it explained a sound change apparently in progress by very precise reference to the social situation in which it was taking place. One finding reported by Labov and relevant here was that a group of young male Vineyarders who had in response to a questionnaire expressed loyalty to the island in its pristine social organization, also showed linguistic behaviour that was analogous to that of some older male speakers, who were admired by the younger groups as typifying values that stood in sharp contrast to the transformation of the island into a holiday destination. These values were connected with the then already largely superseded fishing industry, and were typified by attributes like self-reliance and willingness to face danger. Identification with this 'reference group' by some younger male Vineyarders correlated with use of a centralized vowel in the first element of the diphthong in words like *right* and *house*. In standard US English these are pronounced [ɹait] and [haʊs]; the forms used by the older fisherman in

Chilmark, the south-west area of the island largely unaffected by the tourist influx and part of what was referred to as 'up-island', had a more central first vowel, either [ɹɐit] and [hɐʊs], or [ɹəit] and [həʊs] in its most extreme central realization. The quantification that shows most clearly the convergence of interest here is the one in Table 4.3.

The two left-hand columns in the table show use of the two variables by two young Vineyarders who expressed little attachment to the traditional activities practised on the island and wished to leave to pursue a career on the mainland. The low scores for [ɐi] and [ɐʊ] ((ay) and (aw) in Labov's notation) correlate with this orientation, and contrast sharply with those in the right-hand columns that show high use of the variables in association with the desire of the two speakers to stay and make a living on the island, after having gone to college on the mainland. As Labov remarks (1972b: 32), 'the indexes speak for themselves'. This is certainly true in the context of the article, and the values in the two sets of columns contrast quite dramatically.

Labov's findings show very clearly then a link between a social motivation and the use of a linguistic variable that has a very readily defined social coding. No other study has shown so clearly the social impetus driving a sound change – that is, the impetus elicited by the researcher, as opposed to one suggested post hoc. As Labov himself points out, the results do however raise interesting issues (Labov 1972b: 39):

> There remains a gap in the logic of the explanation: in what way do social pressures and social attitudes come to bear upon linguistic structures? So far we have assembled a convincing series of correlations: yet we still need to propose a rational mechanism by which the deep-seated elements of structure enter such correlations.

This is of course an issue associated with all correlations; indeed it is a commonplace in interpretive statistics. As Butler points out (1985: 149–50):

> [...] even a very significantly high correlation between scores on two variables does not mean that the phenomena are related in a cause-and-effect manner. [A test] will not tell us how such correlations should be interpreted, still less will it give us direct information about causes and their effects.

Table 4.3 Comparison of four young male Vineyarders' treatment of the (ay) and (aw) variables (adapted from Labov 1972b: 32)

Down-island, leaving		Up-island, staying	
(ay)	(aw)	(ay)	(aw)
00	40	90	100
00	00	113	119

Statistical tests, obviously enough, are not designed to explain results, but to assess the degree of confidence researchers can place on them. Arguably, however, the notion of explanation or 'cause and effect' that is implicit in both Labov's and Butler's observations represents an impossible ideal insofar as it relates to linguistics. A correlation in the field of medicine, for example, can in principle be explained by examining the relevant organs of the body and identifying an underlying biochemical chain of cause and effect. What would the equivalent chain be for a sociolinguistic correlation? Presumably some subtle neurological state, resulting from a history of exposure to certain external inputs, which tends to propel the organs of speech in one way rather than another. Discovering and analysing such a state is well beyond the means of neuroscience in its present state of development, and arguably may never be possible. Realistically, then, the most that can be achieved is to establish a clear link between linguistic behaviour and ideological constructs (beliefs, loyalties, interpretations etc.). Labov's study is in fact one of the very few to match attitudes and behaviour directly, and a test performed on a larger sample would no doubt give a value close to unity, suggesting a high positive correlation between the two phenomena of interest here. The problem that remains is one of interpretation rather than any underlying deficiency in the overall approach.

As Labov points out further, this problem is rather more complicated if we take into account his view that the variables of interest in the Martha's Vineyard study were not salient, in the sense of being the object of the informants' conscious awareness. This state of affairs is double-edged, since a variable that is salient, while perhaps convenient for the researcher in its ease of identification, may be susceptible to what Labov calls 'conscious distortions' by informants if they possess a high degree of awareness of its social-stylistic value. That is, speakers may avoid using certain variants of which they have a high degree of awareness. On the other hand, a correlation between social practice of the type discussed here and the use of a linguistic variant that appears to possess little salience raises the question whether we can equate in any close way the cognitive status of an explicitly acknowledged social attitude and that of a linguistic variant whose use seems far from explicit to the speaker concerned.

The concept of salience is of course problematic in its definition – social as well as linguistic salience can be at issue, nor are these two aspects clearly separable – and in its introduction as an explanatory factor the concept can itself be in need of explanation (cf. Kerswill and Williams 2002). Thus a variable may be salient on account of its being associated with a more or less clearly defined social group, or by reason of being in some way linguistically marked; or for other reasons. Nor are these first two aspects easy to distinguish; for instance, variation between apical and uvular /r/ in French is perhaps salient on account of the large phonetic difference between the two variants, but also no doubt because the older variant is associated with an easily identifiable (or salient) social group. Linguists have found no better way of inferring the salience of variables than by the indirect means of studying their social or stylistic distribution. The argument is that sharp patterns of differentiation imply a high degree of awareness by speakers of the salience, or social-stylistic value, of the variables they are using. The motivations behind style shift cannot be elicited by direct questioning, for reasons to do with deontology and epistemology. More plainly, an investigator who enquires of informants why they have produced a given sequence will produce embarrassment and bewilderment, since few speakers have the linguist's hypersensitivity to language. At best, 'conscious distortions' will result, in evaluation in this case, rather than production.

4.4.4 Conclusion to Section 4.4

We have explored in this section the conceptual and methodological difficulties that stand in the way of explaining in a truly accountable way the links between social and linguistic change. These difficulties are apparent at all levels beyond the micro-community, as exemplified by the Martha's Vineyard study. None the less, there is little room for genuine doubt that these links are real. Below, we look at some case studies of language change which illustrate how social indexing (or ideologization) of a given variant is the driver for the diffusion of an innovation, and hence that the locus of the change is social positioning manifested through language use.

4.5 Case studies in language change

4.5.1 /o/-fronting in French

As a case study of phonological variation and change we examine /o/-fronting in French, consisting in the replacement of the back mid-open vowel [ɔ] with a fronted schwa-like sound such as [œ]. Although this phenomenon has only been discussed in systematic terms since the mid twentieth century, it has a long attestation. Vaugelas (1663: 308), for example, already notes and condemns the pronunciation of *commencer* 'begin' as *quemencer*. And Fónagy (1989: 245) points out the pronunciation of *homme* 'man' as *heume* is noted by Desgrange in his *Petit dictionnaire du peuple* (1821). More recently, Gadet (1992: 33) cites examples that seem to indicate fronted /o/ in written modes in which the normative influence of the standard spelling is attenuated, such as notices in shop windows and bars, for example *petit rond* for *potiron* 'pumpkin' and *Beaujelais* for *Beaujolais*. Here the unaccented <e> grapheme in *petit* and *Beaujelais* points to centralization or fronting to a rounded schwa or [œ] in the speech of the writer. These observations seem to suggest a working-class feature (so-called *français populaire*).

Other remarks by researchers apart from the results we present here (see Table 4.4 below), although fragmentary and anecdotal, suggest that /o/-fronting is perhaps now in the process of 'change from below' in the sense of the adoption by middle-class speakers of a working-class feature, one of the commonest diachronic patterns highlighted by sociolinguists. Fougeron and Smith (1993) report /o/-fronting in a short passage read by a young Parisian female who, as Coveney points out (2001: 97), is not described as working class. In addition, Carton (2001: 9) suggests that while /o/-fronting was criticized as a working-class feature in the nineteenth century, it is currently 'snobbish' or 'trendy'.

Martinet (1945) was the first to comment at some length on /o/-fronting. He documented pronunciation patterns in the behaviour of 409 French males who, like himself, were detainees in an officers' POW camp. His analysis of the mid-vowels showed the emergence of a centralized or fronted variant in non-southern speakers in contexts in which the back vowel [ɔ] would be expected to occur standardly. For this Martinet advanced a tentative structural explanation: '[cela] aurait été provoqué [...] par la proximité de /a/ et /ɔ/ dans les parlers qui maintiennent une nette différence de timbres entre les deux 'A'' (1945: 17).[16] Martinet suggests therefore that for speakers for whom the low back vowel [ɑ] and the low front vowel [a] represent distinct phonemes, as in the minimal pair *patte* 'paw' [pat] ~ *pâte* 'paste' [pɑt], [ɔ] is fronted as a result of overcrowding at the back of the vocal tract. This is in line with one of Labov's principles of linguistic change (1994: 116), viz. that back vowels tend to undergo fronting, and indeed /o/-fronting has been reported by several researchers investigating English in the UK (fronted /o/ is a stereotype of Hull) and the US.

Martinet's functional explanation seems to be a variant of the type of approach that we highlighted towards the end of Section 4.3, viz. one that reifies the system and conceptualizes change accordingly. For while the notion of crowding at the back of the vocal tract has an attractively physical quality to it, it does not correspond to anything to which individual speakers can be expected to have any cognitive access (unless they are phoneticians). In other words, a cognitive awareness, unconscious or otherwise, of a structural crowding problem cannot play any causal role at the level of an individual speaker. Therefore if crowding does influence individual behaviour, it must do so via a purely bio-mechanical reflex; that is, the architecture of the vocal tract must militate in some way against the vowel system in question. But this is not plausible either, given that the system actually arose in the first place. The absence of any causal link between /o/-fronting and the vowel subsystem at the back of the vocal tract is further confirmed by the fact that, for most French speakers, [ɑ] now has a very restricted distribution and cannot be regarded as a phoneme (Coveney 2001: 188). When scrutinized closely, then, the functional type of causation adduced by Martinet does not really amount to very much.

More generally, we can say that systemic simplifications or de-clutterings are typically outcomes rather than causes.

The initial observations in Martinet (1945) provided the basis for the well-known book chapter 'C'est jeuli le Mareuc' ['It's pretty, Morocco'] (Martinet 1969) which, to date, represents the single most comprehensive account of /o/-fronting. In the main, the chapter replicates the earlier functional approach, which may be due in part to the absence of sufficient empirical data to conduct a more socially motivated analysis. Martinet in fact states that '[l]es données dont nous disposons [...] se fondent sur des observations personnelles faites sans plan et sur une appréciation subjective' (1969: 197).[17] In this later work, Martinet invokes the functionally weak opposition between /ɔ/ and /œ/ as a further motivation for the change. The vowels serve to distinguish few minimal pairs, and as a consequence, if the two phonemes were to merge, there exist only a small number of contexts where the communicative function of an utterance would be compromised (p. 194). This again appears to ascribe an implausible degree of systemic awareness to individual speakers. In any case, as the exchange below (from Malderez 2000) indicates, minimal pairs based on the /ɔ/ ~ /œ/ opposition are not the only loci for ambiguity stemming from /o/-fronting:

(12) A: Moi, l'homosexualité ça ne me choque pas.
      me, the+homosexuality that NEG me shocks not
      'Me I'm not shocked by homosexuality.'

      B: Quoi, le mot sexualité ça te choque pas?
      what, the word sexuality that you shocks not
      'What, you aren't shocked by the word 'sexuality'?'

What this case illustrates is that system-based explanations, even when anchored in the concept of functionality, do little more than rationalize change. Ultimately any change must be driven by a factor that can plausibly be taken to cause an individual speaker to modify their behaviour (this does not of course exclude the transmission of innovations through the normal channels of language acquisition). The view adopted here is that the causality for change lies in the fact that linguistic usages are typically indexed or endowed with particular social meanings. We know from the concept of branding that behaviour can be manipulated in very powerful ways by the deliberate indexing of commercial products. It seems likely, then, that linguistic indexing should also be a powerful determinant of behaviour. In the case at hand, this does indeed seem to be a factor. For in addressing the diffusion, both social and geographical, of the fronted variant, Martinet makes reference to speech communities being influenced by the capital, an important element in the mesh of ideologies that are linked to linguistic behaviour in France: 'l'expansion d'un trait populaire parisien, horizontalement (dans l'espace) et verticalement (dans la société)' (Martinet 1969: 198).[18] This appears to include both the spread of the variant to dialect communities in close geographical proximity to the capital and the adoption of the variant by those speaker groups who are attuned to a changing linguistic landscape, those termed 'early adopters' by J. Milroy (1992). Martinet's statement thus suffices to qualify his wholly functional explanation of the variation, as it implies a convergence towards a salient Paris-based pattern by speakers for whom the adjustment is not structurally necessary.

With this in mind, consider Table 4.4 (from Armstrong and Low 2008: 448), which shows the proportions of fronted, centralized and back /o/ for individual speakers and speaker groups in the Roanne area (Loire, east central France). Fully fronted tokens of /o/ are assigned a value of 2 on a three-way fronting scale, with 0 indicating back /o/ and 1 a centralized variant. The values were assigned as a function of an instrumental analysis of each token of /o/. Observed frequencies have been suppressed so as not to overload the table with information.

The information given in the rightmost column of Table 4.4, referring to use of the fully fronted /o/ variant, in other words the variant that is the most 'advanced' both phonetically and socially, shows patterns of age and (especially) gender that are of interest here. Although the male informants are not behaving in a homogeneous fashion, the females are, especially the younger group, suggesting that the fronted variant has a determinate

Table 4.4 Degrees of /o/-fronting in French based on formant frequency analysis (Armstrong and Low 2008: 448)

Informant	Percentage fronting		
	(0)	(1)	(2)
m.mb.1942	30.00	34.00	36.00
m.md.1956	43.37	27.71	22.89
Older Males	**38.35**	**30.08**	**27.82**
f.fd.1954	19.39	31.63	44.90
f.ng.1955	25.86	34.48	39.66
Older Females	**21.79**	**32.69**	**42.95**
m.tb.1982	21.82	32.73	39.09
m.jpg.1981	43.90	29.27	19.51
Younger Males	**31.25**	**31.25**	**30.73**
f.md.1981	26.19	27.38	46.43
f.at.1981	35.96	20.18	43.86
Younger Females	**31.82**	**23.23**	**44.95**

social meaning. In this regard it is worth reconsidering Carton's (2001: 9) comments on fronted /o/. In expanded form these are as follows:

> Taxé de 'populaire' au début du XIXème siècle [...], cette avancée a été ensuite considérée comme une variante snob, perçu comme une marque de préciosité inconsciente. Dans des milieux 'branchés', il semble plus chic de prononcer *heume* que *homme*. Prononcer *meunnaie* pour 'monnaie', *eureilles* pour 'oreilles' manifeste un souci de bien parler. [...] Ce trait nous semble en progression dans la [conversation ordinaire] des jeunes femmes.[19]

While these observations are impressionistic, they point in the same direction as the data in Table 4.4. From that perspective, the indexical value of the fronted variant has apparently shifted over time, from a broad marker of non-affiliation to the standard to something that is more gender-specific. More research needs to be carried out to ascertain exactly how this variant fits in to the relevant language ideologies, but it seems clear that a causal account of the phenomenon of /o/-fronting should be based upon factors of this type rather than functional considerations such as those adduced by Martinet.

4.5.2 Variable negation

An interesting instance of possible change, which contrasts both functional and purely structural approaches with the more sociolinguistic approach proposed here, relates to negation in French. In the idealized standard variety, this is expressed via two separate items. The typical pattern involves the preverbal negative clitic *ne* together with either the clausal negator *pas* 'not' or one or more items from a finite class of negative quantifiers or adverbs ('n-words' for short): *jamais* 'never', *plus* 'no longer', *rien* 'nothing', *personne* 'nobody', *aucun* 'no', *ni* 'neither/nor', *que* 'only'. Illustrations are given below:

(13) Eric n'a pas encore terminé.
      Eric NEG+has not yet finished
      'Eric has not finished yet.'

(14) Ils ne fournissent aucune aide financière.
      they NEG provide no assistance financial
      'They provide no financial assistance.'

(15) Personne ne veut y participer.
      nobody NEG wants in-it participate-INF
      'Nobody wants to participate in it.'

(16) Tu ne sais jamais rien.
    you NEG know never nothing
    'You never know anything.'

The above paradigm can be analysed in terms of *ne* agreeing (in the sense of Chomsky 2001) with *pas* or an n-word in respect of a negative feature, which we can represent as [+ Neg]. If we consider for a moment the proto-typical agreement relation between the subject and finite verb, it is notice-able that agreement is usually asymmetrical, in the sense that the relevant feature value (e.g. [+ Plural]) is semantically significant for one of the items but has only grammatical import for the other item. For example, in the sequence *The dogs are barking*, while the fact that the subject *the dogs* is plural is semantically significant – the sentence is only true if more than one dog is barking – the fact that *are* is plural does not determine any additional semantic content: the plurality of *are* is a purely formal reflex of the fact that the subject is plural. This latter point can be seen from the fact that the sentence *The dogs is barking* – deemed ungrammatical in standard English – is equivalent in meaning to the sentence *The dogs are barking*. We can thus say that the feature of number is interpretable (i.e. meaningful) when it is located in the subject but uninterpretable (i.e. purely grammatical) when it is located in the verb. This matching of interpretable and uninterpretable instances of a given feature is claimed by Chomsky and others to be an intrinsic part of grammatical agreement. Accordingly, if negation in French also involves agreement – between *ne* and either *pas* or an n-word – then one item must have an interpretable negative feature and the other a cor-responding uninterpretable feature. Which has which?

This question can be answered by considering which of the two items, *ne* or *pas*/the n-word, is inherently negative. The examples below show that both *pas* and n-words can function as solo exponents of negation (note that (18) would be excluded from the formal literary canon):

(17) Qui est-ce que tu a vu?   Personne.
    who is-it that you have seen   nobody
    'Who did you see?'   'Nobody.'

(18) Il voulait pas que je le sache.
    he wanted not that I it know
    'He didn't want me to know.'

On the other hand, (19) is not a structure that occurs in Modern French, indicating that *ne* cannot be a solo exponent of negation (this was not the case in Old French, however, as we discuss shortly):

(19) Je ne vais au cinéma.
    I NEG go to+the cinema

Ne occurs on its own in (20) but in that type of case it does not have a negative meaning:

(20) Il est moins bête qu'il n'en a l'air.
     he is less stupid than+he *ne*+of-it has the+appearance
     'He is less stupid than he seems.'

We can conclude from the above paradigm that in French it is *pas* or the n-word that is inherently negative and hence bears the interpretable [+ Neg] feature. Accordingly, *ne* is a purely formal item whose negative feature is uninterpretable (in the favoured sense).

The point of interest in terms of the overall discussion in this chapter is that, in speech at least, the overt pronunciation of the purely formal exponent of negation – viz. *ne* – has become largely optional, meaning that examples like (18) are widely encountered (see Martineau and Mougeon 2003:121 and references cited there). If this variability foreshadows a complete loss of *ne* (as is proposed in Ashby 1981, 1991, 2001), then the history of French negation could be regarded as illustrating the so-called Jespersen Cycle of negation (see Larrivée and Ingham 2011), at least insofar as clausal negation is concerned. Jespersen states the Cycle as follows:

> The history of negative expressions in various languages makes us witness the following curious fluctuation: the original negative adverb is first weakened, then found insufficient and therefore strengthened, generally through some additional word, and this in turn may be felt as the negative proper and may then in the course of time be subject to the same development as the original word. (Jespersen 1917: 4)

For French, the 'original negative adverb' is *ne* (< Latin *non*), which at first sufficed on its own to express negation, as can be seen from the early thirteenth-century example below:

(21) Li ostes ne set qu'il vent [...]
     the landlord not knows what+he sells
     'The landlord does not know what he sells.'
     (Jehan Bodel *Le Jeu de saint Nicolas*; cited Ayres-Bennett 1996: 62)

The subsequent development of *pas*, together with now archaic or dialectal items such as *point* and *mie*,[20] would represent the phase in which the original negative adverb becomes 'strengthened, generally through some additional word'. Finally, the optionality of *ne* in modern spoken French would signal that *pas* – Jespersen's 'additional word' – was coming to be seen as 'the negative proper'.

In the kind of framework discussed in 4.3, we could view each stage in the foregoing cycle as corresponding to a particular setting on a more general parameter. Roberts (2007: 75), for example, proposes a parameter that determines whether a language has the negative agreement relation outlined above. This would encompass not just the clausal negation mentioned in the Jespersen Cycle, but also the pattern that involves n-words (*rien, personne, aucun* etc.). Modern standard/written French obviously has this relation, and the same could be said for Italian and Spanish (although these latter languages lack an equivalent of *pas* in clausal negation). On the other hand, a language like English clearly does not have negative agreement (although it does have agreement between the negator *not* and polarity items like *any*). Therefore, from a structural point of view the change currently in progress in French – if it is actually a change – constitutes a resetting of the negative agreement parameter. The present state of variability could then be explained in terms of competing grammars: grammar α, which has a positive setting for the parameter, and grammar β, which has a negative setting. Sentences like (13) to (16) are generated by grammar α, while (18) is generated by grammar β.

However, it is clear that an account along these lines does not really give us a fix on the change *per se* but merely presents two abstract analyses, one describing the situation before the change and one describing the situation afterwards. Moreover, the reification of these analyses as separate grammars that are synchronically available to users would be problematic if it turned out that variable *ne* deletion was not actually a linguistic change in progress. In that case, competing grammars would not be exclusively linked to change but would be a general feature of language. This would lead to the conclusion that learning a language typically involves learning multiple languages (or at least multiple grammars). This is not an indefensible position, but it complexifies our view of language learning in an unnecessary way, given that one could account for the relevant variation more simply by surrendering the idealized view of languages as uniform and stable systems.

Turning to possible functional accounts, the commonest approach to *ne* deletion in French highlights a tendency to treat nominative subject pronouns – which in Modern French are clitics – as morphological affixes. Harris (1988: 231–2), for example, notes that subject pronouns are likely to occur in spoken French even where there is already a full DP subject leftwards in the string: so-called 'subject-doubling', as in sequences like *mon frère il chante* 'my brother he sings'. He states that:

> [...] we may regard French *ils aiment* [izɛm] 'they love' as one polymorphemic word (subject-prefix + stem) in exactly the same way as one regards Latin AMANT, or Old French *aiment*, as one polymorphemic word (stem + subject suffix).

From that perspective, the claim would be that the need for adjacency between the subject clitic and the finite verb in some sense squeezes out *ne*, which is normally placed between the subject and the verb.[21] This view receives some support from the findings reported by Martineau and Mougeon (2003: 140–3), which show that grammatical phenomena that appear to diagnose a single word status for 'clitic$_{Subj}$ + verb' sequences became established only after the eighteenth century, which is the period during which they analyse *ne* deletion as having arisen. Armstrong (2002: 163) treats the linear sequence 'DP + clitic$_{Subj}$ + verb' as a conversational default and proposes that certain instances of *ne* insertion, such as in the following example from a 19-year-old female speaker in a relatively formal speech style, could be linked to a failure to deploy that template:

(22)   Personne ne l'a encore fait. (Amstrong 2002: 162)
       nobody NEG it+has yet done
       'Nobody has done it yet.'

However, even if the correlation between *ne* deletion and the development of affixal subject clitics turns out to be robust, it cannot provide any insight as regards what is happening at the level of the individual speaker. This is because the shift towards affixal subject pronouns is a long-term macro change to which, in the normal course of events, individual speakers have no cognitive access. In other words, even though their own linguistic behaviour may represent an atomistic component of the change in progress, there is no sense in which they can be expected to be aware of the direction in which the linguistic community, as a whole, is moving. In fact, the proposed explanation puts matters the wrong way round, in that it is the diachronic erosion of *ne* that produces – or at least contributes to – a state in which subject pronouns are affixes, rather than vice versa. Thus a putative need for adjacency between the subject clitic and the finite verb cannot be adduced as an explanation either for why individual speakers are adopting the feature of *ne* deletion or for why this feature was originally introduced as an innovation.

On the face of it, the rather mundane fact that *ne* is semantically redundant, in the sense that *pas* and the n-words already have an interpretable [+ Neg] feature, might seem to represent a line of causation that could directly involve the individual speaker, assuming that speaker-hearers have a general preference for economizing time and effort so long as meaning is not compromised. However, a similar redundancy is built into the Spanish system, for example,[22] but in that case there is no tendency whatsoever for *no*, the equivalent of *ne*, to be dropped.[23] Moreover, Martineau and Mougeon (2003) report that the Wallon dialect of French does not have *ne* deletion, although apart from that the relevant facts are analogous. Considerations such as these suggest that redundancy *per se* is not enough to trigger the dropping of an element like *ne*.

In the absence of any clear functional motive for *ne* deletion, it may well be sensible to view the initial innovation as a spontaneous ideologization, by which we mean the introduction of a variant entirely for the purpose of social positioning. It is probably impossible to know with certainty when the innovation occurred, but in their detailed corpus-based study, Martineau and Mougeon (2003: 145) report 'infrequent or incipient *ne* deletion' in eighteenth-century French, suggesting that the innovation phase occurred during or before that century. At this distance any proposal as regards etiology must be speculative, but one possibility would be that the innovation arose as part of the linguistic apparatus for expressing a speaker's orientation towards the standard, or at least towards the salient social groups that could claim ownership of the standard. This would be consistent both with what is known about the genesis of of *ne* deletion as a linguistic variable and with what is known about the standardization of negation in French. As regards the latter process, the *'ne ... pas'* and *'ne ... n-word'* patterns are known to have been embedded in the idealized standard from the seventeenth century onwards. Vaugelas (1663: 292–4), for example, castigates the use of *'ne ... pas ... n-word'* and also lists cases in which *pas* can be omitted from *ne ... pas*, implying that the latter is the basic pattern for clausal negation. *Ne* deletion appears to have emerged not long after this time and appears to have been associated with speaker groups that were not stakeholders in the standard language. This is evident from Martineau and Mougeon's (2003) findings in their survey of literary texts providing data on popular Parisian French in the nineteenth century. These authors report (p. 138) that '*ne* deletion was largely confined to the speech of individuals from the lower strata of society'. Thus, unless it can be shown conclusively that there is some built-in necessity to reduce the multi-word expression of negation to a pattern involving a single word, an explanation along the lines suggested here seems to be at least plausible in terms of accounting for the initial innovation.[24]

We can now turn to the status of variable *ne* in contemporary French. Table 4.5, adapted from Coveney (1996), gives figures for the retention of this item in a corpus of spoken French recorded in the 1980s in children's summer camps, chiefly in Picardy.

Table 4.5 Variable *ne* retention: Coveney's results (adapted from Coveney 1996: 86)

Speaker group	% *ne* retained	Speaker group	% *ne* retained
17–22 years	8.4	Working class	9.2
24–37 years	23.9	Intermediate	16.4
50–60 years	28.8	Upper class	19.3
Female	14.8		
Male	16.1	All speakers	17.0

The informants were for the most part *animateurs* in the camps, and speech was recorded in an informal interview style. One or two familiar sociolinguistic patterns are observable: less retention of *ne* by younger and working-class speakers; against this, the degree of sex differentiation present is negligible.[25] The display also indicates the importance overall of the negative particle as a sociolinguistic variable in contemporary spoken French: the rather low levels of *ne* retention (or high levels of deletion) are distributed across all social groups, so that all speakers, whether differentiated by age, social class or (to a lesser extent) sex, are involved in this area of sociolinguistic variation. In other words, whatever the motivations that originally brought about the deletion of the negative particle, it clearly functions now as an 'ideologized' variable that serves among other things to express aspects of a speaker's social identity.

In this connection, Coveney (1996: 90) identifies 'a pattern of age-grading, whereby each generation of speakers has virtually a zero rate of *ne* retention as children and adolescents, but then as they become older modify their speech under pressure from and in the direction of the written language'. In our framework, this could be viewed in terms of speakers having an evolving social identity, which in turn results in evolving patterns of usage of linguistic emblems. As youngsters they tend towards positioning themselves outside what may be perceived as the conservative mainstream – embodied linguistically in the standard language – but that stance is gradually eroded as they grow older. An analogous spectrum could be posited for the axis of class differentiation, where the crude quantitative data roughly match the pattern of age grading. Here the ideological framework would again involve orientation towards the standard language, but this time expressed in terms of social 'value', with better-educated (middle- and upper-class) speakers deriving more advantage from the use and maintenance of the standard and working-class speakers having little or no stake in it.

According to Ashby (1981), variable *ne* deletion represents a change in progress, meaning it is predicted to become categorical in the future.[26] In fact, Ashby (2001) reports a big increase among older speakers in the rate of *ne* deletion in comparison to his 1981 survey: from 48% to 75%. In our view this highlights one possible route whereby variation – which in itself does not embody change – can result in change. For here we see erstwhile younger speakers maintaining their linguistic habits into middle age and beyond (a phenomenon that presumably reflects a shift in social ideology), with the result that the innovative variant is diffused into social sectors that hitherto were resistant. If this process is sustained, the variant becomes so generalized that its eventual adoption by the entire speech community is to an extent guaranteed, owing to weight of numbers.

To sum up the discussion of *ne* deletion, the structural and functional accounts proposed in the literature capture long-term outcomes rather than the actual process of speaker-led diffusion that constitutes the fine grain of linguistic change. It is this latter process that needs to be clarified if we are seeking the factors that cause one type of linguistic behaviour to be replaced by another (rather then merely diagrammatizing language states before and after a change). The correlations in the surveys mentioned indicate that *ne* deletion has social meaning – which we hypothesize to relate to how speakers position themselves in relation to the standard language and what it represents – and accordingly we analyse the current diffusion of this option as being ideologically motivated. We speculate that a similar account should apply also to the initial innovation, given that there does not seem to be any compelling functional reason why the semantically redundant *ne* should be deleted.

4.5.3 Variable *wh* interrogatives

As has often been observed, French speakers potentially have available a considerable array of variant *wh* interrogative structures, although not all speakers use all of the variants available. Some of these variants are listed below under (23a–g), in roughly descending order of socio-stylistic value. The surface sequence involved in each interrogative structure is indicated schematically after the example, using Coveney's (1990: 117) notation where: Q = *wh* word or phrase; V = verb; S = subject; NP = subject noun phrase; CL = clitic pronoun; E = the interrogative sequences *est-ce que/qui*; k = *que*; sek = *c'est que*.

(23a)   Quand venez-vous?   [QV-CL]
        when come-you
        'When are you coming?'

(23b)   Quand est-ce que vous venez?   [QESV]
        when is-it that you come

(23c)   Vous venez quand?   [SVQ]
        you come when

(23d)   Quand vous venez ?   [QSV]
        when you come

(23e)   Quand que vous venez?   [QkSV]
        when that you come

(23f)   Quand c'est que vous venez?   [QsekSV]
        when it+is that you come

(23g)   Quand que c'est que vous venez?   [QkseksV]
        when that it+is that you come

The variants listed in (23) pose an interesting dilemma for the kind of approach discussed in in Section 4.3. This is because these data imply variation across two parameters. The first of these relates to whether the language in question moves *wh* phrases to the beginning of an interrogative clause or whether it leaves them in situ, in their putative base position. The contrast between (23c) on the one hand and all the other variants on the other indicates that both possibilities exist in Modern French. In situ *wh* phrases are also possible in English, but in that case they have a very specific interpretation, namely as echo questions:

(24)   A: I ran into John this morning.   B: You ran into who?

Apart from that, *wh* in situ is only possible in English when two or more *wh* items co-occur, as in the example below:

(25)   What should we do when?

Here *when* does not (necessarily) have an echo interpretation, but is in situ due to a rule that only allows one *wh* item to be fronted in any given clause in English. The French situation is quite different, in that sentences such as (23c) need not be echo questions. Barra Jover (2004: 112), for example, contrasts the following pair of mini-dialogues, in which only the second involves an echo question:

(26)   — Aujourd'hui je suis allé faire des courses.
       'Today I went shopping.'

       — Et tu as acheté quoi ?
       'And what did you buy?'

(27)   — Aujourd'hui j'ai envoyé mon patron sur les roses
       'Today I told my boss to go to hell.'

       — Tu as fait quoi?
       'You did what?'

Moreover, in his survey of non-standard interrogative forms, Foulet (1921: 323) takes for granted that sentences such as the following are colloquial equivalents to the corresponding structures with *wh* fronting (rather than echo questions):

(28)   Et elle rouvre quand?
       and it re-opens when
       'And when does it re-open?'

(29) Vous avez vu qui là-bas?
you have seen who there
'Who did you see there?'

(30) Vous pensiez à quoi alors?
you thought about what then
'So what were you thinking about?'

Thus the French structure illustrated in (23c) does seem to be genuine '*wh* in situ' rather than simply an echo question.[27] If we assume that the distinction between languages that have *wh* movement (English, Spanish, Italian etc.) and those that have *wh* in situ (Chinese and Japanese, for example) is a parametric one, then modern spoken French appears to have both values for this parameter, which represents a logical contradiction unless contemporary speakers are assumed to have two separate grammar systems at their disposal, say a standard system and a colloquial system (a *français de dimanche* 'Sunday French', to borrow Blanche-Benveniste's (1985) phrase).

However, as was mentioned above, there also appears to be variation in respect of another parameter. This is illustrated by the contrast between (23a) and (23d), which shows that subject–verb inversion is optional in French in main clauses that exhibit *wh* fronting. Following a fairly conventional line of research, we could analyse the inversion pattern in (23a) as a residual verb second (V2) phenomenon. In full V2 languages, the finite verb is to the left of the subject in main clauses whenever an item such as an object or an adverbial is fronted to the clausal edge, as in the example below from Old French:

(31) Itieus paroles distrent li frere de Lancelot.
such words said the brothers of Lancelot
'Lancelot's brothers said such words.'
(*La Mort le Roi Artu* 21; (2b) in Adams 1989)

The parametric approach attributes full V2 phenomena to a positive setting for the so-called 'V-to-C movement' parameter. The implication of this is that in full V2 languages the finite verb in root clauses habitually occupies a position – notated in the literature as 'C' – to the left of the usual subject position. A residual V2 language is one that has a positive setting for a parameter that requires V-to-C movement but only when certain types of item – notably a *wh* phrase – have been fronted. Given the contrast between (23a) and (23d), Modern French appears to have both a positive and a negative setting for this parameter, which would again require the postulation of competing grammars if the assumption of languages as stable and uniform systems is to be salvaged. But now we have two independent axes of variation – *wh* fronting versus *wh* in situ, and V-to-C movement (as a corollary to *wh* fronting) versus its absence – meaning there are three distinct parametric permutations. This would require speakers to in fact have three grammars at their disposal, say standard French and then Sunday French (a) and Sunday French (b). This is not theoretically impossible but, if our thinking so far is correct, it represents the wrong way of looking at matters. Clearly, what the variation in question reveals are different ways of 'doing' French. Our proposal envisages this as a unitary phenomenon, with speakers across the community having access to essentially the same totality of linguistic resources but deploying them differentially as a function of where they are or where they wish to be in social space. In contrast, the multiple grammars approach reifies these different behaviours as idealized systems, each one analogous to the standard language in terms of its fixed and uniform nature and hence different in detail but not in kind. In other words, in the latter approach, the phenomenon of linguistic variation is not analysed on its own terms but rather is forced into a framework that is conditioned by an artifice – the idealized standard – that exists primarily as a counterweight to such variation.

Turning now to the dimension of change, the conventional approach (Foulet 1921; Price 1984: 269–70; Posner 1996: 309) envisages a long-term shift from a system that allowed inversion freely to one that has generalized Subject-Verb order. Foulet expresses this view picturesquely when he writes as follows:

> Une loi rigoureuse domine toute cette multitude de faits, et elle donne un sens à leur variété et même à leurs contradictions. Depuis la fin du XIVe siècle au moins la langue est engagée dans une oeuvre de formidable réorganisation [...] Une âme nouvelle naissait dans ce vieux corps et, mal à l'aise, essayait de le façonner pour un renouveau d'existence. Or nulle part l'ancien système n'avait mieux marqué son empreinte que dans l'inversion. L'inversion était donc condamnée. Là où elle contrariait le plus les tendances nouvelles, elle disparut rapidement. Là où elle rachetait sa tare originelle par de vrais services, elle se maintint plus longtemps. Ce fut le cas de l'inversion interrogative qui, même aujourd'hui, ne semble pas très près de sa fin. Elle est pourtant malade et sa maladie date de loin.[28] (Foulet 1921: 346)

Foulet in fact attributes this 'formidable réorganisation' to the loss of the Old French case system, which is immediately implausible given, for example, that Old Spanish also allowed inversion rather freely (Fontana 1993) but did not have a case system. Nevertheless, the notion of an ever greater preference for Subject-Verb order, now obligatory in almost all declarative clauses, is an attractive one. The SVQ type of sequence (*wh* in situ) in particular is close in structure to its declarative analogue (*vous venez demain* ~ *vous venez quand?*); QSV fuses *wh* fronting with declarative word order (*quand vous venez...*); and while the *est-ce que* sequence is historically derived from the inversion of *ce* 'it/that' and *est* 'is',[29] it is now grammaticalized as an interrogation particle: thus, from one point of view at least, the QESV pattern achieves essentially the same effect as QSV.

However, it is difficult to see how this tendency – essentially an instance of analogical levelling – could actually have a causal role. Residual V2 is stable in many SVO languages, such as English, Spanish and Italian, so it cannot be that the tendency observable in French responds to a universal human impulse. Therefore, if it was indeed the case that French speakers in general were possessed by a desire to level the paradigm of available word orders, this would represent a quite amazing coincidence. Here we can invoke Lightfoot's (1979: 391) observation that '[individuals] do not have racial memories such that they know in some sense that their language has gradually been developing from, say, an SOV and towards an SVO type, and that it must continue along that path'. The explanation of variation in French interrogative structures – together with its apparent directionality – in terms of a drift towards generalized Subject-Verb word order tacitly relies on a similar assumption to the 'racial memory' alluded to by Lightfoot, namely a sense that the French language as a whole has a certain preference, which individual speakers are merely implementing.

A more plausible approach attributes a speaker-based motivation to speaker behaviour. In light of our discussion so far, this can be predicted to relate to the construction of social identity. Such a supposition is borne out by the several sociolinguistic surveys of the phenomenon in question; we give the results of one in Table 4.6.

Table 4.6 Variable interrogation: Behnstedt's (1973) results (adapted from Valdman 1982: 225)

Social class/style	'français populaire'(WC)	'français familier' (MC)	'français soutenu' (MC)
Wh construction	% use	% use	% use
QV-CL	0	3	47
QESV	8	12	3
SVQ	12	33	25
QSV	36	46	10
QkSV	26	0	0
QsekSV	3	4	0
QksekSV	6	0	0

This fragment of evidence provided by Behnsted shows some very sharp patterns of variation, most notably in the distribution of the QV-CL sequence, used only by middle-class speakers, and almost exclusively in formal style (recorded from radio programmes).[30] At the other end of the scale, we find that the 'k' (= *que*) and 'sek' (= *c'est que*) sequences are almost exclusive to *français populaire*. In this pattern *que* is a non-standard equivalent of *est-ce que*, while *c'est que* is (in its origin at least) an emphatic counterpart to popular *que*. The emblematic value of the latter appears to have changed little over the last century, given that Foulet (1921: 345–6), writing in the early 1920s, was able to state that

> les deux particules essentielles de l'interrogation, dans le français parlé, sont aujourd'hui (ɛsk) [i.e. *est-ce que*], souvent réduit a (sk), pour la langue correcte et (k) pour la langue populaire. Ainsi il n'y a entre une forme acceptée et un vulgarisme connu, en bien des cas, que la nuance d'un *s*.[31]

Overall, then, it seems fairly clear that speakers deploy the variant interrogative forms as a function of their orientation to the standard language and the social values it represents. For middle-class speakers, the availability in the survey of two distinct styles enables this to be demonstrated rather spectacularly in the style shift manifested in relation to QV-CL, the most conservative of the variants, and QSV, the least standard item within the middle-class repertoire. In contrast, working-class speakers define themselves linguistically as having little or no ownership of the standard language.

The data shown in Table 4.6 were collected in 1973, and it seems quite likely that the situation has evolved since then. Zribi-Hertz (2011: 18, note 18), for example, states impressionistically that some metropolitan French speakers aged over 50 sometimes produce questions using the QV-CL sequence, and that she personally never uses it. This would suggest that the directionality of any change is away from the patterns that most overtly embody the standard. This may be seen either as a shift in language ideologies, with middle-class speakers embracing a less elitist mode of expressing themselves, or it could signal that the variants in question have become de-ideologized, meaning that speakers whose ideological affiliations differ in the relevant respects can nevertheless converge in their linguistic behaviour. Either way, given that the written code is the ultimate locus of Standard French, we can see here an instance of what Gadet (2007: 209) refers to as the 'lent ébranlement du privilège à la langue écrite'.[32]

The foregoing account assumes that the relevant ideological framework operates at a supralocal or 'global' level. This seems to be the case for contemporary variation in French interrogative structures. However, Foulet (1921: 336–7) suggests that at least some of the non-standard variants arose in highly localized dialects and then spread to mainstream French through what amounts to dialect contact. As one possible cause for such innovations, he suggests *velléité d'indépendance* 'vague longing for independence', which recalls L. Milroy's (2003: 162) concept of a local ideology, in which locally based loyalties and affiliations can be a driver of language change. Foulet's proposal seems to us to be entirely plausible, and the historical trajectory it implies would illustrate the permeability of the dividing line between localized and supralocal social meaning.

4.6   Conclusion

In this chapter we have argued that many theories of language change are covertly ideological, in that they embody a conception of the possible ways in which language can be manifested that is modelled on the idealized construct of the standard. This applies potentially at all levels of linguistic structure, but is particularly noticeable in diachronic syntax. As we showed, a leading assumption in that field is that change consists in changes to parameter settings. From that perspective, change is necessarily abrupt, but this is obscured by the slow process of diffusion. We argued that this puts matters the wrong way round; that any parameter resettings are merely analytical markers, abstracted from the real process of change, which occurs at the level of individual behaviour. We also demonstrated that it was impossible to reconcile the assumption that change is abrupt with the observable gradualness of change without positing competing grammars. While the latter hypothesis is logically consistent in terms of its own initial assumptions, we contend that it too is coloured by the standard ideology. This is because it identifies variable usage with the existence of multiple idealized systems, each modelled on the basic template embodied in the standard.

We also argued against the notion that variation and change result from community-wide 'functional' tendencies, such as analogy. While analogical similarities with existing patterns may set limits to possible innovations – in the sense that speakers do not innovate in a linguistic vacuum – the notion of community-wide linguistic drift describes rather than explains the fact that large numbers of speakers independently converge on the same behaviour.

The view of change that emerges, then, is that it is speaker-based, with any macro outcomes, be these structural or functional, being no more than components in an abstract analysis. Our core belief is that a capacity for change is built into language, in the sense that variation is inherent to it. Linguistic variants are not value-neutral, but occupy determinate positions within the set of ideologies to which a given speaker subscribes. Speakers deploy a particular variant as a function of their ideological projection, which may reflect either a conscious or an unconscious process. When such ideological positioning results in convergent behaviour across the community, linguistic change is likely to occur, which we envisage as the loss of a hitherto competing variant (or variants) and the de-ideologization of the prevailing item. We assume that linguistic ideologies may be localized, as in the case of the Martha's Vineyard data, or they may be anchored at a more general level, intersecting in that case with the conventional categories of class, gender, age etc. Among such generalized ideologies is that which pertains to the standard language, which is particularly relevant to French, as we saw from the case studies considered above. Much contemporary and long-term variation (and possible change) in that language can be considered as a reflex of speakers' divergent and shifting attitudes towards the idealized standard, which in French perhaps more than any other comparable language casts long shadows over the linguistic behaviour of speakers at all levels of society.

Notes

1. Functionalist approaches are less easy to characterize, but in essence they link change to particular aspects of language use. For example, the frequency-based approach posits that linguistic outputs that have a high frequency become stored in the memory as fixed sequences and hence are susceptible to reanalysis as unstructured units. It is not clear whether in such approaches the paradox of change is actually regarded as a genuine problem. Thus the first part of this chapter refers primarily to formalized or 'structural' theories of language rather than to functional approaches.

2. For one thing, a causal link between acquisition and language change has not been demonstrated empirically. Moreover, it is unlikely such a link could in practice be proven. The required type of experimentation would involve interfering with language acquisition by children and hence would be unethical and illegal. In addition, language changes are typically reported only once they have appeared in adult speech and hence there is no sound means of demonstrating that the change arose in infancy. In fact, most changes discussed in the literature are essentially historical and hence can only be studied through the textual record. Here again, any discussion of a possible link between change and acquisition can only be speculative.

3. In using Detges and Waltereit's formulation, we are not implying that these authors themselves are in thrall to the standard ideology. Our comments in the text refer to the paradox itself, which in one form or another animates much theoretical discussion concerning language change.

4. The analogy breaks down to the extent that in principle a language is not restricted to a finite number of states.

5. For morpho-phonological variation in the Middle Ages, see Penny (2000, 2002). As regards syntax, note among other things the variability of clitic placement discussed in 4.2, the availability of OV word order (in addition to the commoner VO pattern), as in example (i) below, and negative concord alternations such as that in (ii) and (iii):

   (i) [...] tantas vegadas le pueda esta pena demandar quantas [...]
   as many times to-him he-can this fine demand as
   'he can demand this fine from him as many times as ...'
   (*Siete partidas*; CDE)

   (ii) puede tomar a todos & ninguno non puede tomar a el
   it-can take ACC all [pieces] & none not can take ACC it
   'it can take any piece but none can take it'
   (*Libro de ajedrez, dados y tablas*; CDE)

(iii) E ninguno deue tomar della otra cosa;
    and nobody must take from+it other thing
    'and nobody must take anything else from it'
    (*Siete partidas* I; CDE)

In examples (ii) and (iii) it can be seen that a preverbal n-word functioning as the subject could appear either in conjunction with the negator *non*, in a relationship of negative concord (see Section 4.5.2), or without it.

6. As we will suggest below, the postulation of multiple grammars may not be the best approach to synchronic variation.
7. Note, for example, Pountain's (2001: 20) difficulties in assigning the famous *Glosas emilianenses* (tenth- or eleventh-century Romance glosses on a Latin codex from the Rioja area in Spain) to any specific 'language'.
8. For a similar view of continuity across early Romance, see Posner (1996: 254).
9. This belief is sometimes expressed overtly, as we see in the following remark from Chomsky and Halle (1968: 3):

    We use the term 'grammar' with a systematic ambiguity. On the one hand, the term refers to the explicit theory constructed by the linguist and proposed as a description of the speaker's competence. On the other hand, we use the term to refer to this competence itself.

10. This is a weighted average of the following rates of preverbal placement: 91.8% for negative objects (N = 49), 63.5% for quantified objects (N = 178), 56.7% (N = 1416) for all other (non-pronominal) objects.
11. Here we are thinking of main clauses. In subordinate clauses it was not always the case that the clitic had to be adjacent to the finite verb (or indeed any verb). The phenomenon of separating the clitic from its verb is known as interpolation (see Poole 2006) and is illustrated in the thirteenth-century example below.

    (i) qualquier que lo non fiziesse auria mi jra
        anyone that it not did would-have my anger
        'anyone who did not do it would face my anger'
        (*Documentos castellanos de Alfonso X - Murcia*)

12. The idea behind *v**P is that the conventional verb phrase VP has a periphery to its left. The latter hosts, among other things, the direct object in OV constructions. This is noticeable, for instance, in those Middle English sentences in which the object occurs between the auxiliary and the main verb, as in the example below:

    (i) whilis he myȝte <u>alle þese synnys</u> do
        while he might all these sins do
        while he could do all these sins'
        Pecock, *Crysten Religioun* (EETS 171), 174.3)

13. 'EPP' originally stood for 'Extended Projection Principle', the idea that all sentences must have a structural subject. For reasons internal to the historiography of linguistics, the notion of EPP has become divorced from its original sense and

Chomsky now envisages EPP as an abstract feature that, when present on one item, attracts another.

14. Chomsky (2001: 34) in fact envisages the possibility of v^* being [+EPP] or [–EPP] in a single language. However, this variation must be associated with an 'effect on outcome', such as a different interpretation of the object depending on whether it moves leftwards (= v^* that is [+EPP]) or does not (= v^* that is [–EPP]). Here we abstract away from this type of 'motivated' variation. What we have in mind is free variation that cannot be correlated with any interpretive effect.

15. Holmes's use of 'macro' to designate a level of linguistic analysis should be distinguished from the sense in which the term is used generally in this chapter (where it typically identifies phenomena that have a community-wide import as opposed to being relevant only to individual speakers).

16. This was most likely caused by the proximity of /ɑ/ et /ɔ/ in speech varieties that maintain a clear difference in vowel quality between the two As.

17. Our data are based on personal observations made in situ and from a subjective perspective.

18. The spread of a feature of vernacular Parisian speech, horizontally (in space) and vertically (through society).

19. Criticized as 'working-class' at the beginning of the nineteenth century, this fronting was later considered as a snobbish variant, perceived as a mark of unconscious preciosity. In trendy circles it seems more fashionable to say *heume* than *homme*. Pronouncing '*monnaie*' as *meunnaie* and '*oreilles*' as *eureilles* indicates a concern for good speech. [...] This feature appears to us to be in progression in the ordinary speech of young women.

20. Price observes (1984: 252) that: '*pas* comes from the Latin *passum* 'a step' and so was perhaps first used with verbs of motion (*je ne marche pas* perhaps meant 'I don't walk a single step') and *mie* comes from *mica* 'a crumb' [...].' The negative particles *pas*, *gout(t)e* 'drop', *mie* and *point*, all used as postverbal 'reinforcing' particles in clausal negation in the history of French, originally denoted small quantities, implying they were minimizers in the sense of Horn (1989: 452) or Krifka (1995). It seems likely that their use passed quickly from literal to emphatic force, although as Price points out (ibid.) 'it is extremely doubtful whether they retained this [emphatic] value even in the earliest texts in which they occur.' As McMahon remarks (1994: 165), there is a parallel with English in phrases like *I don't care a jot/ fig/iota*, where negation is reinforced by an adverbial that includes a noun denoting small quantity or little worth. The difference is obviously that French *pas* has grammaticalized from full lexical noun to become the standard negative adverb (*gout(t)e*, *mie* and *point* are now dialectal or archaic).

21. Note that object clitics as well as partitive *en* 'of it/him/her/them' can intervene between the subject clitic and the finite verb. An account along the lines described in the main text would have to explain why *ne* is 'squeezed' but not these other elements.

22. Although it should be noted that for clausal negation, where French has *ne* ... *pas*, Spanish uses the single negator *no*. With negative quantifiers and adverbs, however, negative concord obtains, as in French.

23. Historically, however, *no(n)* deletion occurred – and became categorical – when the n-word was preverbal. In the thirteenth century, such deletion occurs only when the preverbal n-word is the subject but by the sixteenth century it occurs categorically with all preverbal n-words. In Modern Spanish, then, negative concord only occurs with postverbal n-words.

24. With this in mind, it might not be too presumptuous to suggest that the Jespersen Cycle as currently envisaged is epiphenomenal. Arguably, what Jespersen describes is a series of macro outcomes rather than an actual process that can be localized in individual speakers. Perhaps, in a more fine-grained approach, we would simply see long-term quantitative drifts resulting (in part at least) from social indexing of the kind proposed here in the text for the case of *ne* deletion. From that perspective, the fact that the macro outcomes identified by Jespersen tend to be replicated across many different languages may have a rather trivial cause, viz. that the spectrum of possible negation patterns is in reality highly constrained, in that (clausal) negation seems in general to be expressed via either a single item (e.g. English *not*) or by two separate items (e.g. French *ne … pas*). Assuming that, in innovating, speakers typically build upon or modify what is already in existence, the possible diachronic trajectories that can be taken in regard to negation are thus in practice rather limited: either the single negator can be added to or the two-item construction can be reduced to a single negator. In other words, regardless of the etiology, all (or most) variation and change in clausal negation can be expected to end up fitting the Jespersen template.

25. On the other hand, Ashby (1981) found that working-class women displayed the highest rates of *ne* deletion and attributes significance to this, given that working-class women have often been found to be at the forefront of change away from the standard (Labov 1998).

26. According to Sankoff and Vincent (1977), *ne* deletion is nearly categorical in contemporary casual spoken French in Quebec.

27. See Coveney (1995) and Mathieu (2004) for discussions of possible pragmatic factors that affect the use of *wh* in situ. It seems to us that such factors are neither sufficiently consistent nor sufficiently binding to constitute 'an effect on outcome' in the sense of Chomsky (2001: 34) – see note 14 above.

28. A rigorous law governs this multitude of facts, and gives a meaning to their variety and even to their contradictions. From the end of the 14th century, at least, the language has been engaged in a remarkable operation of reorganization … A new soul was being born in this old body and, ill at ease, tried to shape it for a new lease of life. Nowhere had the old system left a deeper imprint than in inversion. Inversion was therefore condemned. Where it contradicted the new tendencies the most it disappeared quickly. Where it atoned for its original defect by true service it survived longer. This was the case with interrogative inversion which, even today, does not seem too close to its end. It is, however, infirm and its sickness dates from long ago.

29. Price (1984: 267) discusses the *est-ce que* interrogative sequence at some length, pointing out that for a while in Old French, 'each element in the construction probably retained its own value.' He gives as an example *Que est iço que est avenud a Saul?* (twelfth century), translated by him as 'What is this that has befallen Saul?'

30. As the reader will note, the percentages in each of the three columns in the table do not add up to 100. This is due to the fact that, in addition to the constructions shown (corresponding to examples (23a–g) listed above), Behnstedt quantified the two given below in (i) and (ii).

(i) quand viennent les enfants?   [QV NP]
   when come the children
   'When are the children coming?'

(ii) quand Jeanne vient-elle?   [QSV-CL]
      when Jeanne comes-she
      'When is Jeanne coming?'

Clearly, these differ from (23a–g) in having a full DP subject rather than a clitic pronoun or, in the case of (ii), as well as one. Thus whereas all members of the (23a–g) set are in principle interchangeable with one another in certain pragmatic contexts, (i) and (ii) constitute an additional set having only partial overlap with (23a–g). They have therefore been excluded from the display shown in Table 4.6.

31. The two essential interrogative particles, in spoken French, today are (εsk), often reduced to (sk), for correct language and (k) for popular language. Thus there is, between an accepted form and a known vulgarism, in many cases, no more than an *s*.

32. The slow destruction of deference to the written language.

5
Social levelling, or anti-standardization

5.1 Introduction

The previous chapters have been concerned primarily with the relationship between the ideology of standardization and linguistics. Here we consider standardization within the context of a more thoroughgoing analysis of the social conditions and ideological framework that arguably lie behind much current linguistic variation and change. The principal theme of this chapter will be that recent social changes have led to the creation of alternative, ostensibly egalitarian, ideologies that implicitly challenge the hierarchical model built into the conventional standard ideology. The result of this from the linguistic point of view is a degree of convergence in linguistic practice that is perhaps unparalleled in modern history. This seems to go beyond the diachronically well-attested phenomenon whereby standard languages at various points in their histories have absorbed and legitimized previously stigmatized speech patterns. Traditionally, where that has happened, the separateness of the standard vis-à-vis other varieties has continued undisturbed. The contemporary situation appears to present a different model, in which the boundary between standard and non-standard is becoming less well defined, partly, though not exclusively, because categories of speaker who previously might have been expected to be loyal stakeholders in the standard ideology increasingly forswear the elitism that such a stance embodies. We analyse this 'anti-standardization' process as a form of levelling, but one that operates primarily in the social rather than the geographical dimension and one that involves the global speech community associated with a given language as opposed to localized communities.

The process that we have in mind is distinct in principle, then, from 'dialect levelling' in the conventional sense, which is defined by Watt and Milroy (1999: 26) as 'the eradication of socially or locally marked variants which follows social or geographical mobility and resultant dialect contact'. Nevertheless, as we shall see, certain current patterns of change that can and have been analysed as dialect levelling also appear to implement a broadly anti-standardizing ideology. To that extent, our approach differs from that of L. Milroy (2003: 166), who categorizes levelling as an 'ideology-free' process. One of the reasons Milroy treats dialect levelling as non-ideological is because the processes it involves have a 'widespread and rather predictable outcome' (p. 161), making it analogous in some respects to internally motivated change. We argued in Chapter 4 that internally motivated language change is essentially an analyst's construct rather than a real phenomenon. If we are correct in that view, it potentially has implications for the dichotomy that Milroy invokes. In particular, it calls into question whether any linguistic change can be a matter purely of abstract or mechanical process, unmediated by factors that ultimately reflect the way language indexes beliefs and attitudes. We do not pursue the issue in detail here. Nevertheless, we do assume that, on occasion at least, dialect levelling may be an expression of an overarching phenomenon of social levelling or anti-standardization.

The overall structure of this chapter is as follows. First, in Section 5.2, we attempt to contextualize the conceptual issues involved, focusing on certain methodological problems together with recent trends in cultural theory. In Section 5.3 we examine what we term 'social levelling', the erosion of previously well-entrenched hierarchies. In Section 5.4 we look in more detail at the linguistic manifestations of this process. And in Section 5.5 we present some concluding remarks.

5.2 Contextualizing the debate

5.2.1 Methodological limitations

The nature of the social change we examine here can be referred to in various terms, perhaps the least problematic of which are 'convergence', or better, 'levelling'. The term 'levelling' is more suitable as it seems to describe more accurately a symbolic diminution of social distance in certain respects, but without necessarily implying, as the term 'convergence' may, a concomitant increase in social cohesion or solidarity. Levelling in this sense seems more intuitively applicable to what we call below 'vertical' levelling. For clarity of exposition we distinguish below between regional (horizontal) and social (vertical) levelling, although as we shall see the two can hardly be separated in principle. We refer to 'social' levelling because the term 'social', as well as being a hyponym in this categorization, is also the superordinate since the term covers both the regional and (for example) social-class dimensions. Regional origin can most obviously be thought of in spatial or horizontal terms, as represented in Trudgill's well-known pyramid (1995: 30) that relates the social (class) and regional components of UK accent variation. At the same time, the regional axis is 'social' in the sense that regional origin is an ascribed attribute possessed by virtually all speakers and capable of influencing social behaviour.

Regarding social levelling in its hyponymic sense, symbolic divisions between groups that can be thought of as arranged, or having been arranged until fairly recently, in a vertical or hierarchical organization, for example between the middle and working classes, men and women, old and young, seem to have become blurred in recent times, even though certain economic divisions are as sharp as before, or even sharper. To take the French example, it appears that although no spectacular change in the French economic structure has taken place since perhaps the most highly visible recent historical turning point (1968), most notably in terms of the distribution of wealth and income, important *symbolic* social changes have come about. France continues to have a fairly high ratio of inequality between the highest and lowest deciles of wage earners in comparison to other countries in the OECD group. At the same time, decision-makers seem now to feel the need to adopt a consensual rather than a directive approach, and to emphasize solidarity rather than hierarchy. A crucial element in this situation is therefore symbolic social (as opposed to actual economic) levelling, although expressing economic inequality in highest–lowest terms, as above, hardly gives a representative picture, as we discuss below.

The central phenomena of interest here are socio-economic and cultural, since the social drives, or is expressed through, the cultural, the linguistic, etc., while the economic, in very indirect terms, can be argued to drive in turn the social, in the neo-Marxist view that continues to be current in some academic circles. It was noted in Chapter 1 that economic, social and cultural elements and effects can scarcely be separated out in a hierarchical way, since the perspective of an individual or community on their socio-cultural experience forms an integral part of that experience. Thus for example, US citizens' perceptions of concepts like 'freedom', 'democracy' and 'mobility', conveniently summed up in phrases like 'the frontier' and 'the American dream', suggest continuing social mobility in that country. By contrast, the perception of UK society as being 'class-ridden' is still common. This disparity is however not borne out by statistics describing income distribution and social mobility in the US and UK. A recent study of intergenerational mobility (Blanden, Gregg and Machin 2005) found little difference between the two countries. The rather unintuitive measure devised by them, the 'intergenerational partial correlation', gave 0.289 to the US against 0.271 to the UK, where a figure closer to unity indicates less mobility (for comparison, Norway was attributed a figure of 0.139).

A superficial comparison of this kind is relatively uninformative in terms of an understanding of what 'social mobility' is in the UK and US unless a complex nexus of social, economic, historical and geographical factors are also taken into account, but it does show that subjective attitudes are important, not least in shaping some of the social practices we discuss below, and that they are an indissociable element of the situation we describe here. Among other things, the example discussed above shows clearly what one might call 'cultural memory' lagging behind contemporary reality, as well as the continuing ideology that reinforces it. Both are important elements in determining the individual and collective perspectives of a given situation. For example, in the UK the persistence of class-consciousness is perpetuated through the continuing high profile of the monarchy and peerage which, as Adonis and Pollard point out (1997: 141): 'underpins the *perception* of a rigid class system' (emphasis in original). In other words, perception and reality cannot be disentangled, nor is it possible to attribute primacy to either. Armstrong and Pooley (2010: chapter 3) distinguish between what they refer to as the 'substantive' and 'symbolic' social changes that propel language change. Substantive changes in social structure include urbanization, counter-urbanization and professionalization, among many others. We mentioned the example of counter-urbanization in Chapter 1; it seems worth pointing out here that the linguistic changes attendant upon this 'substantive' social phenomenon could not take place unless the accompanying 'symbolic' ideology were propitious; correspondingly, the sheer scale of professionalization (discussed further below) can be presumed to have promoted the ideology of interest here.

It can be noted further that the development in cultural studies referred to as the 'cultural turn' lays stress on the difficulty of teasing apart the various social and economic elements in any cultural phenomenon under examination. The cultural turn is in contrast, say, to a Marxist approach that lays stress on the economic as underlying the social. The following quotation from Brantlinger (2002: para. 6) expresses quite clearly what one might call this 'negative faculty' of postmodernism:

> [...] the British Marxists such as E. P. Thompson and Raymond Williams, who helped establish cultural studies as in some sense a counter-discipline [...] rejected the theoretical reductionisms they saw both in mechanistic applications of the base–superstructure paradigm and in Althusserian structuralist Marxism in favor of a renewed sense of the complexities and contingencies of historical processes and of the indeterminate significance of human agency (summed up in the concept of 'experience').

We share this attitude to the extent that it recognizes the complexity, and indeed ultimately the inscrutability of the object of our study here. As Sankoff has pointed out (1988: 148–50), sociolinguistics possesses a 'hermeneutic, or interpretive, component which is antithetical to positivist criteria'. No social science can replicate the methodological precision found in the 'hard' sciences, quite simply because of the nature of the respective objects of study concerned. We mention this to make clear firstly that we are aware of the limitations weighing on the descriptions and (tentative) explanations that follow, and secondly that we do not share what seems sometimes to be a celebration of obscurity found in some work in cultural studies and allied disciplines, where one seems to detect here and there a reflexive wish to mirror real-world complexity in obfuscation of terms and method. We recognize the complexity of what we are discussing here, but do not particularly welcome it; we wish to achieve clarity of explanation where possible, even though the subject matter rules out absolute certainty. Nor do we share the 'strong' postmodern rejection of rationality, which seems to suffer from an interior contradiction. As Sunstein points out (1994: 126, citing Habermas), postmodernists 'can give no account of the normative foundations of [their] rhetoric' because a rejection of the notion of canonical knowledge seems inevitably to fall within the canon, and because a substantial element of the (itself normative) postmodernist enterprise consists in directing opprobrium against normativism. One should at the same time distinguish between truth relativism, which is logically flawed, and moral relativism, which at least holds water logically; Benn (1998: 12) remarks that: 'the statement that moral relativism is true, is not itself a moral claim. Rather, it is a *claim about morality*' (emphasis in original). We discuss this issue further in 5.2.2 below.

A concern for clarity leads us therefore to include below the informal and sometimes polemical comments of non-academic authors, since in this field, individual insight seems at least as important as formal qualification. A further shortcoming relates to subject matter. Our account is necessarily partial, since we wish to emphasize a group of related social trends; quite obviously, trends by definition admit of exceptions. No total theory is possible: alongside levelling remains hierarchy; example can be matched by counterexample. These caveats need to be borne in mind in the following account.

We consider therefore in Sections 5.3 and 5.4 how levelling is manifested in several areas of social practice, language among them. It is in this way that we can reflect on how linguistic structure can be related to social structure, and beyond that to the ideologies that drive it. This can only be done indirectly, however, by constructing hypotheses about how changing social structure relates to changing cultural or social practice. This point is not new: it was made in cogent terms by Meillet (1921: 17–18):

> [...] le seul élément variable auquel on puisse recourir pour rendre compte du changement linguistique est le changement social [...] et ce sont les changements de structure de la société qui seuls peuvent modifier les conditions d'existence du langage. Il faudra déterminer à quelle structure sociale répond une structure donnée linguistique et comment, d'une manière générale, les changements de structure sociale se traduisent par des changements de structure linguistique.[1]

This determination to link social and linguistic structure was a crucial element in the research programme mapped out by Labov in his Martha's

Vineyard study, carried out in 1961 (see Labov 1963, 1972b: 1–42). As we discussed in 4.3, that study showed very clearly a link between a social motivation and the use of a linguistic variable that had a very readily defined social coding. No other study has shown so clearly the social impetus driving a sound change – that is, the impetus elicited by the researcher as opposed to one suggested post hoc. In the context of the present chapter, an important corollary of Labov's study is that an attempt to replicate his results beyond small communities like Martha's Vineyard can only result in an approximation. The quest for solid evidence in a 'community' of 60 million can hardly be expected to meet the same standards.

5.2.2 Postmodernism and the cultural turn

An interpretive and (especially) descriptive set of concepts that throws some useful light on the issues of interest here is that connected overlapping group whose various components are known as postmodernism, late modernism, the cultural turn, and social constructivism, among others. These are enlightening to the extent that some commentators have described in quite a clear way the blurring between high culture and low culture, along with many other social and intellectual phenomena. The postmodern situation, and the intellectual enterprise that attempts to describe it, are notoriously difficult to define with any degree of precision, but the following formulation by Vattimo (1991: xix) is fairly cogent:

> Progress today no longer possesses its original sense of destination, or of a teleological end-point (such as the Kingdom of Heaven or a classless society) toward which it is directed; it has simply become part of the routine of consumer society [...] Progress no longer seems to lead anywhere except to the creation of conditions in which (more) progress is always possible in an always new guise. This circular process, where progress leads only to more progress, dissolves the very meaning of progress as a forward movement in history and of the new as something qualitatively different from what precedes it, thus producing an experience of the 'end of history'.

In other words, where the programmes of religion and progressive politics are widely perceived to have failed in their goals, a sense of purpose and progress will tend to be lacking. Correspondingly, where canonical ideas lose credence, whether they are concerned with morality or political organization, then intellectual and cultural hierarchies seem to erode and distinctions such as that between high culture and popular culture become blurred. It is clear enough that modernism is associated with the notion of progress, and that religious and socialist programmes can be classed in this progressive category, although of course in rather different ways from a contemporary perspective. This is because the socialist view of progress was until quite recently viewed widely as a rational enterprise (as suggested by the once current phrase 'scientific socialism'), while a rather longer time-depth and a different perspective are needed to chart the transformation of religion from knowledge to belief or ideology. The decline of religion represents in our present analysis a perhaps more fundamental shift, since a religious (certainly Christian) viewpoint presupposes a hierarchy, has indeed given us that word. The view that argued from a religious theory of moral hierarchy to a social hierarchy need not concern us in detail here; for our present purposes it seems sufficient to note a broad association between Christian belief and social conservatism, and indeed this association is far from defunct in developed countries – the US provides an interesting exception to the correlation generally seen between increasing material prosperity and declining religious belief. From a contemporary perspective it is easy to lose sight of the fact, as expressed by Bloom (1987: 28), that it requires 'a great epistemological effort [to assign] religion to the realm of opinion as opposed to knowledge'. We can leave aside the question whether religious 'knowledge' ever did in reality gain widespread acceptance; the point is that in former times, open deviation from the consensus was liable to severe sanction. In a modern view the magnitude of this epistemological effort is often forgotten, because situated in a no longer immediate past. We look below in some detail at the degree and speed of the changes that have differentiated the present time from a past which, if no longer immediate, is recent in a conventional historical timescale.

An important qualification is that the postmodern way of looking at things seems valid only if one assumes a widely shared perception of the attitude that connects lack of purpose, progress, absolute truth, cultural hierarchy, etc.: that is, a perception shared by the population at large, rather than just a section of the academic community. Some fairly convincing evidence is provided by Bloom (1987: 25–43), who points out that the closely related relativist viewpoint, which sees all cultural values, ideologies and belief systems as having equal validity, has been very broadly propagated in the US through the educational system. Relativism clearly informs the contemporary view of popular culture in question here; in the postmodern idiom, 'there are no more grand narratives', a formulation that implies a parity of points of view and an absence of any overarching scheme of things. Bloom suggests that the now very widely held relativist view arose in the United States as a result of the wish to promote tolerance in a country that is truly multi-cultural. Relativism in this sense means a refusal to recognize any nation, culture, race, social group, etc., as superior to another, and within this, the refusal to recognize the superiority of cultural practice of any of these social categories. Bloom points out (1987: 26) that this position is not difficult to criticize, for example by asking whether the British, when administering India, were wrong to outlaw suttee. It hardly needs to be added that relativism in the US sits alongside its diametrical opposite, in view of the multiculturalism referred to above.

In Bloom's model, the large degree of tolerance accorded to a given national, ethnic or racial group will tend towards a levelling effect, since tolerance in this degree implies acceptance that sees no need for improvement or betterment (the meaning of these terms is discussed in what follows). Tolerance then spreads to all other groups perceived as being more or less oppressed. From that perspective, the internalization by the groups concerned of this way of looking at things will result in a sense of more or less categorical equality that differs markedly from the earlier view of equality 'in the sight of God' that accepted immovable and substantial inequalities in the moral and temporal spheres. What distinguishes relativism from earlier accounts of social organization is therefore its non-normative character, at least as popularly thought of. Mention was made earlier of Benn's (1998: 12) distinction between moral relativism as a theory of morality (what he terms a 'metaethic') as opposed to a moral system. In this view, one can logically be tolerant of other moral systems while reserving censure for certain practices judged wrong according to one's own system of ethics. But as Benn points out (p.19), in the popular mind an association holds between moral relativism and near-absolute tolerance: 'although [moral] relativism is strictly speaking a metaethical doctrine, in practice it has usually been taken to justify certain normative conclusions; in particular, that toleration is morally virtuous'.

The normatively anti-normative relativist view stands in sharp contrast to the earlier republican ideas of the Founders of the US Constitution. In Bloom's phrase (1987: 27), 'the old view [as expressed in the Constitution] was that, by recognising and accepting man's natural rights, men found a fundamental basis of unity and sameness'. It can be stressed again that the difference between then and now is that the concept of natural rights belongs in a normative tradition that seeks to prescribe how citizens should behave in order to live virtuously – terminology that seems rather outmoded now. We consider in greater detail below the contrast between 'democratic' and 'republican' views of social and political organization, in a separate chapter on the French situation. Finally, in view of the aim stated here of pointing to concrete evidence of the working of these social processes, the question remains how the US situation described above has transplanted to the UK and other countries, at least in modified form and assuming it has. It is perhaps sufficient to rehearse some well-known factors: cultural traffic is generally one-way in the US–UK direction, owing to the dominance of the only remaining 'hyper-power', in the Gallic phrase; and the language common to the US and UK facilitates this further, in contrast to links between continental Europe and the UK. Seabrook, whose book *Nobrow* we discuss further below, provides a useful historical perspective (2001: 27):

> In less egalitarian countries [than the US; like the UK in this argument] a class-based social hierarchy existed before a cultural hierarchy evolved,

and therefore people could afford to mix commercial and elite culture. Think of Dickens and Thackeray, who were both artistic and commercial successes, or more recently, Monty Python, or Tom Stoppard, or Laurence Olivier. But in the United States, people needed highbrow–lowbrow distinctions to do the work that social hierarchy did in other countries.

Seabrook's argument complements Bloom's in emphasizing the commercialization of culture, which replaces the highbrow–lowbrow distinction with a 'landscape of niches and categories' (Seabrook, ibid.), the cultural counterpart or social equivalent of relativism. What is of interest here is that the US–UK cultural-social distinction that Seabrook describes from a historical viewpoint now seems distinctly outmoded, despite the recent date of his book.

Having set out the broad social context in which our discussion is situated, we look below at horizontal and vertical levelling, describing some social and linguistic manifestations of these processes and trying to bring their underlying characteristics into sharper focus.

5.3 Levelling as a social phenomenon

5.3.1 Studies of social levelling

Studies or discussions of social levelling are not numerous, at least in the Anglo-American context. There is a critical literature on the role of elites of various kinds, which implies the study of democracy, but few scholarly authors have looked as it were from the outside, and from a cultural point of view, at the opposite of elite rule: what might be called rule by the many (using 'rule' here in a symbolic, cultural sense; the economic sense is real). There is however an increasing amount of satirical, polemical or committed literature, some of which we consider below in some detail; for example, the novel *Incompetence* (Grant 2003) takes the relativist premise to absurd egalitarian lengths in a future world where incompetence is no bar to any employment; *All oiks now: the unnoticed surrender of Middle England* (Anderson 2004) is a squib directed, as its title implies, against the adoption by the middle classes of working-class modes of behaviour. There exists also of course a considerable literature on popular culture, but here the perspective generally takes the situation as given, and assumes the view that high and popular cultural practices are generally found in a parallel distribution rather than arranged hierarchically. This non-hierarchical view suggests that the two types of culture (if we accept for convenience a binary opposition) are attempting to achieve different effects, which certainly implies rejection of the view that the one is superior to the other. Further approaches taking democratization as a given are feminism and others concerned with the study of continuing inequalities. A related example is to be found in

Giddens (1992), an examination of 'the democratisation of personal life' (p. 184) as it affects family and sexual relationships. Giddens remarks that 'the democratisation of personal life is a less visible process [than what has occurred in the public domain], in part precisely because it does not occur in the public arena, but its implications are just as profound'. This is true; at the same time this democratization is affected by what happens in the public domain, as the discussion of the culture of marketing below aims to show. A non-hierarchical view is therefore assumed in the approaches mentioned above as a starting-point, and is not examined further as an object of study in itself. But as Walden (2006: 14) expresses the matter, discussing what he sees as the contemporary near-total primacy of the populist, 'it ought to be possible for democracies to stand outside themselves and take an objective look [...] but in the contemporary climate raising a finger at The People will be greeted as disapprovingly as spitting in church'. We explain Walden's views in more detail below, as they are relevant to our argument.

Wouters (1986) discusses various social changes that have taken place in the post-war period from the perspective of the relation between what he calls informalization and the internalization by individuals of self-restraint as a mechanism of socialization, as opposed to its imposition by others. Wouters assumes this latter process to be in the direction of greater civilization, but tends to define informalization in terms that are themselves in need of definition, such as 'permissiveness'. The term 'informalization' is in any event misleading, as it is current in economics in a quite different sense that refers to the informal or 'parallel' economy. The basic assumption here, that social change has been broadly proceeding in the direction of levelling, can however be framed also in terms of formality–informality. These latter terms refer in sociolinguistics to the stylistic or 'intraspeaker' axis of variation: that which differentiates speakers in the short term across different speech situations. These are generally thought of as varying on a formal–informal continuum, and formality in turn is linked to the degree of social distance subsisting between the interactants in a situation.

The relation between social or 'interspeaker' variation and intraspeaker variation is that speakers draw upon socially prestigious linguistic variants in a formal speech situation. This is because in any society above a given level of complexity, division of labour becomes necessary, and social groups come to be (perceived as being) ranked hierarchically, some occupational groups enjoying more overt prestige than others, the prestige deriving from a perceived greater access to power and wealth. The social behaviour (including of course non-linguistic as well as linguistic) of the more highly ranked groups, who are in a position to define the standard language and behaviour generally, comes to be highly prized by all social groups; the next step is that the social behaviour of the higher groups is associated with more formal situations. Thus, the more formal the speech situation, the more prestigious will be the speech variety used, just as for instance more prestigious forms of dress are worn on formal occasions: the tailcoat may on the one hand be worn by members of all social classes at weddings, and on the other forms part of daily dress only at prestigious establishments such as that worn by head waiters in certain expensive restaurants. This at least is the situation that has obtained hitherto.

Speech style (or style in other forms of behaviour) is linked therefore to social structure, seemingly in a derivative way. Speakers respond to the nature of a situation by pitching their speech on a continuum of formality, in response to the perceived social status of the persons to whom they are talking; this is the essence of Bell's (1984) influential 'audience design' theory of style variation. Informalization (in Wouters' sense) used in a society-wide application and referring to linguistic change would therefore entail greater proportional use in more formal speech styles, or more prestigious speech varieties, of variables formerly considered suitable in informal styles or less prestigious varieties.

Social levelling is harder to discuss than regional levelling, because it involves the examination of assumptions that are now very basic, almost to the point of being axiomatic. These assumptions concern concepts like social equality and democracy, now virtually taken as given in the developed societies. More precisely, the phenomenon of interest here is the erosion or denial of the concept of virtually any hierarchy, whether based on class, birth, intellect or other criterion. Perhaps the sole hierarchy that remains important in majority terms derives from the capacity to consume. As we state in more detail below, the sacrosanct status of democracy, and 'ultra-democracy', its modern manifestation (Walden 2006), is reflected in the lack of literature devoted to it, at least written from the perspective we adopt here. Put bluntly, discussion of democracy carries the risk of seeming to call it into question. As stated above, a scholarly literature exists on the role of elites in democracy, and on a superficial view the non-critical consideration of elites, as was characteristic of an earlier literature, can seem anti-democratic. Indeed, anti-elitism is a defining characteristic of 'ultra-democracy', but as Walden points out (2006: 32–7), while the concept of the inevitability of elites in democratic societies is above all associated with conservative political theorists such as Pareto, Mosca and Michels, left-wing thinkers like Gramsci have also discussed the roles of elites in these terms. By contrast, academic discourse that takes democratization as a given is generally left-leaning politically. To describe and discuss concepts like democracy and equality 'from the outside' is not however to question their validity, and while commentators who do so tend to be situated on the political right, it should be possible to approach the subject in a way that is neutral politically, and to set aside any distaste one might feel for the politics of those who set out to explore delicate subjects like anti-elitism. As the French paradox has it, 'il faut souvent un vrai courage pour persister dans une opinion juste en dépit de ses défenseurs',[2] though we have to do here with enquiry rather than opinion.

We are in any event discussing here what one might call 'cultural democracy', and it should therefore be clear that our analysis does not bear on the concept of democracy in the political sense of universal adult suffrage. Walden (2006: 55), for many years a UK Conservative MP but generally characterized as a 'maverick', points out in his explanation of the term 'ultra-democracy' (where the prefix is used in its pristine sense of 'beyond'):

> An ultra-democracy is not [....] a society where democracy is extended to the limit – obviously a desirable state of affairs. It is one where democracy is denatured by taking the notion of the sovereignty and equality of the people to seductive, demagogic lengths, and where the debasement of genuine democratic values is encouraged from above. Ultra-democracy, in other words, is anti-democratic.

Walden seems to be using 'democracy' here in a socio-political sense – something like 'the capacity of citizens to participate in the democratic political process in a mature way'. We shall see that an analogous argument has been put forward by some French thinkers, although in the French context the opposition is expressed as between 'republic' and 'democracy', rather than between 'democracy' and 'ultra-democracy'. Our concern here is therefore with the rather paradoxical phenomenon of top-down initiatives aimed at the opposite of standardization, and driven by a populist ideology.

Walden remarks further that certain elites are currently exempt from the opprobrium directed at most, and suggests that those regarded positively are generally either useful (elite surgeons, elite troops) or providers of entertainment (elite footballers, the royal family). The use of 'elite' as an adjectival noun in these collocations carries no negative resonance. Elites that are neither obviously useful nor entertaining, such as the intellectual elite of the academy, are viewed negatively in the ultra-democratic perspective; this is seen very clearly when universities are periodically urged to combat elitism in their selection procedures. Debates like these show that the term 'elite' has undergone a shift in meaning, or at least has taken on a new sense; a recent dictionary definition is 'a chosen or select part, the pick or flower of anything' (Chambers), implying selection by merit, and indeed 'elite' and 'elect' have a common etymology. Hughes (1988: 191), in the section of his work on semantic change in English entitled 'Democracy and language', comments on the 'deterioration' (in the semantic jargon, 'pejoration') of the terms 'elite' and 'elitism' and notes the irony of 'elite' and elect' being doublets. When the universities of Oxford and Cambridge are accused of elitism, the word must refer to something like 'social elitism', in other words the opposite of social justice understood in the sense of a flatter distribution of economic and social opportunity. One could argue that accusations of this kind levelled at universities are in fact criticisms of social elitism in shorthand, and it remains true that admission to Oxford and Cambridge is skewed in favour of the socially privileged. This debate is complicated by the recent history of higher education in the UK, especially in relation to Oxford and Cambridge which were in fact until fairly recently the preserve of the upper classes without much regard to intellectual merit. Accusations of elitism seem increasingly, however, to be used to reproach any institution or practice not in principle open to all, whether on grounds of merit or social privilege; the same reasoning applies in reverse to the use of the term in response to criticism of popular-cultural products like reality TV and soap operas. But as Walden points out (2006: 14), 'providing they are open, elites are not just defensible but desirable in a democracy'. This seems self-evident, if only from the basic functional viewpoint that desires efficiency in the running of public and other concerns. But the fact that 'elite', as well as opposed terms like 'mass', have become uneasy terms indicates the extent of the social levelling we are discussing. Perkin (2002: xiv–xvi) has a different interpretation of the significance of the new kind of 'entertaining' elite:

Meritocracy has been transmogrified, as merit has come to be defined in non-traditional ways, to include talents no longer dependent on higher education: pop music, fashion modelling, sport, Britart, television presenting, soap operas, and other celebrity vehicles now yield huge incomes and greater wealth than ever. [Celebrities of this kind] are the exceptional beneficiaries of 'jackpot' professions in which many are called but few are chosen, but have the unlooked-for effect of giving hope to those who have missed out in the orthodox educational stakes.

Popular admiration of 'non-traditional' merit is of course by no means wholly new, although its current scale seems unprecedented, as witnessed by the plethora of popular magazines and TV shows exploiting the cult of celebrity. Perkin cites celebrities like David Beckham and Tracey Emin as representative of this trend. The implication latent in Perkin's insight is that media figures like these attract attention because their ordinary qualities enable the public to identify with them, and even cherish the dream of joining their number. In this sense they are a kind of anti-elite, and it does not seem implausible that their high public profile is an influencing element in the situation under discussion.

Walden's book is entitled *The new elites*, and its central argument explores the various implications connected with the fact that political and cultural elites in the UK are currently conforming to, and indeed helping to reinforce, the populist or anti-elitist zeitgeist, to the extent that public affairs are now controlled by 'anti-elitist elites'. Walden distinguishes sharply between 'popular' and 'populist', maintaining that the current unquestioning approval of the populist is in fact oppressive of the majority, and hence anti-democratic in the sense defined above. Although impressionistic and polemical, Walden's analysis contains some useful insights: he suggests that a determination to pursue a populist agenda degrades the public mind to the point where intelligent participation in the democratic process becomes difficult for the majority. This is of course because levelling currently seems to be proceeding downwards, directed by an elite that appears to adhere unquestioningly to the proposition that what is popular is good; at the same time this elite is in a position to define what is popular. As Walden points out (2006: 51): 'critical consumers know that a popular TV programme can be brilliant or imbecilic. The populist will insist that it is brilliant because it is popular'. A further useful insight that Walden proposes is a definition of the problematic term 'the masses'. As he remarks, this is now an uncomfortable term as it implies uniformity in a downward direction, and phrases like 'Mondeo man', 'middle England', etc., are used in preference. Certainly, a book entitled *Musings for the masses* (Derfel 1897), a work designed to popularize political and economic notions for the general reader, would be unlikely to be so entitled today.

A further work that shares characteristics of Walden's examination is by Seabrook (2000), alluded to briefly above and entitled *Nobrow*, with the sub-title *The culture of marketing and the marketing of culture*. The author, a journalist on the *New Yorker*, traces the response of that journal to what he sees as the marginalization of high culture, or its reduction to one form of culture among many. Seabrook uses the metaphors of the 'townhouse' to refer to high culture and the 'megastore' for mass culture. He suggests the following representations of what differentiates the current and former situations (2000: 66):

Identity
Subculture
Mainstream culture

High culture
Middlebrow culture
Mass culture

Seabrook glosses this is as follows. The argument is couched in a past tense, a sort of 'free indirect style', because the train of reflection is represented as having been prompted by a series of daily journeys between the offices of the *New Yorker* magazine and MTV, the pop music channel, in New York:

[...] where the old culture was vertical, the new hierarchy – Nobrow – seemed to exist in three or more dimensions. Subculture served in the role that high culture used to serve, as the trend giver to the culture at large. In Nobrow, subculture was the new high culture, and high culture had become just another subculture. But above both subculture and high culture was identity – the only shared standard, the Kantian 'subjective universality'.

As can be seen, Seabrook's term 'Nobrow' refers to subculture as universal culture. The essence of the situation is a mosaicization and levelling of culture, which the schema shown above does not fully capture, because it is set out in a way that implies hierarchy. Both Walden's and Seabrook's analyses concern the radical reshaping of the hierarchy that placed high culture at the apex of a pyramid. By contrast, the essence of mass culture, or popular culture, is that it should be open to all; high culture is therefore no longer high but elitist (not 'elite'). Because it is disprized therefore, it is ranked as one form of culture alongside others. At the same time, there is a certain dislocation of the moral from the cultural; perhaps the most extreme example of this is the popularity of rap and hip-hop forms of music, which represent one cultural choice among others despite their sometimes misogynist or homophobic lyrics. This is in contrast to the earlier state of affairs where high culture was regarded as in some degree transcendent or appealing to one's higher nature. In the new order, identity is expressed through consumption; the line between cultural and consumer products is blurred through an aestheticization of the latter, by means of advertising among others. Marketing is important in this process, because the 'marketing of culture' both drives and is driven by the levelling we are attempting to describe here. A striking example is the UK marketing campaign for the clothes shop 'French Connection', centred on the 'fcuk' logo: an acronym for 'French Connection UK' but also obviously an anagram of a word that still carries powerful taboo value for many. In this argument, corporations therefore contribute, for marketing purposes, to a symbolic process of subversion of high-cultural values, on the analogy of the role of the cultural-political elites referred to above but in a way that arguably influences individual behaviour in a more powerful way, given the importance, referred to above, of self-expression through consumption. Subculture now feeds quickly into mainstream culture owing to the instant accessibility of electronic media – Seabrook illustrates this using the example of the pop-music youth TV channel MTV. The ready and copious availability of subculture and mainstream culture (which is increasing the derivative nature of both) has the effect of marginalizing high culture, and as a result the hierarchizing effect of high culture is attenuated further. Again, this process is not new: big business was quick to exploit the first large-scale manifestation of youth culture, the pop music that emerged in the late 1950s. But the process has the characteristic of pushing further in the direction of symbolic outrage as each initiative is assimilated; an obvious example is the Rolling Stones, in the early 1960s the 'rebellious' counterpart to the likeable Beatles. The acceptance by Mick Jagger of a knighthood can be thought of as representing assimilation of this kind. And yet the power of symbolic subversion continues to hold sway even when the object of subversion has long since assimilated (again symbolically) to the values of the 'subverter'.

In summary, the essence of social levelling seems to stem from an implicit denial (implicit because the subject is delicate) of a hierarchical social organization; that is, one based on any attribute that is by its nature unequally distributed. This generalization is of course too broad, and needs to be qualified, as Walden points out, according to the attribute in question; thus a footballing or show-business hierarchy is acceptable, owing to the influence of the populist ideology discussed above, while the corresponding logic applies to unacceptable hierarchies, those deriving from orthodox values. In the interests of balance, it is perhaps worth citing the left-wing sociologist Daniel Bell:

> A post-industrial society reshapes the class structure of society by creating technical elites. The populist reaction, which [began] in the 1970s, raises the demand for greater 'equality' as a defense against being excluded from society. Thus the issue of meritocracy versus equality (Bell 1999: 410)

The argument is that social mobility proceeds through education in the knowledge-based post-industrial society. Access to education is however unequal in a meritocracy, since 'merit' in this sense is unequally distributed. The unfairness comes to be widely perceived and a reaction sets in. The unfairness is more keenly felt because it is not 'ascriptive', i.e. ordained by God or some other non-human agency. This analysis can be thought of as complementing the other accounts of populism already discussed.

Again, these remarks appear justified so long as one assumes that they have some wider psychological reality, as opposed to being confined to academics. Direct evidence of this is lacking, although a literary description by George Eliot of the earlier state of affairs is revealing. In *Silas Marner*, she draws a striking parallel between the common view of the social order and the weather, commenting on the village parson:

> whose exclusive authority to read prayers and preach, to christen, marry and bury you, necessarily co-existed with the right to sell you the ground to be buried in, and to take tithe in kind; on which last point, of course, there was a little grumbling, but not to the extent of irreligion – not beyond the grumbling at the rain, which was by no means accompanied with a spirit of impious defiance, but with a desire that the prayer for fine weather might be read forthwith.

The picture is no doubt idealized, even sentimental, but striking nonetheless as a portrayal of the earlier 'organic' state of affairs.

5.3.2 The timescale of social levelling

It is perhaps worth pointing out how recently the contemporary assumptions of democracy (or ultra-democracy) have become totally prevalent, at least in the public mind. We shall have occasion to quote in the following chapter some recent French pronouncements concerning non-standard language. In the UK context, what is arresting is the open expression of linguistic correlates to anti-democratic sentiments that were common fairly recently, when formulated at the time by scholars of language. For example, J. Milroy (2002: 12) cites the linguist G. P. Marsh (1865: 458) to the following effect:

> In studying the history of successive changes in a language, it is by no means easy to discriminate [...] between positive corruptions, which tend to the deterioration of a tongue [...] and changes which belong to the character of speech, as a living semi-organism connatural with man or constitutive of him, and so participating in his mutations [...] Mere corruptions [...] which arise from extraneous or accidental causes may be detected [...] and prevented from spreading beyond their source and affecting a whole nation. To pillory such offences, [...] to detect the moral obliquity which too often lurks beneath them, is the sacred duty of every scholar.

As Milroy remarks (ibid.), 'the belief that some forms of language (such as urban dialects) are not valid forms, and that changes observed in them are not legitimate changes, has persisted until very recently and may still be current in some quarters.' This attitude is exemplified most clearly where changes in the dominant variety led by its speakers are scarcely visible as change; the loss of post-vocalic /r/ in standard UK English, for example, or the adoption of back /a/ in the *bath* word set. One cannot of course with justice expect Marsh to have observed before its time had come the non-prescriptive view now axiomatic in linguistics. Nevertheless, the mismatch between his scholarly activity as a student of linguistics and his views as expressed in this passage – which are of course anti-democratic at one remove – remains striking. We have already cited in Chapter 1 the counterpart to this view, expressed sixty years later by Wyld, the historian of English.

The anti-democratic view openly prevalent in the nineteenth century, which Marsh's statement expressed indirectly and which is so repugnant in a contemporary perspective, must be seen in an intellectual context (at least among some thinkers) that then saw the possibility of progress through education: as Wright Mills states (1956: 301), 'if looking about them, nineteenth-century thinkers still saw irrationality and ignorance and apathy, all that was merely an intellectual lag, to which the spread of education would soon put an end'. These optimists felt free therefore to point out 'irrationality and ignorance and apathy' among the masses.

The contrast between what we have just described and the present situation is very great; in fact, the situation now is more or less a mirror image of the previous state of affairs. Put another way, cultural hegemony is to some extent inverted compared to the previous state of affairs. As Seabrook remarks (2000: 24): 'hegemony [...] is the idea that power becomes embedded in cultural distinctions as common sense.' It is widely agreed that social change has proceeded rapidly in recent years; terms like 'the century of the common man', 'increasing egalitarianism', etc., etc., are common, indeed almost commonsensical. The 'ultra-democratic' view cannot however yet be regarded as hegemonic, if we accept what is implicit in Seabrook's definition, namely that hegemony is an ideology that is powerful because unspoken. Nevertheless the scale and rapidity of the near-reversal remain striking. There is perhaps a basic human tendency to overestimate the rate of social (and other) change, possibly because of a golden-age mentality, possibly also because of a need to feel that one has lived through a momentous epoch. Certainly there is a tendency among laypersons to consider language change as abrupt and catastrophic and to continue to regard innovations as more recent than they in fact are. For instance, Amis (1998: 94) points out that the term 'happening', commonly perceived (in its sense of an informal or unstructured artistic performance) as a term first current in the 1950s or 60s, is attested in the (pre-1910) Edwardian era. This attitude is allied to the common habit of telescoping successive events in time, especially with increasing age, with the result that they appear to succeed each other more quickly than they in fact do.

Despite these tendencies, the fact, as implied above, that not much more than a century separates the sharply anti-egalitarian sentiments expressed by Marsh and others from the present time of writing, gives an indirect indication of the pace and recency of change in this period. The date from which one begins to track the process of what one might call symbolic egalitarianism or 'ultra-democracy' is a matter of the theoretical and practical optics adopted. Most immediately, one looks to changes consequent principally on the social upheavals of the 1960s and 1970s, typified most spectacularly by the events of May 1968 in France and elsewhere. Earlier significant dates are 1945, 1918, and further back, the French Revolution and the influence of Romanticism, with its prizing of the individual. The period following 1918 saw authority questioned on a scale that had perhaps been unprecedented in the modern era, while in the post-1945 years, as we argue below, a certain social solidarity was present, at least for a time. In a practical perspective, accountable linguistic data have become available only relatively recently, since about the beginning of the 1960s when portable recording equipment began to be used in sociolinguistic enquiry. This starting-point is convenient because it coincides more or less with the social revolution of the 1960s and 70s, which is generally agreed to have produced greater relaxation in many directions. Walden (2006: 27) remarks that the 1960s meant 'a thawing of frozen hierarchies, a freeing of thought, the liberation of women and the breaking down of repressive social codes'. Incidentally, a comment by the novelist Aldous Huxley (1894–1963) made in 1949 after listening to a recording of his own voice, whose accent would now be described as hyperlectal RP, provides further (weak) evidence of the relatively recent base-line of the change we are discussing (Smith 1969: 609):

> Language is perpetually changing, the cultivated English I listened to as a child is not the same as [that] spoken by young men and women today. But within the general flux there are islands of linguistic conservatism; and when I listen to myself objectively, from the outside, I perceive that I am one of those islands. In the Oxford of Jowett and Lewis Carroll [the middle-to-late 19th century], the Oxford in which my mother was brought up, how did people speak the Queen's English? I can answer with a considerable degree of confidence that they spoke almost as exactly as I do.

Impressionistic and non-scholarly comments like these have their limitation, but Huxley's suggestion, firstly that younger RP speakers had a pronunciation different from his own, and secondly that the pronunciation of his generation was conservative, contrasts sharply with the seeming pace of recent linguistic change. In particular, we shall see below that 'the Queen's English', in the literal sense of the term, has changed according to a quite different pattern from that sketched by Huxley.

It is in many ways convenient to take the post-1945 years as one watershed among several, since many economic, social and political factors coincided at the time. Some factors that were notable in the UK were:

- the after-effects of the social levelling that was inevitable in wartime, at least in the UK where 'total war' was prosecuted, both among the armed forces and others contributing to the war effort, notably women who had done factory work
- the admiration strongly felt for Soviet Russia, of course an Allied power at the time and perceived then as a proponent of egalitarian values
- the virtual disappearance of domestic service after 1945, partly as a result of increased taxation on income
- the effects on the post-war economy of the effort of total war
- the introduction of the Welfare State by the post-war Labour government.

Some factors that came to prominence a short time later, and having comparable effects, were:

- the increased purchasing power of the population generally, and notably of young people

- related to this, the increased regard in which the young are held, consequent in part on their being fewer and in part of their being an immensely important consumer group
- the promotion of popular culture, initially by influential cultural commentators like Williams (1958) and Hoggart (1957).

This list cannot of course pretend to be exhaustive. It should be pointed out too that certain processes are capable of reversal: social levelling in wartime, the reflex of an increased cohesion resulting from external threat, is likely to recede when the threat disappears. Similarly, admiration for the Soviet Union evaporated rather rapidly with the onset of the Cold War. In view of the large number of factors in play, and of the complexity of their interaction, we can hardly hope to provide a complete, or even a particularly coherent account here: it will be seen that a congeries of economic, political, social and intellectual factors is listed above. The relative weight of these factors is equally difficult to judge. The imponderable nature of the 'spirit of the age', determined by a nexus of attitudes and influencing factors and analogous to that enumerated above, was recognized by William Cobbett in the early nineteenth century, when he referred to 'THE THING'. As Walden (2006: 50) expresses it: 'to [Cobbett] THE THING seemed powerful, unyielding and irremovable precisely because it was so difficult to put your finger on.' This articulation of this intuitive notion anticipated by some time the 'cultural turn' discussed in 5.2.

Nevertheless it is perhaps justifiable to isolate in these lists two broad groups of factors, the economic and the socio-cultural, and to attempt to explain the causation of what we are describing here primarily in terms of interactions between them. In the following section we discuss them together, as they cannot usefully be separated. What is equally important for our present purposes is to try to determine whether the changes in question have taken place in essentially similar ways in the UK and France; and if so whether they have developed at similar rates. A further important element is the influence on the UK and French situations of economic and socio-cultural developments in the US.

5.3.3   Economic influences on socio-cultural behaviour: real or symbolic levelling?

We hazarded above the observation that although no substantive change in the economic structures of the countries of interest here has taken place in recent times, most notably in terms of the distribution of wealth and income, very important symbolic social changes have come about. The first part of this proposition could be qualified endlessly; certain substantive economic changes have of course taken place, like the massive shift from secondary to tertiary sector employment, which indeed can be thought of as potentially important in its impact on changing speech patterns. We focus here however on changes and continuities in the level of income distribution, since it is these factors that are germane to our argument.

Looking at extremes of income, it is undeniable that economic differences have been widening rather than narrowing in recent years. Table 5.1 shows how the income distribution has changed in the UK over the 15 or so years to 1994–95, essentially the Conservative administration of 1979–1997.

Table 5.1 shows divergence in this 15-year period between the top and bottom deciles of the income distribution. The ratio of inequality, about 12:1, between the highest and lowest deciles, is close to that characterizing other developed countries. There is undoubtedly a substantial gap between the highest and lowest earners, but a fairly high degree of homogeneity in the middle of the distribution; the four deciles from the fourth to the seventh, in particular, show degrees of inequality that are not gross. Even the large share taken by the top decile is distorted by the small number of very high earners, and one consequence of this is the fairly large difference between the mean salary (the 'average' in everyday usage, that is the sum of observations divided by their number), which in April 2004 was £519 per week, and the median or mid-point, which was £422 (Incomes Data Services, November 2004). The distribution is therefore skewed leftwards in relation to the 'normal' or 'bell' curve, towards the lower end of the range of values. Another way of expressing this is by saying that the income of almost two-thirds of employees falls below the mean (61.6% in 2002; Incomes Data Services, ibid.).

Tables like 5.1, which indicate relative distribution of income, do not of course reveal absolute increased general prosperity, driven by factors like technological and economic advances (improved infrastructure, higher industrial productivity and efficiency) and the fall in real prices produced by globalization, all factors that benefit the greater majority of the population. Of particular significance is the fact that UK wage inflation in recent

Table 5.1 Changing distribution of income in Britain (adapted from Hobson 1999: 692)

Deciles	Share 1979	Share 1994–5
Top tenth	21.0	27.0
Second	14.0	16.0
Third	13.0	12.0
Fourth	10.0	10.0
Fifth	10.0	9.0
Sixth	8.0	8.0
Seventh	8.0	8.0
Eighth	6.4	5.7
Ninth	5.6	4.1
Bottom tenth	4.	2.2

times has far outstripped price inflation (excluding the recent high inflation of house prices); on average prices rose sixty-fold in the twentieth century, while wages increased by a factor of 200 (*Guardian*, 11 June 1999). This standard conservative argument needs of course to be nuanced by acknowledging that at the same time, the incidence of relative poverty, however quantified, remains substantial. It is a commonplace of recent discussion that an uneducated 'underclass' has not participated in this general bounty. But these facts, and the relative material similarities in the middle of the income distribution shown in Table 5.1, lead one to question the validity of the income- and occupation-based contemporary social-class categorizations generally used until very recently by government agencies like the UK Office for National Statistics, sociologists, market researchers and indeed by many sociolinguists.

We leave aside the minutiae of these categorizations. Class is of course a construct, and as Cannadine argues (1998: 188), 'class is best understood as being what culture does to inequality and social structure: investing the many anonymous individuals and unfathomable collectivities in society with shape and significance, by moulding our perceptions of the unequal social world we live in'. In this view, class is a conceptual organization of inequality, although like many concepts it undergoes widespread objectification. Cannadine suggests further (pp. 19–20) that 'three basic and enduring models' of class have prevailed in Great Britain since the eighteenth century: 'the hierarchical view of society as a seamless web; the triadic version with upper, middle and lower collective groups; and the dichotomous, adversarial picture, where society is sundered between "us" and "them" '. In this perspective it hardly matters that in comparable countries official classifications differ, since these are primarily designed to reflect economic rather than social organization. Thus the British ONS employed until recently an essentially four-way distinction that recognized lower-middle and upper-working groups, while the three-way grid used by INSEE, the French equivalent, collapses these into one 'intermediate' category. Sociological models of class are generally based on occupation, since this feature accounts best for generational social reproduction, while cultural reproduction of the type of interest here seems to operate in different ways.

Cannadine's three broad models of social class throw further light on the issue. The ascriptive, organic, seamless-web conception of society seems tenable only where an exterior, i.e. divine, ascription is commonly accepted, as discussed in relation to Bell's populist model. The triadic model needs qualification because the middle class has expanded, and because the opposition, hitherto important in sociolinguistic enquiry, between lower-middle and upper-working, no longer appears pertinent. The anti-elitist zeitgeist now prevalent seems closer to Cannadine's 'dichotomous, adversarial picture, where society is sundered between "us" and "them"' than the other two models he evokes. A further formulation of Cannadine's (1998: 13) summarizes one more important theme that is relevant. He refers to 'a broader change in the conventional vocabulary of political discussion and social perception: namely the shift from the traditional preoccupation with people as collective producers to the alternative notion of people as individual consumers'. At the same time, of course, the discourse of class-as-collectivity continues to be employed to mobilize anti-elitism.

A further relevant factor is that recent adjustments to social-class attitudes in the UK and elsewhere reflect a shift in economic terms towards tertiary activity, which now represents about 70% of mature economies. The decline of the manufacturing sector is a commonplace of economic debate in the countries of interest here. This change is reflected in the increased 'social mobility' which Fabricius (2000:10), for example, identifies as an important factor in language change, but the nature of this mobility remains in need of more precise definition as it relates to our present concerns, for reasons we discuss below. The introduction of the concept of the 'tribe' rather than the social class in some French sociological literature (Maffesoli 1988) emphasizes the type of non-hierarchical atomization we have been examining here. Perkin's analysis (2002), entitled *The rise of the professional society*, suggests that class stratification has in the twentieth century been replaced by 'a congeries of parallel career hierarchies' (p. 398). The distinction between stratification and hierarchy suggests mobility versus its opposite, but a 'career hierarchy' might evoke the possibility of upward progress, slow and secure in the public sector and potentially more rapid and remunerative in the private, if more of a 'jackpot'. This is in contrast to the earlier, broader opposition between manual and non-manual occupations and the limited social mobility associated with it. Indeed, Perkin suggests that the public–private distinction is now the 'master conflict', exploited still in contemporary politics because it superficially resembles the outmoded right–left (capital–labour) opposition. Perkin points out further that even if much 'social mobility' from secondary to tertiary occupations is scarcely upward in the acquisition of much skill or prestige as normally thought of (a point we return to below), many occupations have taken on at least superficial professional attributes or secondary benefits like monthly salary and the right to paid leave and pension schemes.

Perkin's analysis is valuable in emphasizing that contemporary division of labour is now so complex as to blur something of its hierarchical organization. The notion of a congeries of 'parallel' career hierarchies needs of course to be nuanced, and Perkin does so by stating (ibid.) that 'some of the hierarchies are indeed more powerful than others'. This is undoubtedly true if we define power in any conventional sense, like the ability to control narrowly distributed resources, but as Perkin himself points out (2002: 4), 'we can envisage society [...] as an *equi-valent tetrahedron*, its faces labelled [...] class, power and status' (emphasis and hyphen in original); 'equi-valent' is so spelt to stress that the three faces are 'of equal worth, at least till one of them wins out in the competition' (ibid.). Perkin argues further (pp. 5–6) that 'a good case could be made (though it is unlikely to hold for all historical societies) for the primacy of the socio-ideological face [of the tetrahedron, i.e. status]'. This is because:

> Socio-ideological persuasion is an enviable form of power [...] since its devotees give freely and enthusiastically what they yield only grudgingly to military force or superior purchasing power. Political and economic elites pay it the compliment of emulation in propaganda and education.

This is an admirably concise summary of what we have been arguing so far. To illustrate the force of 'socio-ideological persuasion', we may cite the findings of a survey conducted by the polling organization MORI in 2000 which found that 58% of respondents ($N = 603$) answered 'working class' to the question: 'Most people say they belong either to the middle class or to the working class. If you had to make a choice, would you call yourself middle class or working class?' This contrasts with the 'objective' figures shown in most class categorizations where some 45% of the working population is commonly defined as middle class. A result such as that obtained by MORI is manifestly open to criticism regarding its methodology; perhaps the most obvious shortcoming of a question framed in this way is that the terms 'middle class' and 'working class' do not distinguish clearly between present social class and previous social trajectory. In the second definition, many respondents might regard their social origins to be as important as their present status, or more so if they feel their upward mobility is a matter for congratulation. A comparison between reported and 'objective' or ascribed social class would also have been enlightening. Nor can we estimate the seriousness of the responses offered. More straightforwardly, informants unversed in sociological terms may feel that they are working class for the simple reason that they go to work every day. At the same time, when the MORI survey was reported in a newspaper (*Metro*, August 21 2002), a Labour MP remarked; 'If you're a bloke [i.e. working class] you have got an army of friends who live off their skills and their wits and don't live off their education'. This remark epitomises one aspect of the nexus of ultra-democratic attitudes described above, with its implication that to 'live off' one's education is somehow parasitical.

The term 'inverted snobbery' can to some extent be applied to what we have been discussing here, although the term generally refers to individual attitudes, and the scale of the present phenomenon seems unprecedented. Straightforward snobbery and the inverted kind are complex attitudes, if only because their inflections depend on the social status of those who profess them. Convoluted attitudes to social class and social origin such as that quoted immediately above complicate discussion about 'social mobility' as one of the vectors of recent language change. This can be seen, for example, in relation to the observation by Karen Corrigan (a scholar of English linguistics) that 'at the moment [language] is changing faster than it ever has done because of increased opportunities for social and geographical mobility' (*Guardian*, April 1 2004: 7). The reference to geographical mobility is uncontroversial here, as it is almost commonsensical that under this constraint, speakers will modify their most localized accent features in the interests of short-term and long-term accommodation. However, the term 'social mobility' at first seems oddly applied in the same connection, because it evokes (or has done hitherto) 'upward' social mobility, with the implication of the latter's frequent effect of *embourgeoisement*, accompanied in many if not most cases by an adjustment by individuals of their speech and other behaviour 'upwards' (that is, towards more overtly prestigious norms). The type of downward levelling characteristic of the UK situation is, however, hard to describe in these terms: the title of the *Guardian* article that quoted Corrigan was 'Dialect explosion signals decline of BBC English'. Although typical of the hyperbolic journalistic idiom, this does capture the situation in its essence. Similarly, when Fabricius (2000: 10) mentions increased access to higher education as a factor propelling increased social mobility, it is in the context of a linguistic trend that might be regarded as instantiating 'downward levelling', viz. increased glottalling in RP, whereas under an older conception access to higher education would imply language change in the opposite direction.

We need therefore to understand 'social mobility' in a rather counter-intuitive sense, and one that requires an articulation that is only latent in the explanations cited above. In the example given by Fabricius, increased access to higher education, within the current levelled situation, brings with it a redefinition of higher education and its products. A linguistic reflex in secondary education is perhaps the increasing tendency to call pupils 'students'; in semantic terminology, the term has undergone 'amelioration' and has therefore been extended to a larger group, the counterpart of the pejoration of the term 'elite' mentioned above. While social mobility in its pristine sense of *embourgeoisement* is a factor in the current situation, one needs to look more radically to an adjustment of the entire framework of values in which social mobility works itself out. In schematic terms, Trudgill's pyramid, referred to previously, no longer seems to capture the situation; the distribution is now broader in the middle. One might wish to say that higher education (in the present example; others could be mentioned, and will be below) has modified in part because of increased access to it, such that a majority effect is at work which transforms behaviour that was characteristic formerly of an 'elite' sphere of activity. It is unlikely that mutations of this kind are contributing in a truly primordial way to language change; figures cited in the *Times Higher Education Supplement* (2 July 2004: 1) show that working-class access to higher education increased very little between

1994–95 and 2001–02, despite government initiatives designed to promote it. On the contrary, it is the higher-placed social classes who have benefited from the most recent university expansion; the proportion of students entering higher education from households with twice the mean income rose from a third to a half in this period; the proportion from households with the mean income (this was given as £20,890, so it is more likely to be the median) rose from 10% to 19%; while the proportion from households with half the 'mean' income rose from 0.89% to 1.77%. In other words, middle- and lower-middle class participation increased most sharply. Clearly therefore, higher education is no longer, and indeed has not been for some time, the preserve of the upper-middle classes: the most recent very large expansion relevant here, in proportional terms, was no doubt that prompted by the Robbins report of the early 1960s.

This example shows therefore a broadening of the social base in a sector of activity that was formerly highly exclusive, socially if not necessarily intellectually. We can perhaps see this is an instance of the broadening of the middle class, since a graduate is normally thought of as belonging in this class (despite the MORI results discussed above) and much employment in the burgeoning tertiary sector is definable as such. As Fabricius suggests (2000: 59), this is an example that is analogous to 'the new availability of more prestigious forms of employment to a larger part of the middle class than was the case before World War Two'. This is perfectly true, and data to support the statement come easily to hand. To cite Perkin again (2002: 269–70), 'The middle class as a whole has expanded in the twentieth century, from about 25 per cent in 1911 to [...] 43 per cent in 1971' [expansion in the intervening period has been omitted]. Since 1971 the middle class has no doubt expanded further; there is genuinely 'room at the top' aside from the perhaps spurious social mobility discussed above, in the transfer from relatively unskilled secondary to tertiary activity. Many recently created professional jobs are in the public sector, representing the continuing expansion of the government's share of GDP.

In the preceding paragraph we discussed the suitability of the term 'social mobility' from the perspective of those experiencing upward mobility. From the point of view of these speakers, the majority effect referred to above would however most plausibly take effect within the broad context of levelling we are discussing here, which places emphasis on mass values while disprizing behaviour carrying connotations of the elite, unless defined in Walden's and Perkin's populist senses as described earlier in this chapter. 'Upward' social mobility in its effect on language change can therefore be thought of in two ways which are not mutually exclusive; in the example of employment, an increase in the availability of middle-class or at least service-sector jobs, having the effect of broadening the middle-class social base, but operating within the wider social context of the vague, complex and multi-faceted levelling ideology: 'THE THING' discussed on p. 180.

A further, even clearer example than university expansion is that of employment in call centres. These currently employ more than a million people in the UK (reported in a BBC news item in 2011), representing the shift from the production of 'labour' to 'services' This is mobility in the 'spurious' sense described in the previous paragraph, but it is of interest because it illustrates linguistic behaviour rather directly. Looked at in the abstract, the 'classic' sociolinguistic analysis would be that the effect upon language change of a shift from employment in 'labour' to 'services' would tend to be towards the standard. This analysis, reconciling occupation- and income-based social class with social network and allied to the linguistic-market approach, stresses the importance of the standard language in an individual's working life. Teachers, secretaries and other people in jobs that entail a wide range of superficial contacts with strangers, including call-centre operatives, would therefore be thought of as middle-class, even if their jobs are not highly remunerative. By contrast, working-class speakers will tend to be employed in places where the standard language is less important because the range of social contacts is less wide but more intimate, or 'close-knit' in the social-network terminology. The service sector is of course as disparate as it is large, but employment in a call centre does comprise in very large measure the use of language in this 'middle-class' sense. In this perspective one would have expected until quite recently that the present burgeoning of tertiary-sector employment of this type, requiring a successful approximation to the standard language in the context of face-to-face and (increasingly) telephone service encounters, would entail a lessening of the possibility to express the finer nuances of social-regional diversity through accent. Against this, in the UK the call-centre sector seems increasingly to exploit the positively perceived social information encoded in these regional accents (even if they are less finely differentiated) perhaps partially in the interests of lessening the tensions inherent in service encounters, which by definition take place between non-intimates and often involve a conflictual element. It appears that those responsible for locating call centres rely on informal (non-academic) linguistic research on perceptual dialectology. In this connection, in 2002 the *Economist* reported research by the Aziz Corporation, a 'spoken communications consultancy', which gave the findings presented in Table 5.2.

The table shows a sample of UK accents perceived by a sample of company directors as being very or fairly honest. (A further finding reported in the same survey was that a strong regional accent was considered by 31% of the informants to be a disadvantage in business. A possible conclusion from this is that perceived honesty is considered a disadvantage to success in business.) The findings shown below more or less echo the classic ones reported by Strongman and Woosley (1967) and subsequent scholars: it will be recalled that the qualities of honesty, reliability and generosity were attributed to regionally accented speakers, by both northern and southern UK informants. The results shown can be regarded as an extrapolation in

Table 5.2   UK accents perceived as being very or fairly honest (Aziz Corporation: adapted from the *Economist*, 7 December 2002, p. 37)

Accent	Percentage of informants judging accent to be very or fairly honest
Scottish	27
West Country	25
Welsh	21
Newcastle	21
Home Counties (RP)	18
Birmingham / West Midlands	15
Liverpool	11
Cockney	9

more regional detail of one the standard results: regional and urban accents apart from Liverpool and London are in relative terms regarded as fairly trustworthy, while the accent of Birmingham, as so often, fares rather badly for reasons that are unclear. As suggested previously, the regional stereotype underlies the linguistic; thus the low rating accorded to the working-class London accent is perhaps unsurprising in view of the untrustworthy 'Jack-the-lad' image attaching to the stereotypical Cockney, while similar remarks can be made of Liverpool.

No rigorous real-time comparison can be attempted between the results tabulated above and those reported earlier, since the latter were in general qualitative not quantitative, and where quantities were shown, they related to other attributes like the 'prestige' or 'competence' attributed by some informants to RP speakers. Strongman and Woosley's informants were undergraduates, so one would hardly be justified in proposing that the attitudes tabulated above have in the interim been adopted by informants who are more highly placed socially. To the extent that there is a link between the results shown and our previous discussion of call centres, we can suggest that there is a rather remote parallel with the 'marketing of culture' discussed previously, whereby popular attitudes to language varieties are exploited for commercial reasons. A reflexive element continues in turn to reinforce these attitudes, since call centres are comparable to the broadcast media in diffusing language widely from a fairly narrow base. We discuss further examples of this kind of 'informal language planning' in a final section devoted to reflexes of social levelling that are not the direct outcome of socio-economic mutations of the type of interest here.

To what extent are some of the changes and attitudes described above prompted by economic factors beyond those that have restructured employment patterns? It is plain from the foregoing that the influence on social relations of economic developments is hard to measure, or even describe in a rigorous way. It is nevertheless tempting to draw parallels between high levels of prosperity and the social levelling that has taken place in certain countries. To look again at developments in the post-war period, we listed above the effects on the UK post-war economy of the total-war effort. It would seem at first sight that such an effort would have a negative rather than positive effect on a nation's economy, and this is indeed the classical view of the economic consequences of war. The problem can be formulated as follows, in the words of Milward (1984: 15): 'Is the extra expenditure entailed by war wholly a loss to the economy, or is some part of it actually beneficial in so far as it generates income by stimulating new employment and production?' In the case of the US, the view is widespread that the opposite of the classical negative analysis is true; for example, Chomsky (2003: 329) points out that it was the Keynesian effects of the war effort, rather than Roosevelt's New Deal, that were chiefly responsible ultimately for the recovery of the US from the Depression of the 1930s. Obvious negative effects of war are loss to the workforce and damage to infrastructure, as well as indebtedness. In the case of the UK, the classical negative view needs to be nuanced; while the loss to the workforce through war casualties was considerable, as was damage caused by bombing and general wear and tear, positive effects were provided by post-war aid from the US and the possibility of converting to other uses the industrial plant devoted to wartime military production. We need not examine this issue in much detail, beyond suggesting that post-war economic recovery started earlier than might be thought, so that the timescale of the changes in question here is longer than a superficial view might suggest. In another perspective, to cite Perkin again (2002: 409), 'the war prepared the way for a more state-interventionist, more equal and caring society after it had ended. It produced a revolution in expectations [...]'. This recapitulates some of the elements listed above. The term 'revolution' is a strong one and we must presume that it was used advisedly. Perkin himself (1926–2004) lived through the experience as an adult.

One can question whether these expectations of a 'more equal and caring society' were fulfilled. We have argued throughout this chapter that the term 'social levelling' is being used here in a sense that refers to symbolic social equality but not solidarity. It is somewhat of a commonplace, indeed almost a commonsense view, that increased prosperity has the effect of dissolving cohesive social networks of the kind that promote solidarity. We have already cited Frankenberg (1969: 232) to the effect that 'the less the personal respect received in small group relationships, the greater is the striving for the kind of impersonal respect embodied in a status judgment'. Our concern here is of course with social levelling, which implies, or at least brings in its train, the anti-elitism mentioned earlier, but not social solidarity in the intimate sense that is found in Milroy's descriptions of the Belfast communities she studies. Impersonal respect embodied in a status judgment can of course refer to status expressed through many social attributes, for example level of education, but the obvious consequence of increased prosperity is greater individualism, since prosperity decreases economic interdependence, with the conformity that can entail. Labov's (1972b) and Milroy's descriptions of the sometimes oppressive capacity to enforce norms inherent in a very cohesive community are too well known to need recitation here. While impersonal respect depends quite obviously, among other things, on the power to earn, spend (or employ credit) and consume, at the same time spending enhances subjectively the ability of individuals to express their social identity through the consumption of products that are increasingly aestheticized to the point where everyday consumer goods shade into products hitherto more generally thought of as cultural. The tension between individualism and conformity stems in this perspective from levelling in a different sense. Where no substantial differences exist between consumer products, as a result of continual refinements in the production process that produce technical upward levelling, subtle differentiation becomes important, always however with the proviso that the products in question are in principle available to all in the social strata concerned. Upward levelling in this sense, implying increased access to commodities and practices formerly confined to the upper and middle classes (foreign holidays, durable goods that were initially designed as luxuries), contribute further to the compression of the pyramidal social structure referred to earlier.

5.3.4 Other expressions of social levelling

In the following sections we look at some tabulated results produced by the variationist method that are 'accountable' in the sense of issuing from reasonably rigorously constructed speaker samples and elicitation methods. These are in contrast to impressionistic or informal observations, which can of course be misleading or provide only weak evidence. This is especially true of observations of sound change, but other types of language change are capable of unambiguous attestation: most obviously, those that find expression in writing. One very clear example is the telephone directory, which now bears the conversational label 'The Phone Book' on its front cover, reflecting the modern tendency to adopt into writing forms that hitherto were exclusive to speech. Different in detail but analogous in its inspiration is the employment by the BBC and other broadcasters of continuity announcers with regional accents, in sharp contrast to the prevalence of RP until not very long ago. This is a contemporary expression of the charge laid upon the BBC to promote impartiality. There has persisted however, until fairly recently, a broad division of labour that mostly has seen standard accents associated with serious topics, and regional accents with sport, reality shows, etc. Linguistic changes such as those initiated by telecommunications firms, operators of call centres and broadcasters are what we might call 'second-order' phenomena, in the sense that they are allied to more or less conscious language-planning initiatives that have arisen in response to the social changes we describe here. There is of course an element of reflexivity in processes of this type, if one accepts that they reinforce the underlying phenomenon as well as reflecting it. As previously stated, they produce an exaggerated effect, because they are diffused widely. Other instances like reality TV programmes differ in stemming, at least in part, from an anti-elitist ideology, although economy in the cost of production seems to be at least as weighty a factor. Reality TV can be assumed to be of some influence in raising awareness of non-standard language, but unlike the initiatives of the BBC and others referred to above, it seems likely that this is an unintended consequence.

Other, more 'spontaneous' examples (in the sense of being uninfluenced by quasi-conscious initiatives of the types listed above) are not far to seek: for instance, the increasing use between acquaintances of first name rather than title plus last name stands in very marked contrast to the former habit of indicating informality by using last name only, rather than title plus last name. To quote an example of the latter from *Born in exile* (1892b: 350), a novel by the Victorian novelist George Gissing (1857–1903), an ex-schoolfellow of a character called Peak addresses him as follows, having initially used the appellative 'Mr Peak': 'How can you ignore it, my dear Peak? – Permit me this familiarity; we are old fellow-collegians'.

Table 5.3 shows a trend that is analogous to language change of the type that we discuss here.

Although rather difficult to analyse in linguistic terms, the changing fashion in boys' names over fifty years shows a tendency towards 'informalization' to the extent that the pet names Jack and Harry (and Tom, Josh, Max, Archie, etc.) are now regarded as birth names in their own right. This is informalization in more or less the same sense as that discussed above, namely a greater use both on the inter-speaker and intra-speaker levels of variants formerly considered suitable only in informal styles. In other

Table 5.3 Top 10 names for England and Wales – Male (Source: Office for National Statistics)

1952	2001
David	Jack
John	Thomas
Michael	Joshua
Peter	James
Stephen	Daniel
Robert	Harry
Paul	Samuel
Alan	Joseph
Christopher	Matthew
Richard	Lewis

words, we can draw a fairly close parallel between (say) the increasing use of glottal stops in formal speech styles or prestigious speech varieties and the adoption as 'formal' names of what were formerly pet names. It is worth noting too the probabilistic or percentage-wise nature of the change shown in the table, which in miniature mimics other types of language change (at least in vocabulary), not all items being affected in the same way. Lexical change is ephemeral and reversible, since it takes place at the most superficial linguistic level, and fashions in children's names are subject to several factors, for example the passing influence of celebrities.

Nor are non-linguistic signs of levelling far to seek. Clothing is an obvious example; as Adonis and Pollard (1997: 242–3) point out, items of working and sports wear like t-shirts, jeans and trainers are now increasingly acceptable in more formal contexts. The authors speculate, following Perkin (2002: 431–2), whether trends like these reverse

> the sociologists' 'principle of stratified diffusion' (the theory that trends in dress, music, entertainment, and lifestyle always begin at the top and work their way down through society). If it had ever been wholly true – and the past history of the upward trajectory of trousers, the lounge suit, and casual wear generally [...] suggest otherwise – the 1960s turned it upside down, with the young of the upper and middle classes emulating the denizens of Liverpool and the East End of London.

The 'language of clothing' is a complex subject, but a glance at photographs of earlier periods suggests at once greater uniformity and hierarchy (upper- and middle-class clothing imitated by working-class) in contrast to the present fragmented situation.

5.3.5 Conclusion to Section 5.3

The subject of this chapter so far has been the zeitgeist that seems currently to be at the root of much language change. The term is of course a German loan-word, which like most borrowings has undergone a shift in meaning: 'zeitgeist' is now a journalistic term that more often means in English something like 'latest trend', rather than the more philosophical 'spirit of the times', its more literal translation. The ambiguity reflects one aspect of what we have discussed above. Is what we have been discussing the latest trend, with the reversibility that implies, or does it reflect a more fundamental shift in the framework of what Perkin calls the 'socio-ideology' of class organization? Much language change is ephemeral, especially in vocabulary, but the tendency among linguists is to assume that change in pronunciation is usually structural and permanent. Perkin's informal anecdote (2002: 431–2) recounting that in the 1960s 'public school [pop] groups like the Hollies had to fake a working-class accent to become acceptable' is of little relevance as a datum for the present argument, as indeed is a remark from a professional linguist, such as McMahon's (1994: 246): 'a pronunciation of *house* as [haɪs] [the hyperlectal RP form] surfaced briefly in the 1980s among workers in the City of London, was stigmatised as a feature of the then-prevalent 'yuppie' culture, and seems to have all but gone.'

It seems therefore that some pronunciation variants can ebb and flow fairly rapidly, and the [haɪs] example is no doubt unrepresentative of most variants in being an upper-class stereotype whose sociolinguistic value is very readily apparent to many if not most speaker-hearers. The linguistic data that we discuss in the next section have for the most part been gathered using robust variationist methods, and if their limitation is a lack of time-depth, so that change cannot be inferred with certainty, many of the patterns they show are capable of being interpreted as indicative of change. This limitation needs, however, to be borne in mind in the discussions that follow.

A related question is the cognitive status of variable language, compared to other kinds of social behaviour that are capable of variation and change. It is notable that Adonis and Pollard (ibid.) included class-variable language along with other elements of what they term 'lifestyle'. The term implies choice as well as a certain superficiality, and an obvious difference between variable language and other types of variable behaviour is that we are all producers as well as 'consumers' of language. A common consensus in sociolinguistics is that language change proceeds in the context of face-to-face interaction, such that, for example, UK English shows no sign of adopting US pronunciation features despite the considerable exposure of its speakers to these. This is in obvious contrast to the adoption of other US cultural artefacts, including variable lexis. As Trudgill points out (1990: 11), the acquisition of new lexis is a simple matter, since it is in any event a continual process, whether importations are from within or without the speech community, whereas an imported pronunciation feature goes against speech habits acquired very early in life, and needs to be learned at a structural level, as it affects word-sets that can be structured in a complex way. At a deeper level, pronunciation seems to be linked to social identity in a more personal and intimate manner. Change in pronunciation is only possible through the accommodation associated with face-to-face interaction, if then. And as Coveney expresses it (2001: 1): 'Pronunciation is particularly closely linked to identity, more so on the whole than lexis and grammar. [...]', on account of its concrete character, which is allied to other physical aspects of behaviour like gesture and dress. Further, (ibid.): 'The connection [between pronunciation and identity] is also due to the fact that speakers use relatively minor differences in pronunciation to signal aspects of their identity, while generally maintaining intelligibility with speakers of the same language.' The implication is that the high processing cost of often subtle phonological adjustments is offset by the social advantage gained by alignment to the desired reference group. To reiterate, accommodation takes place where social advantage is perceived as being gained thereby. This is in contrast to the 'imitation' of other accents, of which most speakers are capable over short sequences. Exposure to variable language, via the broadcast media, from outside the immediate speech community may however have a 'softening-up' effect, with the result of increasing what Trudgill (1986: 55) calls 'passive' sociolinguistic competence, perhaps bringing with it the *potential* to change productive speech habits, if not with immediate effect.

Analogously, we have described in this chapter a range of social effects that can be thought of as having the kind of 'softening-up' effect capable at least of increasing passive competence in a wider range of non-standard accents. This is in part due to the magnifying effect of the broadcast media, of the few speaking to the many, which again until recently has worked to increase awareness of prestigious accents, in contrast to the present de-standardizing tendency. If a good deal of space has been devoted here to phenomena of this kind, as well as to concepts like social mobility, which seem to increase active as well as passive competence of the type discussed above, it is because they seem to have been rather sketchily explored and analysed in most recent accounts of language change, and because the social mutations impelling them seem quite radical, if not momentous. At the same time it can appear invisible, like the 'elephant in the room' of recent cliché. Initiatives to promote large-scale social levelling in planned societies have always failed, but the largely unplanned levelling seen recently in the societies of interest here seems at the present time irreversible. In what follows we consider how these processes are shown in language change.

5.4 Linguistic manifestations: the erosion of the standard

The obvious linguistic corollary of social change in the direction of symbolic convergence is the attenuation of 'prestige' language features and the promotion of 'change from below': the adoption by middle-class speakers of working-class language features. This latter is a phenomenon attested in UK English by a considerable number of quantitative results. One of the substantial findings of quantitative sociolinguistics is indeed that most language change proceeds from below, in the sense just used. Social-regional stereotypes underlying UK urban vernaculars seem to be exploited increasingly in opposition to traditionally 'prestigious' language varieties, and hence of course the social values they represent. The best-known example in English is probably the increasing use by upper-class speakers, and by many speakers in formal styles, of the glottal stop.

In this section we consider some linguistic manifestations in English of the social processes discussed in 5.3, attempting to show how this social theory can be married to language as 'the construction of social identity'. We look first at what we referred to previously as horizontal levelling, turning subsequently to the more difficult issue of social levelling.

5.4.1 Horizontal dialect levelling in UK English

The issue of levelling is currently the focus of attention of several scholars (Foulkes and Docherty 1999; Jones and Esch 2002; Britain and Cheshire 2003). In the introduction to their edited volume, Foulkes and Docherty (1999: 13) suggest that several linguistic changes currently in progress in English can be analysed from the perspective of social processes having the effect of reducing dialect differences:

> Levelling differs from standardisation (or dedialectalisation) in that speakers do not automatically abandon their local forms in preference for the standard. Rather, there appears to be a tension between speakers' desire to continue signalling loyalty to their local community by using local speech norms, and a concurrent urge to appear outward looking or more cosmopolitan.

Simplifying somewhat, at least three broad processes can be identified as currently taking place in the UK:[3]

(i) Throughout the UK, certain consonantal features of 'Estuary English' are spreading: glottal stop, labialized /r/, (th)-fronting. This is not currently linguistic levelling in the sense of diminution of difference, as the process is still in an intermediate stage that increases differentiation, but falls more neatly into the category, distinguished initially by Labov in the 1960s, of 'change from below'. It can however also be thought of as dedialectalization in some UK regions, since it is affecting highly localized linguistic features there. A further, more neutral term sometimes used is 'diffusion'.

(ii) In the north of the UK and elsewhere, high localized features, perhaps mostly vowels, are giving way to variants distributed over a wider region. This corresponds more neatly to the definition of levelling quoted above.

(iii) In certain towns, of which perhaps the most notable (certainly the most studied) case is Milton Keynes (Kerswill and Williams 2000), levelling has taken place as a result of town-planning initiatives that have brought together speakers from widely scattered localities in SE England. This is perhaps the best example of socially neutral levelling towards a widely shared localized dialect, although within the wider context of levelling it is of course socially loaded in rejecting standard variants.

A further term that is current in the literature and covers the first two of these processes is 'dialect borrowing'. The term is suitable to the extent that it emphasizes 'dialect' over 'standard'. At the same time, we are dealing in all cases with the borrowing of dialect features from regions or localities either larger in size, or considerably removed in space, from the borrowing communities; or in cases like Milton Keynes, with a process of 'dialect blending' that is fairly easy to explain, in mechanical if not ideological terms. The social mechanisms driving these processes are described by Watt and Milroy (1999: 26) as follows:

> One view of levelling is that it is a linguistic reflex of the large-scale disruption, endemic in the modern world, of those close-knit, localised networks which can be shown to maintain highly systematic and complex sets of socially structured linguistic norms.

Watt and Milroy (ibid.), citing Auer and Hinskens (1996: 4) suggest that the large-scale disruption referred to above comprises processes such as:

> industrialisation, urbanisation, mobility and increased ease of communication at regional, national and international levels, [which] have brought about dialect contact to an extent hitherto unknown. To this list of precipitating factors we might add the more recent phenomenon of *counterurbanisation*, or the movement of urban populations into surrounding rural areas.

Fabricius (2000) has a more detailed description, which embeds recent dialect levelling within the wider social context:

> The last half of the twentieth century has wrought many changes in British society. These include changes in individual social mobility, through increased access to higher education [...]. Contact between different parts of society has increased, through the new availability of more prestigious forms of employment to a larger part of the middle class than was the case before World War Two. The same period has also seen a change in demographic patterns, as the migration of large numbers of people from London led to the establishment of new towns such as Stevenage and Milton Keynes. People living in many parts of Britain have also had increased contact with London speakers because of improved transportation reducing travelling times to London.
>   Linguistic studies are beginning to show that these recent changes have also had a profound influence upon British English speech. Accents are beginning to reflect new patterns of contact. We are now seeing a levelling of previous class and regional differences in speech, and this is perhaps most visible in the South of England [...] At the same time [...] it has become unfashionable to flaunt a privileged background in the form of a 'public school' accent. The signs seem to be unmistakable: the former bastion of RP in the public domain, the BBC, has recently changed its policy to include 'more energetic and vigorous voices from the regions' (Culf 1994). (Fabricius 2000: 10).

Developing the approach implicit in the Fabricius quotation, it would appear that the overall tendency of current levelling processes is towards the erosion of the status of the standard language. Rather than an accidental side effect of koineization, however, we see this as a further manifestation of the social processes discussed in Section 5.3. From that perspective, it is important to distinguish mechanism from motivation. Some of the social mechanisms that are currently bringing about dialect levelling are listed in the quotations given above from Watt and Milroy and Fabricius. While some of these, like counter-urbanization, are subject to individual choice or participation, others, like the disruption of close-knit, localized networks, are less so. Nevertheless, a common theme in these changes is an implicit rejection of the standard variety, implying that accounts framed purely in terms of process (simplification, blending etc.) may be missing an important component of the underlying aetiology.

With this in mind, we examine below some of the relevant quantitative findings that have been reported in the literature. Table 5.4 shows an example of the tendency outlined in **(i)** at the start of this section.

Table 5.4 shows a pattern in Tyneside English in which middle-class (especially female) speakers seem to be promoting a linguistic change in the direction of the replacement of glottalized stops, transcribed as [ʔt] below, by full glottalling. The figures in bold in the table illustrate this tendency (these are raw figures, not percentages). So the standard realization of intervocalic /t/ in words like *butter* is an alveolar plosive [bʌtə]; the non-standard supralocal realization is a glottal stop [bʌʔə]; and the local non-standard realization is an alveolar plosive reinforced by a glottal stop, transcribable as [bʌʔtə]. Full glottalling, originally a working-class phenomenon until fairly recently associated stereotypically with the speech of working-class London and Glasgow, appears currently to be spreading very rapidly in the urban centres of the UK. The process shown in Table 5.4 suggests therefore the regional and social promotion of a variant that is both supralocal and non-standard. Unlike the middle-class speakers, the other groups seem to be resisting the introduction of the innovating supralocal form, preferring the glottalized form [ʔt], which is very highly localized to NE England, more specifically to Tyneside.

Table 5.4 Glottal reinforcement [ʔt] and glottal replacement [ʔ] of /t/ in Tyneside English (adapted from J. Milroy *et al.* 1994: 348)

Sex/Class	[ʔt]	[ʔ]	Sex/Class	[ʔt]	[ʔ]
WCF	112	59	WCM	52	28
MCF	66	130	MCM	82	70

Legend: WCF = working-class females; MCF = middle-class females; WCM = working-class males; MCM = middle-class males.

Glottalling has a long history and, clearly, synchronic results like these give no definitive evidence of change in progress,[4] although support from other results endorses the notion, if only impressionistically, that t-glottalling is spreading. Other findings are quite copious, and have been surveyed recently by Marshall (2003), who asserts that 'the spread of the glottal stop as a variant of /t/ in British English has been well documented in the recent literature' (p. 89). This strong statement needs to be qualified by reference to the fact that no comparable diachronic results are available, except for Scots English; the closest comparison is between the results reported by Macaulay and Trevelyan (1973) and Stuart-Smith (1999), for Glasgow English, which certainly show increased use of the glottal stop. The results in Table 5.4 conform to Labov's principle (1998: 7) that 'in the majority of linguistic changes, women use a higher frequency of the incoming forms than men'. It is worth noting also the frequent use of the glottal stop by the younger females in the most socially differentiating linguistic context, between vowels, implying that glottal replacement is now well established in the most linguistically favourable environment, before a consonant.

We look now at an example of the tendency described in **(ii)** above, where localized features are receding in favour of variants distributed not necessarily nation-wide, but beyond the local environment. Some relevant data are given in Table 5.5.

Table 5.5 again shows raw figures, not percentages. Speakers of Tyneside English have at least three variants of the /o/ vowel in the lexical set exemplified by *home, goat*, etc. One of the most localized variants is [ø]; the variant distributed over the north of England is [o:]; while the standard supralocal realization is [oʊ] or [əʊ]. The results show that the most localized variant (and one that is almost exclusively the property of males) seems to be receding. The same gender-based pattern is incidentally also apparent in

Table 5.5 Social distribution of variants of /o/ in Tyneside in *goat* word-set (adapted from Watt and Milroy 1999: 44)

Linguistic variant	[ø]	[o:]	[oʊ]
Sex/Class/Age	N	N	N
WCF 45–65	1	188	0
WCF 16–24	1	196	0
MCF 45–65	2	176	18
MCF 16–24	6	126	34
All speakers F	10	686	52
WCM 45–65	55	55	3
WCM 16–24	53	113	2
MCM 45–65	27	127	0
MCM 16–24	59	76	30
All speakers M	194	371	33

Table 5.4, such that female speakers are promoting the non-local variant. The difference in sociolinguistic structure is that in Table 5.5 the non-local variant, while non-standard in the sense of not being distributed nation-wide or being a feature of the prestige or dominant variety, is non-innovating in the sense of not being wholly foreign to the region.

Watt and Milroy (1999: 25), setting up a comparison between vocalic chain-shifts occurring in some of the northern cities of the US (Labov 1994) and the vowel changes in progress on Tyneside, express the problem as follows:

> It appeared to us as we examined our data that the Newcastle vowel system was indeed [...] undergoing change. However, a chain-shift model does not capture the evident patterns, namely that variants characteristic of a larger area than the Tyneside region appear to be spreading at the expense of extremely localised variants.

In other words, Watt and Milroy suggest that a socially based explanation that refers to change reflected in the linguistic system, rather than a system-internal mutation prompted by linguistic factors, seems more suitable in this case. What is very striking is that very few Tyneside speakers indeed favour the southern, standard, supralocal variant. This is therefore levelling in the double sense that differences between localized varieties narrow and that 'speakers do not automatically abandon their local forms in preference for the standard', in the formulation of Foulkes and Docherty (1999: 13) quoted previously. This invites the question what exactly is meant by levelling in any given instance. While the concept of linguistic diversity seems both intuitive and capable of being used in a specialized linguistic sense, the opposing term 'levelling' can be understood in several senses. A definition of the latter concept in the sense of homogenization, or the reduction in the number of linguistic features that distinguish speaker groups differentiated by the customary social criteria (age, sex, class, region), seems hardly to correspond to the UK situation, at least so far as the linguistic features discussed above are concerned, since the recession of localized forms in favour of more widely distributed (but not standard) features implies not necessarily linguistic homogenization, but rather greater diversity in the form of more competing features available to speakers, at least in the medium term. This is at least true of glottal replacement and other consonantal changes. A social interpretation of the promotion of wider regional forms at the expense of the standard suggests levelling in a quite different sense: a process of social rather than linguistic levelling, taken in the sense discussed above, sees the standard transformed from its status as the metonymic variety to one among others. This therefore is levelling in a sense opposed to standardization; that is, levelling as anti-standardization. The term 'process' needs to be emphasized; it would be wrong to suggest that the standard is no longer superordinate. It will be recalled that the further element of Foulkes and Docherty's definition (ibid.) was as follows:

> there appears to be a tension between speakers' desire to continue signalling loyalty to their local community by using local speech norms, and a concurrent urge to appear outward looking or more cosmopolitan.

The more neutral term 'outward-looking' certainly seems apposite. As we suggested above, horizontal and vertical levelling interlock in that the abandonment of local forms is not reinforcing the standard variety. At the same time, it is not clear how current levelling processes are explicable by the 'reference group' theory discussed in Section 4.3, if only because, as previously stated, these are operating on a large scale and in a complex way.

To what extent is the Tyneside situation typical of other UK urban speech communities? Tyneside or 'Geordie' speech is regarded by other speakers of UK English as highly distinctive, owing no doubt to the large number of pronunciation variables in Tyneside English not found in other varieties, so that Tyneside is a remarkable in vivo laboratory for researchers wishing to demonstrate the processes listed under **(i)** and **(ii)** above, the replacement of localized features by non-standard supra-regional and more widely regional variants. The results presented in Table 5.6 show a comparable example of the same process; these are drawn from the study reported by Llamas (1998) on variation in the speech of Middlesbrough in NE England.

Table 5.6 shows essentially the same tendency as that discussed above in relation to Table 5.4, although with a further level of social complexity. A consonantal variable is again in question, this time /r/, which in standard English is generally realized as an alveolar approximant in initial position (transcribed as [ɹ] in the table), as in *real* pronounced [ɹɪəl]. The incoming variant in Middlesbrough is 'labial /r/', a labiodental approximant, in IPA notation transcribed [ʋ]. This phenomenon, referred to as '/r/-fronting', has been reported in several UK cities. Of further interest to our purposes is the fairly recent emergence of the labiodental variant, at least with its current value; it is of course caricatured as an upper-class stereotype in the works of such authors as P. G. Wodehouse and Frank Richards (in the *Gem* and *Magnet* stories): 'you fwightful wotter!'. Jones (1956: 109) treats the variant as 'defective' and offers recommendations for its correction. Trudgill (1988) reported

Table 5.6 Variable use of (r) by gender in Middlesbrough (NE England)

	Total	[ɾ]		[ɹ]		[ʋ]	
	N	N	%	N	%	N	%
Male	479	103	21.5	293	61.2	83	17.3
Female	480	23	4.8	407	84.8	50	10.4

that he noticed the use by one speaker of labiodental /r/ during his first field investigation in Norwich, but assumed that it was a speech defect. Use of the variant had increased dramatically by the time of Trudgill's second field trip to the city some twenty years later. Speculation in this regard would focus on the developmental correlate to the variant's current status. The standard alveolar approximant is acquired relatively late in children's speech, and one might suggest that the normativism prevalent at the time when Jones stigmatized the labiodental variant as defective, has been replaced by a quite widely generalized attitude of greater tolerance, connected with the egalitarianism described previously, such that many parents may now be less ready to correct this variant as defective in their children's speech.

5.4.2 Vertical dialect levelling in UK English

The second type of convergence is harder to discuss than the first, but not because the examination of concepts like democracy and equality is particularly delicate. The problem is rather that the study of vertical dialect levelling ideally entails the study of the most socially prestigious language varieties, to ascertain whether such varieties are seeing increasing use of non-standard variants, and this has rarely been done. One reason is no doubt that highly placed social groups are in a position to resist sociological enquiry, as a result of interacting in relatively tightly knit social networks, or more plainly, in more exclusive social circles. As Fabricius remarks (2002: 116), 'sociolinguistic studies of elite varieties are rare, Kroch's (1995) study of the speech of the upper class of Philadelphia standing almost alone in the literature'. To Kroch's study we can add that of Malécot (1976), who recorded upper-middle-class Parisians surreptitiously in a spontaneous conversational style.

The alternative to studying upper-class speech directly is of course the recording of the formal speech, generally scripted, of speakers who are less highly placed socially; or of upper-class or highly educated speakers, for example politicians and journalists, in public situations. It is plain that most speakers draw upon socially prestigious (and hence older) linguistic variants in formal speech situations: the phenomenon known as style shift or 'intra-speaker variation'. A well-known study (Harrington, Palethorpe and Watson 2000) combined both principles – upper-class speech in a highly public setting – in a survey of how the speech of Queen Elizabeth II evolved between the 1950s and 1980s, as shown in her annual Christmas address broadcast to the nation. This is a convenient reference point, as the monarch is by definition at the apex of the social hierarchy, as least as defined in any book devoted to defining social precedence, or other manuals of etiquette. Harrington, Palethorpe and Watson found that ten out of 11 vowels they studied in the Queen's speech had modified over this period, in the direction of what they called the 'standard southern-British' accent.

The authors discuss several factors as possibly at work in the modification of the Queen's speech: ageing (which they reject); 'hyperarticulation' or a 'change in the style of delivery [...] to produce a perceptually clearer style of delivery of broadcasts in later years' (p.79); and more plausibly, accommodation to more widely distributed speech norms. This latter explanation conforms to the results of other studies, most recently that of Fabricius, which shows RP speakers adopting certain features like glottalling and so-called 'happy-tensing' that are characteristic of less narrowly distributed social dialects.

We suggested above that the effects of social mobility, often cited as an explanation for recent changes in UK English and other languages, need to be understood in a sense which is perhaps not customary. Social mobility in this sense modifies the dominant accent, perhaps because of the large scale on which it operates. An example of social mobility of this type was discussed in the *Economist* (7 December 2002: 33–4), where it was pointed out that the social origins, as expressed by educational background, of the members of what is sometimes referred to as the 'power elite' of the UK have changed quite markedly in the past thirty years or so. This is shown in Table 5.7.

Table 5.7 shows a sharp change in the pattern of educational background of 100 influential decision-makers (drawn from politics, business, academia, sport and the arts) over the last thirty years. Stable between 1972 and 1992, the large shift occurs between the latter date and 2002, when recruitment from the endowed fee-paying 'public' schools and the ancient and highly-regarded universities of Oxford and Cambridge ('Oxbridge' in the table) drops sharply. This shift is explained in the article by reference to several factors: globalization, with the consequence that several currently prominent politicians and (especially) business leaders were educated outside the UK; allied to this is the fact that the Labour government at the time contained several Scots. A further factor is that many members of this elite (average age 57) were educated in state grammar schools, to which free admission was guaranteed by the 1944 Education Act and which were abolished, at least in recommendation, in the mid-to-late 1960s following 'Circular 10/65' that requested local education authorities to replace the tripartite secondary system with comprehensive schools. The selective state grammar schools recruited some 20% of pupils through the 'eleven-plus', a competitive examination taken in the final year of primary school, and for three decades or so were the route by which many pupils of modest social origin gained access to the universities. An effect of this kind is clearly one among many,

Table 5.7 Educational background of 100 members of the UK 'power elite', 1972–2002

	1972	1992	2002
Public school	67	66	46
Oxbridge	52	54	35

and it is unprofitable to speculate on the effects on, and consequences for, language change of for example, the presence in high office of a figure such as the former Deputy Prime Minister John Prescott, who left school at 15 and retains a fairly strongly marked north-west accent. Greg Dyke, the first Director-General of the BBC not to be a public-school and Oxbridge product, retains a fairly noticeable London accent. Other prominent examples outside the power elite and the 'jackpot professions' could be multiplied: the most notable is perhaps Jamie Oliver, the seemingly ubiquitous 'celebrity chef' whose unreconstructed (and perhaps exaggerated) London accent has been the object of much comment. The authors of the piece in the *Economist* speculated incidentally whether the abolition of the grammar schools, which had the unintended effect of increasing the fee-paying schools' share of the secondary sector, would result in a reversal of the pattern shown in table 5.7. We are now in a position to see that this is so, in politics and some other areas of public life. The results detectable in the accents characteristic of the new 'power elite' are interesting to observe, given the virtual demise of marked RP among the privileged young. We discuss post-war Prime Ministers immediately below, but it is of passing interest that David Cameron, born in 1966 and PM since 2010, stands in sharp contrast to his near contemporary, Boris Johnson (b. 1964). While both are products of Eton and Oxford, Johnson retains a marked or 'hyperlectal' reflex of RP that attracts some derision in certain sections of the press, unsurprisingly in view of the zeitgeist we have been at pains to describe here. A study of the contrast between the language of Cameron and Johnson through an investigation into their respective social networks would be of some interest.

To pursue further the matter of the formerly increased openness of social access to high office, all but two British Prime Ministers since Douglas-Home (1963–64) have been products of grammar schools. This is in very sharp contrast to the other post-war Prime Ministers (Attlee, Churchill, Eden, Macmillan, Douglas-Home) who were all products of major public schools. The minor exception to the post-1964 pattern is Callaghan (1976–9), who like Prescott left school before sixteen and rose through the trades-union hierarchy. Of more interest to our present purposes is Blair, who attended a prestigious Scottish fee-paying school and falls therefore outside the grammar-school pattern. It seems worth pointing out that while Heath (1970–74), Callaghan and Thatcher (1979–90) had a more or less close approximation to RP (at least in intention, a crucial point), Major (1990–97) a standard southern accent and Wilson (1964–70; 1974–76) a standardized northern accent (all of which could be described using Honey's (1989: 143) term as 'paralects' of RP), Blair's accent sometimes appears designed to repudiate his privileged background, although his accent varies markedly depending on the formality of the speech event. The son of a barrister and himself called to the Bar, Blair had and has accent features that sometimes evoke a more demotic speech variety; his use of t-glottalling seems quite

clearly motivated, but a curious distribution of schwa in unstressed syllables gives the impression of an uninstructed desire to approximate to a
non-standard variety, if none in particular. Brown (2007–10) stood apart
from the dialect pattern by reason of his educated Scottish accent. The
speech of prominent people of the kind tabulated and discussed above is
mediated largely through radio and TV, and it seems implausible that they
serve as models capable of causing changes of the type discussed here. They
are rather the reflection of the wider changes under discussion. As Honey
remarks (1989: 133): 'television and technical advances have brought [into
politics] the new factors of immediacy, visibility, spontaneity, informality,
and saturation coverage.'

The influence of television and other electronic media in promoting
linguistic change has been the object of some controversy among sociolinguists. Fasold (1990: 236) expresses the predominant assumption as follows,
in relation to the pronunciation level: 'it is more important to conform
to what people in your network expect than to what you are taught in
school or hear on television.' More recently and generally, Chambers (1995)
has suggested that while the electronic media have little influence on the
promotion of sound change, which operates in the context of face-to-face
interaction, more superficial change such as that operating in the lexicon
can be brought about through contact with impersonal sources such as
television. But in the opposing perspective, the factors cited from Honey
above quite obviously bring the speech of prominent people under intense
scrutiny and may lead them to modify their speech as a result, if the social
conditions are thought to be propitious. An example often cited is the
advice that led Margaret Thatcher to adopt a less 'hectoring' tone (while her
accent remained unchanged). The situation is not new; an earlier example is
the US President John F. Kennedy (1960–63) who famously had the prestigious Boston accent, characterized impressionistically by Honey (1989: 136)
as 'the Boston hyperlect, the American equivalent of the poshest form of
British (marked) RP'. Honey points out that Kennedy, following advice from
his political advisors, attenuated his accent in order to gain wider acceptance among voters, showing again how a highly marked upper-class accent
is capable of arousing hostility in an egalitarian age.

We can summarize the situation discussed above by stating that while
Blair's tendency was to adjust his privileged accent downwards, those who
held office before him followed the opposite trajectory, characteristic of social
mobility as traditionally thought of. There are various ways of considering
this sharp contrast; one is by evoking the years of their birth: Blair 1953,
Major 1943, Thatcher 1925, Callaghan 1912, Heath 1916, Wilson 1916. At
the age of 43, Blair became in 1997 the youngest Prime Minister since Lord
Liverpool in 1812. He was manifestly of a different generation from those
of his predecessors; one for whom the post-war mutations discussed above
are a given, as shown for example by his involvement in rock music when

a student. It should also be pointed out that several of the post-1964 Prime Ministers mentioned above were educated at Oxford or Cambridge, an experience that might well have led them to adjust their accent in the direction of RP. A further important, non-personal factor is the style of politics characteristic of recent years, itself arguably a reflex of the social levelling we are discussing; this 'consumer-led' approach sees political parties now appearing to follow public opinion rather than overtly leading it as formerly.

We can suggest, extrapolating beyond the prominent products of the grammar schools, that the greater social mobility these schools promoted has contributed in large measure to the erosion at least of the more highly marked prestigious English accents in the higher professions that these grammar-school products chose. As Walden (1996: 201) puts it, in a discussion of the comprehensive system that superseded the grammar schools:

> In the more hierarchical society of the past there was no problem about such [elitist] attitudes. Physically separate and socially exclusive, public schools were nevertheless an organic part of the nation, in a feudal sense, and were seen as its finest expression. It was accepted without question that their purpose was to produce a ruling caste: the better the schools, therefore, the better for the country. Wars were won and empire governed under the leadership of an elite educated to a standard not available to others. In more democratic times, identifying the national interest with that of a moneyed and social caste is neither possible nor desirable.

Tom Brown's universe (Honey 1977) is a book-length account of the Victorian public school, widely agreed to be the seed-bed of RP, and identifies, among the many factors that shaped the development of that institution, the need for the recruitment, in response to the growing need to govern the Empire, of an administrative cadre by competitive examination rather than patronage as formerly. The social features of the members of this group seem to have come to be defined very narrowly, and to have included mastery of RP. Looked at in this way, RP is a quirk of British colonial history. What is striking is that although Walden's depiction refers to the Victorian era, it evokes a more recent situation. Striking also is the speed of the change from a 'caste-based' system to a state of affairs presented as a meritocracy, and beyond that (and in consequence, if Daniel Bell's analysis is accepted) in a more populist or egalitarian direction. But it seems worth emphasizing once more that the need to eschew 'identifying the national interest with that of a moneyed and social caste' operates at a symbolic level in the context of a system which, if no longer 'caste-based', continues as what has been described as an 'elective oligarchy'. Meritocracy in any event notoriously mutates into oligarchy, as first-generation meritocrats exploit the advantages they have gained so as to promote the privileges of their offspring.

5.5 Conclusion

In this chapter we have proposed that much current linguistic variation, and hence perhaps change too, results from an overarching process of social levelling, understood in linguistic terms as a form of anti-standardization. Thus, rather than seeing the current 'democratization' of the standard in terms of its absorption and legitimization of hitherto working-class variants, the view embodied in this chapter envisages a gradual repositioning of the standard within the mesh of ideologies that can be assumed to determine linguistic behaviour. In support of this, we adduced an array of non-linguistic phenomena that illustrate the profound changes, tending cumulatively towards a symbolic levelling of the societal playing field, which have taken place in the UK in recent years. It would be surprising indeed if the standard ideology, in many ways one of the most important ingredients in the social matrix, had somehow remained aloof from these changes and hence escaped their effect.

L. Milroy (2003:166–7) draws an important distinction between global and local processes of change:

> [...] both internally motivated changes and dialect levelling appear to operate globally, in the sense that their effect on a wide range of speech communities is similar and cannot readily be explained by reference to local social structure. Ideologically motivated changes, on the other hand, can be understood only in relation to details of local social structure, as shown by the examples of Martha's Vineyard, Corby and inner-city Detroit.

and further:

> Crucially, if social boundaries become permeable and ideological systems disrupted as a result of migration or mobility, ideology-free changes will take their course, uninhibited by social barriers [...]

The argument advanced in the present chapter implies an alternative perspective, from which linguistic changes that arise when 'social boundaries become permeable and ideological systems disrupted' are not always neutral in terms of their social meaning. In the present case, we have suggested that a phenomenon that interacts with, and in some instances may be responsible for, disturbances to existing social and ideological structures is the emergence of an ideological framework that implicitly undermines the conventional standard ideology. As a motor for change this framework is global, in that it encompasses the maximal speech community of the language, and yet it nevertheless appears to be ideological in character.

Notes

1. [...] the only variable element available to account for linguistic change is social change [...] and it is changes in social structure alone which can modify the conditions governing the existence of language. We need to determine which social structure corresponds to a given linguistic structure and how, in general, changes in social structure find expression in linguistic structure.
2. One often needs real courage to persist with a just opinion in the face of its defenders.
3. In this discussion we mostly leave aside Wales, Scotland and Northern Ireland, although some results are available on levelling in Glasgow (Stuart-Smith 1999).
4. In fact, in light of Chapter 4, 'change in progress' can only be identified once the change has been completed.

6
Away from the Anglo-Saxon model: the case of French

6.1 Introduction

So far we have not considered whether what might be referred to as the 'generalized Western' social situation, previously described, applies uniformly across different countries. Although it appears plausible on a superficial view that recent social change has proceeded in essentially similar ways in most Western industrialized liberal democracies with standardized languages, the different social and political traditions in the UK and elsewhere make a comparison worthwhile. In this chapter we consider the French case because it is often cited as a highly standardized one. Notable differences in social organization in France are the *dirigisme* and sense of cultural uniqueness characteristic of the country, reflected quite vividly in the example of 1994 legislation designed to prohibit the use in official documents of Anglicisms by French state employees; and the republican attitude widespread in France that sees democracy in the light of upward rather than downward levelling. Against this, it certainly makes sense to assume that the youth-driven changes discussed previously are at work in France; for example, the 'events' of May 1968 are above all associated with their French manifestation.

6.2 Cultural conservatism

As with the UK situation, a large descriptive-analytical literature looking at the opposition between hierarchical and egalitarian ideologies seems to be lacking in France, although the more interpretive, hermeneutic or non-empirical tradition found in French sociology and other disciplines has seen some French scholars approaching the subject, often in a committed way, either criticizing the erosion of hierarchy (Finkielkraut 1987) or celebrating it (Maffesoli 1988). The nexus of attitudes that is of interest here, which tends towards the levelling of hierarchical structures, emphasizes the individual over the collective, promotes the values of youth and the 'decline of deference', deplores 'elites' and 'elitism', emphasizes emotion at the expense of reason, etc., has been described by Maffesoli (1988; and in several other works), who highlights what he sees as the positive aspects of the situation. His 1988 work *Le temps des tribus* (translated 1996 as *The time of the tribes*), lays stress, as previously discussed, on a social organization that is mosaicized in a non-hierarchical way. The full title of Maffesoli's book in translation is *The time of the tribes: the decline of individualism in mass society,* and its thesis is similar to that of Seabrook examined in a previous chapter: the expression of social identity through adherence to what Maffesoli calls 'micro-groups', reminiscent of Seabrook's 'landscape of niches and categories'. The book's subtitle refers to the 'decline of individualism', and this might seem at odds with what has been one thread of our argument so far. Whether individualism is in decline in mass society is of course a matter of individual interpretation, and all researchers are confronted with the problem of 'objectivity' that has dogged Marxian analysts especially. Maffesoli is perhaps especially vulnerable to this charge, since his approach is non-empirical; indeed, he claims at one point to have an 'artistic' viewpoint on his subject. We can perhaps best summarize Maffesoli's analysis, and synthesize it with Seabrook's, by suggesting that a social organization in self-selecting 'micro-groups' may confer on the members of those groups a greater impression of individuality than hitherto, irrespective of the researcher's analysis.

What is notable in several French commentators whose stance is on the political left is an attitude of social or cultural conservatism. This is in contrast to the UK situation, where, as Wheatcroft suggests (2005: 271), the right has won the politico-economic debate while the left has triumphed in cultural matters. Wheatcroft's formulation is worth quoting in full: 'Both in academic discourse and in practical politics, class conflict has been superseded by 'culture wars'; and the other great truth of the age is that the right has won politically while the left has won culturally.' This invites the question what exactly it means to be left-wing in culture; the 'cultural victory of the left', admittedly a vague phrase, refers presumably to an obligation on those who have access to public media to promote working-class or majority values and attack the 'establishment'. Wheatcroft illustrates this by the recent ban in the UK on fox-hunting, promoted by the politico-cultural 'left' but arguably not in essence a political issue, or at least not one that can be usefully analysed in traditional left–right terms, and hence an initiative that is part of the 'culture war'. This is not centrally a political issue, because the left–right divide opposes proponents of greater and lesser state spending designed respectively to increase or lessen equality. Opponents of fox-hunting often express surprise when told that Engels was a devotee. This state of affairs was discussed at length previously, by reference to concepts like populism and anti-elitism, which were suggested to be in the process of promotion, at least in part, by the political-cultural elite having a symbolic leftist tendency. The obvious socio-historical explanation of the politico-economic victory of the right is to be found in the economic history of the past thirty or so years, which saw monetarism mobilized in response to the oil shocks of the 1970s. The doctrine has not been successfully challenged since, and it is a commonplace that political debate in the UK is now located in the centre-right. That the left has 'won culturally' can perhaps be interpreted simply as the irreversibility of the post-war socio-cultural developments discussed above. Further, Wheatcroft points out (2005: 167) that 'throughout the 1980s there was an undercurrent of hostility toward the prime minister [Margaret Thatcher], even on the part of those who voted for her' and this hostility was more or less unanimous among the cultural elite, sometimes referred to as the 'left establishment', who conducted a large part of the socio-cultural-political discourse in the broadcast and print media. These factors seem to go some way towards explaining why the cultural march leftwards has proceeded independently of the rightward economic and political restructuring of recent times. In this perspective the culture wars operate on a platonic level and have to some extent supplanted political debate; such that, for instance, aesthetic judgments are notoriously influenced by the politics of the critic.

In contrast to the UK situation is an attitude of 'cultural conservatism' noticeable in France. This phrase, like 'the cultural victory of the left', is rather vague but implies an ability to distinguish between politico-sociological and cultural judgments. This ability was noticeable in George Orwell's writings; he was a man of the left but had strong artistic preferences that were independent of his politics, and contemporary figures like him are far to seek in the UK. The French situation shows the obvious fact that the political terms 'left' and 'right' are in large measure nation-specific. Almost the entire political landscape in France tilts 'left', if by this is meant, as implied above, 'characteristic of greater state intervention', in all major matters: political, economic, social, cultural. Thus the former French President, Jacques Chirac, while commonly described by the British media as centre-right, can certainly be seen as left-leaning in his opposition to free-market reforms; he went on record as stating, in *Le Monde* of 23 April 2004: *'Je ne suis pas un libéral'* where *libéral*, a misleading cognate, refers to free-market economic liberalism, or 'neo-liberalism' as it is sometimes currently termed.

Perhaps the most striking example of a French intellectual who situates himself on the political left but who has attacked 'cultural democracy' is Alain Finkielkraut; the title of his book, *La défaite de la pensée* (1987), speaks for itself. He is very vocal in his opposition to cultural levelling of the kind that, for example, refuses to distinguish between the artistic quality of Mozart and rap music (his examples). The well-known left-wing writer Régis Debray (1992: 18) has an analogous approach, as shown by the following quotation:

La République, c'est la Liberté *plus* la Raison. L'Etat de droit, *plus* la Justice. La Tolérance, *plus* la volonté. La Démocratie, dirons-nous, c'est ce qui reste d'une République quand on éteint les Lumières.[1]

The pun in the last phrase is untranslatable without a gloss, and turns on the double sense of *lumière*, so that the phrase can be rendered more or less literally as 'We might say that democracy is what remains of a republic when the lights are switched off'. At the same time 'les Lumières' is an elliptical reference to 'le siècle des Lumières', the eighteenth-century Enlightenment. This line of thought shows clearly the element of the republican tradition that lays stress on the republic as a rational enterprise and on duties as well as rights, including the citizen's obligation to participate in the polity. The sub-title of Debray's book is *Eloge des idéaux perdus* 'in praise of lost ideals'. While the UK context does not of course lack discussion of 'dumbing down', especially of institutions like the BBC, which in the Reithian tradition has or has had an educational and even morally improving role, the idea of upward rather than downward levelling, with the aim of full and responsible participation by the citizen in the democratic process, seems more central to the French republican concept. Thus for example, *civisme* (citizenship or civics) has long been taught in French secondary schools, while the French republican ideal disprizes ethnic identity by refusing to recognize any national identity other than 'Frenchness'. One result of this among many, admittedly a perverse one, is that social data (for example, rates of educational underachievement) are not gathered together along with demographic correlates such as ethnic group or origin, since these latter are not officially recorded in exercises like the census. The French ideal is therefore in intention an inclusive and uplifting one; in practice, one might say coercive.

The concept of the republic is of course capable of several interpretations. Etymologically a 'public affair' with the implication that all citizens are involved in principle, it is most intuitively defined negatively, in opposition to monarchical, autocratic or oligarchic types of organization, and does not necessarily imply a very wide degree of direct participation in the democratic process, although this association tends to be closer in the contemporary era. A striking characteristic of the republican concept is the tension between the promotion of liberty and the civic duties expected of citizens, which in principle range widely. Rather than attempting to define what constitutes the essence of a republic that distinguishes it from other types of political organization, it is perhaps more pertinent to look to the origins of the French republic as they affect the state's role today. As Brugger (1999: 49) points out, in the context of a modern (Enlightenment) sceptical attitude towards republicanism: 'in France, republican ideas were only vigorously pressed into service during the tensions of the early 1790s.' It is tempting to see a continuity here with the centralizing tendency which was characteristic of pre-revolutionary France, and which is discussed below. We are therefore perhaps less concerned with the formal properties and concepts underpinning the French republic than the historical and social forces that shaped it. Nevertheless, mention may be made of the concept of 'virtue' (in the etymological sense of 'manly force' in opposition to the arbitrary dispensations of Fortune, traditionally personified as a woman) as one of the central voluntarist elements of classical or early modern republican thought. Virtue in this sense is exercised to promote the greatness of a republic in the face of the vagaries of fortune, and may be thought of as an obligation laid upon all citizens, not just those who govern them.

Modern France is of course a democratic republic, and the principles enshrined in the Constitution of 1958 and germane to this discussion are formulated as follows: 'La France est une république indivisible, laïque, démocratique et sociale.' The secular (*laïque*) character of the Republic reflects the long association between republicanism and anti-clericalism; the French Catholic Church was disestablished in 1905 and the republican view opposes the immutable hierarchical social order traditionally associated with a Christian perspective with the meritocratic idea of a 'social republic', one aspect of which is summarized in the well-known phrase attributed to Napoleon: 'la carrière ouverte aux talents'. Bonaparte was responsible for overthrowing the first French republic, but was eclectic in his choice of assistants, as Thody (1989: 36–7) points out: 'he made it quite clear that no tests of belief or social origin would be imposed on those prepared to serve the state.' This eclecticism operated mainly in an upward social direction, since it concerned *ancien régime* aristocrats like Talleyrand, but the able from the middle classes were also recruited. The French paradox consists then in the existence firstly of the social republican ideal, reinforced by the exclusion from the polity of any formal involvement by the Church and perhaps too of a monarchy and peerage which, as was suggested in the previous chapter, 'underpins the *perception* of a rigid class system'. Alongside these elements coexist a centralism and dirigisme, inherited from pre-revolutionary times and reinforced since then, and rigid in principle, though flexible in practice, as we shall see.

Walden (1999: 166), whom we have already cited in relation to 'ultrademocracy' in the UK and who spent five years in France as a senior Foreign Office official, describes France as an 'authoritarian democracy and monarchical republic'; this formulation seems to capture the paradoxical combination of democratic idealism (France regards herself as the cradle of democracy, at least in continental Europe) with a more pragmatic centralizing voluntarism rooted in a long history. In view of his long residence in France and his high-level diplomatic experience (he was posted to Paris as 'first secretary for internal affairs', with the brief of informing the FCO on political and cultural developments in France), it is difficult to dismiss Walden's view as superficial, even if its formulation is slightly facile. The characterization of France as an 'authoritarian democracy' finds support from other writers; Thody (1989: 11) cites Finer (1962) to the effect that France is not or was not among the countries of the type capable of being termed a 'mature political culture', defined (by Thody) as one 'where public sanction for a military take-over would be unobtainable'. In this categorization France is defined as 'developed' rather than mature. Thody's book, an examination of French Caesarism, discusses the tendency for a military or otherwise charismatic figure to assume power at times of crisis (Napoleon I and III, Pétain, de Gaulle). A rather generally accepted view is therefore that France has come late (relative especially to the UK) to mature and confident parliamentary democracy. Thody illustrates this (1989: 106–7) through a discussion of the French term *alternance*, in the political sense of the peaceful transfer of power between left and right through due electoral process. The compact encoding of the French term shows its cultural importance, in the weak version of the Sapir-Whorf theory of linguistic-cultural relativism. Certainly no compact English equivalent appears readily available, as is shown by the circumlocution just used. If the term is or was the object of exhaustive debate it is because *l'alternance* was by no means a given in France until fairly recently – in Thody's argument, 1981, when a socialist president and government, having being duly elected, succeeded a centre-right administration. It is not difficult to see how an authoritarian and centralizing current in government both contributes to and results from such a situation.

As with our discussions of relativism and populism, it is desirable to show how French centralism finds expression in concrete actions. The student of French and France soon becomes acquainted with the notion of French *étatisme* or statism: interference by the State in the lives of individual citizens. As suggested previously, the tradition goes back a long way, although the Revolution was a catalyst that intensified the process and increased its efficiency through the apparatus set up by Napoleon. A key date in the history of French government intervention in language is 1635, when Cardinal Richelieu, chief minister of Louis XIII, established *l'Académie française*, the body that was later given the task of creating an official dictionary and grammar. The connection between nationalism and standardization in intention is apparent even at this early date, since Richelieu regarded the Rhine, the Alps and the Pyrenees as the natural frontiers of France. The general point here is obviously that France has a long history of State initiatives to regulate what we have referred to as social practices, including of course language, and parallels in the UK and elsewhere are notably absent. The French tradition of laying down the law about language is true not only figuratively, but also literally. For instance, a recent hostile official response to the perceived flood of Anglicisms into French was the *Loi Toubon* of 1994, which obliged French state employees to use, when composing State documents, officially approved alternatives to UK and US English terms. Once one has got used to the idea of the French State using the law to regulate language in this way, this does not seem too odd, but an earlier version of the law was thrown out by the *Conseil Constitutionnel*, the legal body responsible for ensuring that new legislation conforms to the provisions of the Constitution. The first version of the *Loi Toubon* sought to ban the use of all Anglicisms in the public sphere. The *Conseil Constitutionnel* ruled that this first draft of the law limited the freedom of expression enshrined in the Constitution, since it concerned private citizens as well as State employees. It is however worth pointing out that French is defined in the Constitution as the language of the Republic.

Clearly, in France and in all countries having a highly developed sense of being a nation-state, that is where political and cultural boundaries are expected to coincide, much stress is laid on the relationship that citizens have to the centralizing State as well as to their fellow-citizens. This dual relationship is in turn connected with the outward- and inward-looking aspects of nationhood; in its outward-looking aspect, a nation defines itself in contradistinction to other nations, and this can call for a patriotic or nationalistic response from its citizens. The inward-looking aspect implies a concern with internal cohesion and the diminution of difference, the counterpart of external distinction. In times of crisis, external distinction can turn into external threat: a state of war is the most obvious example. At these times internal cohesion is also of paramount importance, and anyone who dissents from this cohesion is likely to be thought of as an 'enemy within'. A recent and striking example is cited by Coveney (2005: 98), of one French writer (Renaud Camus) castigating another's speech:

> Redoublement du sujet, redoublement du complément, incapacité de prononcer juste une seule voyelle, prononciation de bout en bout pégreuse, inculte: voilà entre quelles mains, entre quelles lèvres, est le sort de la culture en France. Voilà les «intellectuels» qui nous sauveront.[2]

The quotation contains the essence of the language-crisis mentality characteristic of any contribution to the standardization debate, with its mention of the need to save the language. What seems typical often of the French debate, however, is the continuing contemporary virulence of tone, recalling that of Marsh (published in 1865, however) in its equating linguistic and moral practice. To call someone's pronunciation *pégreuse* ('thuggish' or 'Mafia-like') seems a disproportion. Other contemporary examples could easily be multiplied. The striking aspect of France is therefore that in linguistic matters, the State, or at least some of its representatives, as well as laypersons, quite often show a siege mentality, as if hostile outsiders and insiders were threatening the very existence of the French language. This is curious because France is a mature, autonomous, prestigious nation-state, and its language is a *langue de culture* with a rich literature. One obvious explanation for this attitude is the French sense of having been relegated to the second rank of nations in the course of the twentieth century. But this is true of the UK also, and this sense does not in Britain find expression in alarm among officials and others about an Apocalypse threatening to engulf the language through external threat and internal perfidy. Indeed, one would expect the British sense of decline to be keener if one accepts that Britain has fallen further, from its former status as a major colonial power. The real issue here is of course not linguistic, but socio-cultural and political, and one element that is reflected in this debate is the sense of cultural uniqueness that is prevalent in France at the political level and elsewhere, and is summed up in the phrase *l'exception culturelle*. The French response can also be explained in part by the nation's sense of itself as a beacon of culture and civilization – phrases like *le rayonnement de la culture française* 'the world-wide influence of French culture' are still common. The counterpart to this is that some French people regard as humiliating the perceived invasion of France by Anglo-American popular culture, including of course language. This invasion is summed up in the phrase *la coca-colonization*.

As Thody, Evans and Pepratx-Evans point out (1995: 82), '"la querelle du franglais" can sometimes be seen as an example of what the French themselves call "les guerres franco-françaises", quarrels among themselves about what kind of society they ought to have.' As they remark, what is distinctive in the French situation is the ferocious and polarized nature of these quarrels, with battle-lines drawn up along predictable ideological lines. In contrast to the political centre, which seemed fairly indifferent to the *franglais* issue and which no doubt includes most French people, the reactionary Right and the *étatiste* Left expressed strongly favourable views when the *Loi Toubon* was being debated in parliament. One Gaullist senator expressed his opinion in the following terms (in the translation of Thody, Evans and Pepratx-Evans): 'when I see all these American words on the walls of Paris, I want to join the resistance'.

This issue is relevant to our discussion, not only because it illustrates broad differences in institutional attitudes to language change across France and the UK, but also because the first version of the *Loi Toubon*, if adopted, would have banned the use of all Anglicisms in advertising, the media and business, and this would have affected radio stations broadcasting to young people, for example, with implications for the diffusion of non-standard lexis. The adoption of Anglicisms is one component of the rapid turnover of non-standard lexis, in its turn an aspect of language change, which we discuss below. Clearly, legislation can be applied relatively easily to superficial aspects of a language like lexis, but pronunciation and grammar are in France subject to the same standardizing pressures, at least in intention.

Examples of the statism characteristic of France can be multiplied. Walden (1999: 159–60) discusses the operation of the organization known as the *renseignements généraux* (RG), part of *la Police nationale* and responsible for gathering internal intelligence. There is no UK equivalent, and Walden describes as follows his experience of the RG in the *département* to which he was seconded as an observer:

> The *renseignements généraux* are an extraordinary organisation. The local representative [...] was amazed to discover that there was no British

equivalent. Imagine a government spy, whose function and identity everyone knows, residing in every local authority and reporting by cypher telegram to London. Every week the [French] Home Office would receive its bundle of reports [...] keeping the Home Secretary abreast of the local temper: the activities and relative popularity of the political parties, the state of the economy, the mood of the employers, the workforce and farmers. [...] No wonder the French writer and professor Jean-Marie Doumenach later described *la douce France* as a sort of Soviet Union that worked.

Perhaps the closest UK equivalent to the RG is MI5, two obvious differences being that the latter organization has a narrower scope, and until recently had no official existence. To the openness of French statism corresponds the citizen's response: the French term *système D*, where 'D' stands for *débrouille* or *démerde*, refers to a Gallic conception of the relationship between individual and State that 'resourcefulness', a typical dictionary translation, by no means fully captures. Using the *système D* often means solving a problem, typically one that involves conflict with authority, in a lateral or non-standard way. Walden (ibid.) again has a useful formulation:

No country that is centralised to the extent France is supposed to be could function at all. On the one hand, the state, seat of order and rationality, pulls the nation together. On the other, events on the ground in a country more than twice the size of Britain and with far greater regional differences pull it apart. The solution lies in a kind of constructive tension. The government must appear to be all-powerful, even when it is not. The compromise entails the formal acknowledgement of the authority of the state, while in practice each region or department makes the necessary adjustments.

Walden's example and generalization concern 'tension' between central and local government, but the remarks can be applied equally to the relations between State and individual. We shall see below how these work out in linguistic terms. One striking difference between the UK and France in this regard is the wider 'republican' attitude to schooling in the latter country. Highly normative, 'teacher-centred' methods continue to be concentrated quite largely in the private education sector in Britain, where some 7% of pupils are taught, in contrast to 'pupil-centred' methods that, at least in caricature, are associated, or have been until recently, with the promotion of empathy and self-expression and correspondingly the disprizing of rote learning and the acquisition of canonical knowledge. The private–public divide characteristic of UK schools is largely absent from France, where private schools exist but are mostly denominational and enjoy no particular prestige. The most highly regarded secondary schools are in the state sector, even if the most celebrated of these are in the prosperous districts of central Paris and quite probably operate selection in informal ways. An obvious conclusion is that in sharp contrast to the UK, the French governing class has a vested interest in maintaining in state schools teaching methods that emphasize the transmission of the canon, including its linguistic element, since their children will benefit along with the rest. Public debate in France about a crisis in educational standards is more or less permanent. Normative teaching methods are applied, at least in principle, to the greater majority of French school pupils, including primary. A telling anecdote concerns Jean-Pierre Chevènement, admittedly a contrarian but who, when Minister for Education in a Socialist government, spoke out in 1981 against innovative teaching methods, of the type described above. His language from our point of view was instructive: he called for a policy of *élitisme républicain*, perhaps translatable by reference to our earlier discussion as 'elitism for all'. The formulation summarizes a great deal of what has been discussed so far.

In this connection, a recent article by Stewart (forthcoming) on language ideologies reported that of 136 Parisians who were asked to rate 21 towns in the greater Paris region according to desirability, reputation and linguistic correctness, 15% refused to do so. Reponses to the latter element were elicited by inviting respondents to agree or disagree with the proposition that 'In this city the children will learn to speak French well'. This apparent 'linguistic relativism', or refusal to recognize an overarching standard, appears at first sight to derive from the ideology that propels social levelling of the type discussed in Chapter 5, but Stewart reported that:

> While the respondents in the current study refused to evaluate the linguistic correctness of cities, their reactions suggested that they did not do so because 'each area supports a standard' but because one standard language unifies all areas. One subject, for instance, explained that: 'the problem does not exist because all children have access to education and thus to learn French, regardless of their ethnic or socio-cultural origin ... we have no linguistic ghettos'.

This last remark does not square with the facts, but it suggests the internalization among 'ordinary' French people of the *élitisme républicain* referred to above. The low number of responses of this kind was most likely a result of the elicitation method.

6.3 The ideology of French

6.3.1 Introduction

The aspect of the French statist attitude to language corresponding to the response to perceived external threat discussed above is obviously the inward-looking one that emphasizes internal cohesion. We have already cited Renaud Camus's quite blistering attack on the speech of a fellow-writer. A neatly contrastive example of how this attitude finds concrete expression in teaching concerns France and the US. Walden (1999: 215) describes an incident concerning his daughter Celia that took place when he was on sabbatical leave at Harvard from the UK Foreign Office:

> Being French speakers they [the Waldens' children] went to a bilingual school, and after a while we noticed a glaring dichotomy in Celia's French and English performances. When she brought her work home, at the top of a page of higgledy-piggledy writing in English full of mistakes was her American teacher's drawing of a smiling sun and the inscription, 'Well done!' Her French work was immaculate, the lines straight as a die. Such grammatical mistakes as she made were crossed out and she was required to mug them up. When we asked cheery little Celia how come she was making a mess of her English and doing so well in French, she came up with a reply that deserves to be fed into the education debate: if they want me to do it right, I'll do it right. If they don't care, then neither do I.

Clearly, this example concerns writing rather than speaking, but it does show the normative intent of the French school system very clearly. Furthermore the French system incorporates exercises like dictation, recitation and reading aloud that explicitly relate the spelling to a standardized pronunciation and that 'surely has a standardising effect on children's pronunciation' (Coveney 2001: 5).

The reverence of the French towards their standard language on the one hand, and on the other their deviance from it, have been much commented upon. Le Page's formulation (1989: 12) is worth quoting at length:

> [...] French seems to be among the most reified, totemized and institutionalized of all languages. [It has been suggested that] the stereotype of a standard unifying language perform[s] the same function for France as the monarchy for Britain. It was decreed as the symbol of national unity in 1539, and again after the Revolution. By the end of the 17th century the written language of the intellectuals among the bourgeois of the Île de France, which was seen as having reached a stage of near perfection, was held up as a model for speech. It has been held up as a model ever since.
>
> Nobody actually speaks 'correct French'. The directives about what is to be taught in schools, and in grammars, come from unknown bureaucrats in the Ministry of Education, and when a new Minister of Education wants to make his mark he licenses some new grammatical change. [...] School teachers have strict instructions about what it is they are to teach.

Aidan Coveney [...] reported how a trainee primary school teacher claimed she would correct her children's French – the example she chose was the subjunctive of an irregular verb. Coveney added: 'I strongly suspect that teachers leave uncorrected many other non-standard grammatical features which are well-established in the speech of even well-educated adults.'

Le Page (ibid.) goes on to describe the idealized view of French as follows: 'a rule-system for a highly focussed approved written language, from which people deviate to the extent that they are not properly educated'. This definition coincides closely with that of any standard language, although the association between writing and formal speaking is perhaps closer in French than in comparable languages. As we have often pointed out here, a standard language is the expression of an ideology rather than a reality, and French speakers do of course deviate considerably from the norm in lexis and grammar. An idiosyncratic result of the standardization process in France is however that the pronunciation of the principal variety of French of interest here – what might be referred to as 'urban *oïl* French' (as opposed to the southern *oc* varieties), or 'supralocal French', is homogenized but not ideologized in the way that, for example, British Received Pronunciation is (on these two types of standardization, see J. Milroy 2001). Reference was made above to the close association in the classroom between speaking and writing through dictation and other exercises.

Armstrong and Pooley (2010) have an extensive discussion of the substantive non-institutional factors that have promoted the curious hybrid of standardization and anti-standardization that is characteristic of French. Discussion of these factors would be out of place here, given that we are focusing on the symbolic or ideological aspects of language change. But it is worth reiterating that factors like urbanization, counter-urbanization, professionalization, increased access to education, the shift to tertiary employment, etc., although of course quite real, are experienced through the prism of the ideology examined here, as much as they shape it.

6.3.2 Homogenization in French pronunciation

In the previous chapter we evoked a situation where the UK 'standard' is assimilating certain non-standard regional features, while highly localized regional varieties are losing some of their distinctiveness by absorbing either more widely distributed regional or non-standard and national features. Trudgill (2002: 179–80) has a very wide-ranging summary of the UK 'levelled' pattern as follows, linking it to Europe-wide trends:

The geographical spread of 'Estuary English' is part of a much bigger trend. What is happening in Britain, and probably not only there, as far as regional variation is concerned, is rather complicated. On the one hand, much regional variation is being lost as the large number of traditional dialects covering small geographical areas gradually disappear from most, though by no means all, parts of the country. The dialects and accents associated with these areas are much less different from one another, and much less different from RP and Standard English, than the traditional dialects were. However, and this is crucial, in terms of phonology they are for the most part currently diverging, not converging. The work of the European Science Foundation Network on Dialect Divergence and Convergence paints a very similar picture Europe-wide. Work in large urban centres such as Liverpool, Newcastle and Cardiff shows that, although these places are adopting some nationwide features such as labio-dental /r/, /t/-glottalling and th-fronting, they also demonstrate independent divergent developments [...]

However this may be (and Foulkes and Docherty's comments, cited previously, appear to stress increasing convergence rather than divergence in the UK), without attempting to theorize the situation further from a social point of view, we now turn to the French situation with a view to examining its distinctiveness from the situation sketched by Trudgill.

Armstrong and Pooley (2010, chapter 7, from which the following paragraphs are adapted) suggest that any ongoing levelling in French pronunciation could perhaps be seen as a sort of 'upward levelling' towards the 'standard', this latter term understood here in the sense of a set of linguistic forms that are nationally distributed, non-innovating and socio-stylistically neutral. The term 'supralocal French' is sometimes used to refer to this variety, which is distributed over at least 70% of France (Pooley, 2006). As we have already remarked, this can hardly be thought of as a standardized situation in the sense of a near-universal distribution of a prestige accent, since prestige has by definition a limited distribution.

While there remains considerable variability in French, the degree of levelling shown through comparison of oral data over the twentieth century is by any measure considerable, and arguably greater than in any historically multilingual parts of Europe. This applies particularly to the regional dimension of variation, where the historical *oïl* areas, with some notable exceptions such as the Nord–Pas-de-Calais, now seem to show little distinctive variation that would be readily recognized by ordinary francophones, even if careful linguistic investigation does reveal specific features. This latter qualification is crucial, since phonetic variation that is undoubtedly present but too subtle to be readily detectable without instrumental analysis, such as that reported by Hall (2011) in Normandy, is unlikely to be socially diagnostic, at least outside a circumscribed area. It may be that Brittany and Alsace are further exceptions to the generally levelled situation, particularly the latter, but convincing recent evidence is lacking, and as far back as World War Two (Martinet 1945) a large sample of male middle-class speakers showed few if any regionally distinctive phonetic characteristics. In the south, easily recognizable regional accents are still much more socially respectable, and in Provence informants have been shown to perceive their way of speaking as preferable in some respects even to Parisian pronunciation. That conceded, evidence of levelling in southern France is considerable, particularly among educated young people, and ordinary 'judges' are hard put to discern subregional differences even among older speakers.

The picture we have of variable pronunciation has undoubtedly been distorted by the prevalence, indeed until quite recently the dominance of perceptual studies, which have tended to exaggerate the perceived vitality of older and stereotypical varieties. More recent behavioural studies strongly suggest that while marked regional and social varieties have flourished principally among the lower classes, and to some extent still do, increased social levelling has reduced the differences between the usage of people from other social groups, while in the collective memory these varieties continue to be defined by terms which seem less and less suitable in a post-industrial society pervaded in numerous ways by the individualism we have described earlier.

While studies like that of Boughton (2005) suggest that ordinary subjects can reliably identify the social origins of speakers when invited to do so in no doubt over-simplified binary terms like working and middle class, other research like Hansen's (2000) suggests an ample range of stylistic variation among educated speakers, compared to the less well-educated. This reinforces the notion of the diglossic or quasi-diglossic nature of contemporary French, if by these terms is meant a situation where style variation is more important than social. This presupposes a state of affairs that sees most variable features available to all speakers, such that they become 'more a feature of register than of social dialect' (Lodge 2004: 247). Lodge's remarks bear upon informal vocabulary but they seem to apply to pronunciation too. In this hypothesis the loss of regional pronunciation forms, which by definition are not available to all, have been largely replaced by widespread features like mute-e and liaison, the stylistic value of which is reinforced by universal and still quite highly normative education. We discuss this further below, in relation to lexical variation.

In social terms the demographic dominance of the median classes means that the majority of speakers seek to sound neither too '*pointu*', i.e. precise or pedantic, nor too '*plouc*', translatable as 'bumpkin' and evoking the rural past of France, still an important element in the cultural memory. For most French speakers the regressive distinction between /œ̃/ and /ɛ̃/ will be felt to be too *pointu*, and it may be felt to be either too *pointu* or too *plouc* to distinguish /a/ from /ɑ/, depending on the region or lexical items concerned, given the complex social distribution of the /a/ variable. In general it is certainly *plouc* to use dialect-influenced forms, although highly marked forms of regional languages are enjoying reinvigorated valorization, in most cases without any accompanying adoption as social practice. As Lodge (2004: 14) has pointed out, very few French terms exist to refer to urban vernaculars, in contrast to those current in UK English (Cockney, Scouse, Geordie, etc.). Indeed, it is sometimes said that the very term 'accent' connotes for many French speakers a rural accent, and the only well-known informal terms for urban accents are *chtimi*, referring to the Lille conurbation and reflecting the true 'counterweight' status of the area, and *parigot*, which, however, as its form implies, refers to lexis rather than pronunciation (*Paris* + *argot*).

While the French language remains a respected, indeed a totemic institution, and is certainly less vehemently decried than other social institutions, the reference variety has undergone some degree of levelling through simplification, exemplified by the virtual loss of distinctions such as /œ̃/ ~ /ɛ̃/ and /a/ ~ /ɑ/, and some de-standardization as described by Willemyns (2007), seen most notably in the middle-class adoption of fronted /o/ (see 4.5.1). It remains to be seen whether further markers of de-standardization will emerge; the only other candidate seems at the moment to be affrication of /t, d/. The ideology of the standard, along with the dominance of Paris in every aspect of public affairs as well as in demographic weight, has favoured levelling far beyond the Île-de-France. What is more, as Singy (1996) has rightly observed, Paris remains the main source of linguistic innovation, as in the case of prepausal schwa, seemingly the most recent variable feature to emerge.

In a recent volume (Durand, Laks and Lyche 2009) issuing from the large-scale ongoing corpus-based linguistic survey entitled *Phonologie du français contemporain: usages, variétés et structures* (PFC), mention is made of the principal French variables of interest to the project: these are what are referred to as 'the two As' (/a/ ~ /ɑ/), the mid-vowels, fronting of [o], schwa, and variable liaison, discussed here in this volume (pp. 62–5). Most of these features are distributed very widely in the urban *oïl* area, in contrast to the localized UK pattern. What is noticeable too is the rather limited range of variables, and the fact that they are system-internal in the sense of all being distributed in supralocal French, rather than being in the 'dialects' in the English regional sense. Further variables, like deletion of /l/ and /r/, are motivated by ease-of-articulation processes. As was mentioned in Chapter 1, vernacular French is characterized therefore by its minimal vocalic system and tendency to delete weak consonants, and as such responds to only two of the three related characteristics of the vernacular as defined in L. Milroy (1987a: 57): it is the first variety to be acquired, that most likely to be used in unmonitored speech, but little localization is to be found.

6.3.3 Variation in French grammar

While in the UK and other countries sociolinguistic phenomena seem broadly to track the zeitgeist which encourages informalization, as witnessed by the decline of RP, what is happening in French calls for description and theorization that seem less intuitive, since despite the presence of similar though not identical macro-social factors, the linguistic tracking is harder to fit into patterns or sub-patterns attested both in the UK and in other parts of Europe. This seems to be because, as was suggested above, the social-regional dialect pattern in France has been levelled to a large extent already, where the term 'levelling' is used in the sense of the erosion of low-value dialect features in favour of a homogenized quasi-standard variety. In contrast to what is happening elsewhere, we appear to be witnessing, in French pronunciation, particularly in France, a process of modified change from above and below that sees the supralocal variety supplanting most of the others to the point where the social patterning manifested in variable pronunciation in other languages appears to be shifting to the grammar and lexicon.

We discussed two important cases of variation in French grammar in Sections 4.5.2 and 4.5.3, viz. negation and interrogatives. We also touched on a further area of syntactic uncertainty, the *que* → *qui* transformation, in 2.4. Finally, we considered the shibboleth of past participle agreement in 3.3.3.3. What emerges from these cases is a very clear sense of the reified nature of the standard French grammar, which tends to condition patterns of variation that are broadly reactive to the standard ideology.

6.3.4 Style variation in French

Lodge (2004: 248) expresses as follows quite a commonly held view of the French sociolinguistic situation: 'if the label *le français populaire* designated some sort of social dialect in the first half of the [twentieth] century, during the second half it has come to designate only a style'. Gadet (2003: 105–6) has framed the view as follows: 'Pour le français de France [...] après une domination diatopique ayant suivi l'achèvement de la francisation, puis une saillance diastratique correspondant à l'industrialisation et l'urbanisation, il serait actuellement dans un primat diaphasique [...].'[3]

The suggestion here is that geographical and social differences have become less marked than stylistic. Gadet proposes further that increased style variation is linked to more highly specialized divisions of labour, but the changes in question can also be thought of in relation to dialect levelling, which affected firstly geographical (diatopic) then social (diastratic) features, leaving the intra-speaker or stylistic (diaphasic) dimension as the most 'noticeable' area of variation at the turn of the twentieth and twenty-first centuries in French. This situation may be analysed as a consequence of linguistic levelling because in French this means the attenuation of regional, and to some extent social, marking. In this argument, the variable features remaining after levelling are available to all speakers (because they are not regional), such that they become 'more a feature of register than of social dialect' (Lodge, 2004: 247). Lodge's remarks bear upon informal vocabulary but they seem to apply to pronunciation and grammar too.

The question here is in what sense style variation in French has 'primacy', or is more 'important'. It may be that the primacy of style variation in French, if it exists, is due to more lexical variation being present in the language: 'more' in the double sense of a larger number of lexical variants, and of greater salience reflected in steeper degrees of style shift in vocabulary. It certainly seems that French speakers have available a very copious stock of informal words. Steep degrees of style shift in lexis are explicable by reference to salience in a way that seems less vulnerable to the circularity accusation that usually applies to explanations involving salience. Lodge suggests (1993: 256), in the course of a discussion whether contemporary French may be characterized by a form of diglossia: 'it is probably in the lexicon that style-shifting in French is indicated most obviously'. Whether by this 'obviousness' is meant sociolinguistic salience in respect of the speech community's awareness of it (as opposed to the linguist's) is not made clear, but the involvement in semantic content of full lexical words especially, in a way that does not obtain on the levels of variable phonology, morphology and perhaps grammatical words, makes this notion plausible. Linguistically naïve speakers typically exemplify variation using vocabulary, partly perhaps because the word is the most intuitive linguistic unit, partly because words, as suggested above, have more salience on account of their semantic content, and partly because folk-linguistic judgments are easier to apply to words. Thus, the unsuitability in formal speech of a word like *merde* can be readily 'explained' by reference to its taboo value, while the use of *bahut* for *lycée*, for instance, is open to commentary of the type that criticizes as disobliging the comparison of an educational establishment to a box. Judgments of the latter type require no meta-linguistic knowledge concerning (in this case) the use of metaphor.

Lodge suggests (2004: 242) that French is 'over-lexicalized', in the sense of possessing a large stock of non-standard vocabulary. For instance, Calvet (1994: 44) notes that a recent dictionary of slang lists 71 terms for money and 63 for sexual intercourse. To cite Lodge again (2004: 247), 'the popularity of [dictionaries of slang] attests, at the very least, to the rise in salience of lexical variation, perhaps as phonetic and grammatical differences between the sociolects were levelled.' These remarks are applied to the nineteenth century, but the flow of works on slang, both popular and learned, continues steady to this day. If style variation were more prominent, this would be a rather tortuous example of the weak Sapir-Whorf state of affairs, such that the variable structure of a language influences its speakers' perceptions of variation in that language, and perhaps reinforces their use of the salient variable structures. If this state of affairs does hold for French, then it demonstrates a highly distinctive sociolinguistic situation. In this hypothesis, the displacement of variation from phonology and grammar to lexis has increased the salience of style variation, not just in the eyes of linguists but of ordinary speakers too if 'hyperstyle' or steep style variation is a reliable guide to salience. But this hypothesis must remain tentative in the absence of any cross-linguistic comparison.

We cited Lodge above to the effect that non-standard vocabulary in French has now become 'more a feature of register than of social dialect' (Lodge 2004: 247). We suggested further that Lodge's observation, while applied by him to informal vocabulary, seems to apply to pronunciation and grammar too. To reiterate and expand the argument sketched above at the outset of 6.2.3, the levelling of regional variation which seems a prominent feature of French leaves behind variable features that are available to all speakers, such that they become principally style markers. It seems implausible that a language-plus-dialects situation, i.e. one where regional variation is present, will see hyperstyle variation between unscripted speaking styles, because audience design presupposes accommodation, which serves the purpose of attenuating social distance. Hyperstyle variation is that which sees style variation exceed social variation, and this relation is in sociolinguistics generally accepted as being aberrant. Preston (1991) applied a statistical analysis to the factors governing variation in findings from several languages, concluding that the maximum range of social variation constitutes an 'envelope' within which stylistic variation is inherently delimited. On a commonsense view it seems plausible that social variation will generally exceed stylistic, because of the social networks that govern everyday interactions: no single speaker or speaker group will command with full confidence the entire range of linguistic variables that are socially sensitive in a given speech community, since no single speaker or group will interact at all regularly with representatives of all members of the community. Therefore the stylistic compass of a speaker or speaker group will be circumscribed within the social range of the people with whom they interact regularly. To take a UK example, a middle-class speaker whose everyday speech is a form of (more or less) standardized Liverpudlian, and who is capable of reverting to this vernacular, will plainly not, when speaking to a working-class Yorkshire speaker, try to imitate a Yorkshire accent, as this would be both difficult and unnecessary – difficult because, gifted mimicry aside, the prolonged adoption of an unfamiliar accent is hard to sustain, and unnecessary because most speakers construe imitation of their accent as mockery. The middle-class speaker will rather adjust his or her accent in a more Liverpudlian direction, to convey solidarity. Adjustment is likely to be fairly subtle, again in the interests of allaying any suspicion that derision or obsequiousness are intended. The UK English situation is one composed of the standard and the regional dialects, such that variation will concern the social-regional variety of the speakers in question. This seems to argue further against hyperstyle, which would suppose mastery by all speakers of all dialects.

The case of the French 'diglossic' situation, at least in pronunciation, seems essentially similar. Regional differences in non-southern French have been largely lost, as argued above, and what remains is an array of variables shared by all speakers. These are mute-e, liaison, /l/ and /r/, and fast-speech reductions like *expliquer* pronounced [ɛsplike] (standard form: [ɛksplike]). Apart from mute-e, Zribi-Hertz (2011: 6–7) mentions these, and only these, in her discussion of diglossia in French. That these variables are largely 'quantitative' or characterized by presence/absence does not seem important for the purposes of this argument; nor does the fact that the standard variants are clearly indicated in spelling, since there is no evidence that links hyperstyle variation to representation in spelling. Nor has the universal availability of the variables any influence on their distribution across unscripted speech styles; the fact that speakers control a variable confidently will not prompt them to use it in a greater measure, since use beyond the social norms that have been set will produce 'over-accommodation' effects akin to those described in the Liverpool–Yorkshire example above. The remaining assumption is therefore the rational one, that style variation in French phonology is governed by audience design. The exception seems to be a scripted style internalized by most speakers and affecting schwa and variable liaison; this is most likely a product of the normative teaching methods, like dictation and reading aloud, mentioned earlier.

6.3.5 Diversity in French

In the preceding section we have emphasized a striking degree of uniformity in pronunciation in the dominant northern urban region of France, along with some evidence of convergence towards the dominant variety, but it should be pointed out again that at the same time rural varieties persist vigorously, as shown by the PFC survey referred to above, based in Toulouse (see Durand, Laks and Lyche 2009). Coveney remarks (2001: 3) that what he calls in inverted commas 'French' (supralocal French) 'comes in many different varieties – stylistic, social, geographical and historical', and further, that SF 'is characteristic of the well-educated middle classes from the northern two-thirds of France'. Diversity is present in regional and rural varieties, and in *banlieue* French. Again, Armstrong and Pooley (2010) discuss this at length.

Regarding social diversity, the hostility to Anglo-American culture or *coca-colonization* is less likely to be found among the general population than among its leaders, and a representation of the French school system that suggests the universal transmission of the canon is a sanguine one, to say the least. The social malaise that is rife in the *banlieues* is now common knowledge outside France. Nor does France show any reluctance to participate in recent technical innovations like texting and blogging, which show in a feedback loop the influence of speech on a lightly edited genre of writing. This in its turn can be seen as weakening the highly normative influence of writing on speech, hitherto especially prevalent in French. The French dirigiste intention is not in doubt, but its results need to be nuanced endlessly.

We may remark finally that the dual-pronoun system may to some extent be responsible for increasing informalization in French and other languages. While the dual-pronoun system has remained intact as a structured system, its social distribution has changed in response to less rigidly hierarchical conditions. Non-reciprocal *tu–vous* usage has now largely disappeared; for example, while formerly the relations between master and servant, army officer and private, customer and waiter would find expression in non-reciprocal *tu–vous* exchanges, these will now be characterized by reciprocal *vous*; the major exception remaining is the adult–child relationship. At the same time, some groups having a 'shared fate', such as students and teachers, now largely use reciprocal *tu*. As was stated previously, the social relations expressed by the *tu–vous* opposition now articulate principally social intimacy versus distance rather than 'power and solidarity', in Brown and Gilman's well-known phrase (1960). This is somewhat of a simplification, but it suffices for the present broad discussion and is in line with the levelling hypothesis of interest here. It illustrates the fact of language reflecting society in a fairly clear way. Non-reciprocal *tu–vous* reflects hierarchy quite straightforwardly, while any erosion of reciprocal *vous* can be thought of in terms of Brown and Levinson's analysis (1987: 198–9), which suggests that use of the *vous* form, which is of course also the 2nd-person plural form, allows the hearer the interpretation of being addressed as a representative of his or her social group. The obvious corollary is that the *tu* form individualizes the hearer.

Coveney (2010: 127) suggests that 'the choice between *vouvoiement* and *tutoiement* [...] is possibly the most salient of all sociolinguistic phenomena in French.' The *tu–vous* alternation is certainly a sociolinguistic phenomenon, and is a variable in the sense of offering a choice between two variants, but it is not probabilistic like phonological variables, since once a choice is made in the *tu–vous* system, it is generally fixed. But the decision to select either *vouvoiement* and *tutoiement* has a high degree of salience because its (more or less unavoidable) use prompts the obligation to choose a pronoun plus verb form as a function of the relationship one has with one's interlocutor, which in turn depends on a perception of that person's social status, as well as other factors such as the degree of intimacy or solidarity subsisting between the speakers. The unavoidable obligation to choose between pronouns seems to represent an example of the weak form of Sapir-Whorf, whereby one area of the variable structure of a language influences its speakers' perceptions of the social practice underlying that area, and perhaps in a feedback loop contributes to the mutation of the social practice, if one accepts that the relative salience of the form can heighten a speaker's awareness of the mutation.

6.4   Conclusion

In summary, the distinctiveness of the French situation seems to reside in its diversity in grammar and vocabulary, rather than in pronunciation.

The phonology is simplified in the sense described in Chapter 1, where we saw that a minimal vowel system is found in ordinary speaking styles. It is important to note in this connection the difference between a 'standard' French or English accent, and RP. This latter accent is now controlled by relatively few speakers, at least in its highly marked form, whereas at the pronunciation level, it can be stated again that 'standard' French appears to be the property of the majority of urban *oïl* speakers, in more careful styles at any rate. Moreover, even in less monitored styles, the non-standard features observable are most often unlocalized.

The lexical level appears to obtrude most obviously on conscious awareness, and impressionistic observation suggests an informalization of some vocabulary, for example in an increase during the period in question in the acceptability of taboo words and expressions hitherto labelled 'vulgaire' by French dictionaries: those referring to parts and functions of the body. The lexical level is sometimes described as being the most superficial, perhaps because much variation in vocabulary proves ephemeral. The lexicon is of course open-ended, unlike pronunciation and to some extent grammar, and speakers continue to learn words in a way that contrasts sharply with sounds and grammatical structures. Words referring to the taboo subjects of sex and excretion naturally undergo variation, but the core terms are of long attestation and appear to be in process of change from below.

Some changes in grammar can be thought of in terms of a gradual loss of deference towards the reified standard. The grammatical level is the most susceptible to speciously rational arguments (whereas pronunciation and lexis usually attract pseudo-aesthetic judgments, as has been seen), and it may be that the perception of the superior 'rationality' of the standard is weakening in France. If we have concentrated as much in this chapter on linguistic matters in French as on other social phenomena, it is no doubt because of the totemic character of the language, as discussed above. The French language is an institution in a way that other standard languages are not.

Notes

1. The Republic is liberty *plus* reason, the rule of law *plus* justice, tolerance *plus* will. We may say that democracy is what remains of a republic when the lights have been switched off.
2. Repetition of the subject, repetition of the complement, inability to pronounce accurately a single vowel, pronunciation totally thuggish and uneducated: these are the hands, the lips, holding the fate of French culture. These are the 'intellectuals' who will save us.
3. For the French of France [...] after the prevalence of regional variation following the imposition of French, then the dominance of social-class variation corresponding to industrialization and urbanization, the language seems now to be in a phase where style variation has primacy [...].

References

Adams, M. (1989) 'Verb second effects in Medieval French.' In C. Kirschner and J. DeCesaris (eds.), *Studies in Romance linguistics. Selected papers from the 17th Linguistic Symposium on Romance languages*. Philadelphia: John Benjamins, pp. 1–31.

Adli, A. (2005) 'Gradedness and consistency in grammaticality judgments.' In S.Kepser and M. Reis (eds.), *Linguistic evidence: empirical, theoretical and computational perspectives* (Studies in generative grammar). Berlin: Mouton de Gruyter, pp. 7–25.

Adonis, A. and S. Pollard (1997) *A class act: the myth of Britain's classless society.* London: Penguin.

Aissen, J. (1974) 'The syntax of causative constructions.' PhD dissertation, Harvard University.

Aitchison, J. (2001) *Language change: progress or decay?* (3rd edn). Cambridge: Cambridge University Press.

Alarcos Llorach, E. (1994) *Gramática de la lengua española*. Madrid: Espasa Calpe.

Amis, K. (1991) *The Amis collection.* Harmondsworth: Penguin.

—— (1998) *The King's English*. London: HarperCollins.

Andersen, H. (1973) 'Abductive and deductive change.' *Language* 49: 765–93.

Anderson, D. (2004) *All oiks now: the unnoticed surrender of Middle England*. London: Social Affairs Unit.

Armstrong, L. (1932) *The phonetics of French*. London: Bell & Hyman.

Armstrong, N. (1996) 'Deletion of French /l/: linguistic, social and stylistic factors.' *Journal of French Language Studies* 6 (1): 1–21.

—— (2001) *Social and stylistic variation in spoken French*. Amsterdam: John Benjamins.

—— (2002) 'Variable deletion of French *ne*: a cross-stylistic perspective.' *Language Sciences* 24 (2): 153–73.

Armstrong, N. and J. Low (2008) 'C'est encoeur plus jeuli, le Mareuc: some evidence for the spread of /o/-fronting in French.' *Transactions of the Philological Society* 106 (3): 432–55.

Armstrong, N. and T. Pooley (2010) *Social and linguistic change in European French*. Basingstoke: Palgrave Macmillan.

Ashby, W. (1981) 'The loss of the negative particle *ne* in French: a syntactic change in progress.' *Language* 57 (3): 674–87.

—— (1984) 'The elision of /l/ in French clitic pronouns and articles.' *Michigan Romance Studies* 1 (11): 1–16.

—— (1991) 'When does variation indicate linguistic change in progress?' *Journal of French Language Studies* 1 (1): 1–19.

—— (2001) 'Un nouveau regard sur la chute du *ne* en français parlé tourangeau: s'agit-il d'un changement en cours?' *Journal of French Language Studies* 11 (1): 1–22.

—— (2003) 'La liaison variable en français parlé tourangeau: une analyse en temps réel.' Paper presented at the Conference of the Association for French Language Studies, Tours.

Auer, P. and F. Hinskens (1996) 'New and not so new developments in an old area.' *Sociolinguistica* 10: 1–30.

Ayres-Bennett, W. (1993) 'The authority of grammarians in 17th-century France and their legacy to the French language.' In R. Sampson (ed.), *Authority and the French language. Papers from a conference at the University of Bristol.* Münster: Nodus, pp. 33–45.

—— (1996) *A history of the French language through texts.* London: Routledge.

Baltin, M. (2001) 'A-movements.' In M. Baltin and C. Collins (eds.), *The handbook of contemporary syntactic theory.* Oxford: Blackwell, pp. 226–54.

Barra Jover, M. (2004) 'Interrogatives, négatives et évolution des traits formels du verbe en français parlé.' *Langue Française* 141: 110–25.

Bell, A. (1984) 'Language style as audience design.' *Language in Society* 13 (2): 145–204.

Bell, D. (1999) *The coming of post-industrial society: a venture in social forecasting.* New York: Basic Books.

Belletti, A. (1982) 'Morphological passive and pro-drop: the impersonal construction in Italian.' *Journal of Linguistic Research* 2: 1–34.

—— (2001) '(Past-)participle agreement.' MS. Università di Siena. Subsequently published (2006) in M. Everaert and H. C. Van Riemsdijk (eds.), *The Blackwell companion to syntax vol. III.* London/New York: Blackwell, pp. 493–521.

Bello, A. (1984/1847) *Gramática de la lengua castellana destinada al uso de los americanos.* Madrid: EDAF Universitaria (first published 1847).

Benn, P. (1998) *Ethics.* London: UCL Press.

Bentivoglio, P., L. De Stefano and M. Sedano (1999) 'El uso del *que* galicado en el español actual.' In E. M. Rojas Mayer (ed.), *Actas del VIII congreso internacional de la ALFAL.* Tucumán: Universidad nacional de Tucumán, pp. 104–11.

Bergh, G. and A. Seppänen (2000) 'Preposition stranding with *wh*-relatives: a historical survey.' *English Language and Linguistics* 4 (2): 295–316.

Behnstedt, P. (1973) *Viens-tu? Est-ce que tu viens? Tu viens? Formen und strukturen des direkten Fragessatzes im Französischen.* Tübingen: Narr.

Biberauer, T. and I. Roberts (2005) 'Changing EPP parameters in the history of English: accounting for variation and change.' *English Language and Linguistics* 9 (1): 5–46.

Blanche-Benveniste, C. (1985) 'Coexistence de deux usages de la syntaxe du français parlé.' In J.-Cl. Bouvier (ed.), *Contacts de langues: discours oral.* Aix-en Provence: Université de Provence, pp. 201–14.

Blanche-Benveniste, C. and C. Jeanjean (1987) *Le français parlé.* Paris: Didier Erudition.

Bloom, A. (1987) *The closing of the American mind.* New York: Simon and Schuster.

Bošković, Ž. (1997) 'On certain violations of the superiority condition, AgrO and economy of derivation.' *Journal of Linguistics* 33: 227–54.

Bosque, I. and J. Gutiérrez Rexach (2009) *Fundamentos de sintaxis formal.* Madrid: Ediciones Akal.

Boughton, Z. (2005) 'Accent levelling and accent localisation in northern French: comparing Nancy and Rennes.' *Journal of French Language Studies* 15 (3): 235–56.

Bourdieu, P. (1982) *Ce que parler veut dire: l'économie des échanges linguistiques.* Paris: Fayard.

Blanden, J., P. Gregg and S. Machin (2005) *Intergenerational mobility in Europe and North America.* London: Centre for Economic Performance, London School of Economics.

Brantlinger, P. A. (2002) 'Response to "Beyond the cultural turn".' *The American historical review* 107 (5), http://www.historycooperative.org/journals/ahr/107.5/ah0502001500.html, date accessed November 2010.

Britain, D. and J. Cheshire (eds.) (2003) *Social dialectology: in honour of Peter Trudgill.* Amsterdam: John Benjamins.

Brown, P. and S. Levinson (1987) *Politeness: some universals in language usage.* Cambridge: Cambridge University Press.

Brown, R. and A. Gilman (1960) 'The pronouns of power and solidarity.' In T. A. Sebeock (ed.), *Style in language.* Cambridge, MA: MIT Press, pp. 253–76.

Brugger, B. (1999) *Republican theory in political thought: virtuous or virtual?* Basingstoke: Palgrave Macmillan.

Bruhn de Garavito, J. L. S. (1999) 'The *se* construction in Spanish and near native competence.' *Spanish Applied Linguistics* 3: 247–95.

Brunskill, R. W. (1981) *Traditional buildings of Britain.* London: Gollancz.

Burzio, L. (1986) *Italian syntax: a Government-Binding approach.* Dordrecht: Reidel.

Butler, C. S. (1985) *Statistics in linguistics.* Oxford: Blackwell.

Butt, J. and C. Benjamin (2000) *A new reference grammar of modern Spanish* (3rd edn). London: Arnold.

Calvet, L.-J. (1994) *L'Argot.* Paris: Presses Universitaires de France. Collection *Que sais-je?*

Cameron, D. (1990) 'Demythologizing sociolinguistics.' In J. E. Joseph and T. J. Taylor (eds.), *Ideologies of language.* London: Routledge, pp. 79–93.

Campbell (2008) 'Sarkozy and the past participle: accord . . . ou pas d'accord?' *French Studies Bulletin* 29 (1), no. 106.

Cannadine, D. (1998) *Class in Britain.* London: Penguin.

Carton, F. (2001) 'Quelques evolutions récentes dans la pronunciation du français'. In M.-A. Hintze, T. Pooley and A. Judge (eds.), *French accents: phonological and sociolinguistic perspectives.* London: AFLS/CILT, pp. 7–23.

Chambers, J. K. (1995) *Sociolinguistic theory.* Oxford: Blackwell.

Chen, M. (1972) 'The time dimension contribution toward a theory of sound change.' *Foundations of Language* 8: 457–98.

Cheshire, J. (1982). *A sociolinguistic study: variation in an English dialect.* Cambridge: Cambridge University Press.

Cinque, Guglielmo. 1988. 'On *si* constructions and the theory of *arb.*' *Linguistic Inquiry* 19: 521–81.

Chomsky, N. (1977) 'On WH-movement.' In P. Culicover, T. Wasow, and A. Akmajian (eds.), *Formal syntax.* New York: Academic Press, pp. 71–132.

—— (1980) 'On binding.' *Linguistic Inquiry* 11 (1): 1–46.

—— (1981) *Lectures on Government and Binding.* Dordrecht: Foris.

—— (1995) *The Minimalist Program.* Cambridge, MA: MIT Press.

—— (2001) 'Derivation by Phase.' In M. Kenstowicz (ed.), *Ken Hale: a life in language.* Cambridge, MA: MIT Press, pp. 1–52.

—— (2003) *Chomsky on democracy and education,* C. P. Otero (ed.). New York, London: Routledge.

—— (2004) 'Beyond explanatory adequacy.' In A. Belletti (ed.), *Structures and beyond: the cartography of syntactic structures, vol.3.* Oxford: Oxford University Press, pp. 104–31.

—— (2008) 'On Phases.' In R. Freidin, C. P. Otero and M. L. Zubizarreta (eds.), *Foundational issues in linguistic theory.* Cambridge, MA: MIT Press, pp. 133–66.

Chomsky, N. and M. Halle (1968) *The sound pattern of English.* New York: Harper and Row.

Chomsky, N. and H. Lasnik (1977) 'Filters and control.' *Linguistic Inquiry* 8 (3): 425–504.

Conseil supérieur de la langue française (1990) 'Les rectifications de l'orthographe (Rapport).' *Journal officiel de la République Française, édition des documents administratifs* 100 (December): 7–18.

Coseriu, E. (1958) *Sincronía, diacronía e historia: el problema del cambio lingüístico*. Montevideo: Universidad de la República.

Coveney, A. B. (1990) 'Variation in interrogatives in spoken French: a preliminary report.' In J. N. Green and W. Ayres-Bennett (eds.), *Variation and change in French*. London: Routledge, pp. 116–33.

—— (1995) 'The use of the QU-final interrogative structure in spoken French.' *Journal of French Language Studies* 5 (2): 143–71.

—— (1996) *Variability in spoken French. A sociolinguistic study of interrogation and negation*. Exeter: Elm Bank.

—— (2001) *The sounds of contemporary French*. Exeter: Elm Bank.

—— (2005) 'Subject doubling in spoken French: a sociolinguistic approach.' *The French Review* 79 (1): 96–111.

—— (2010) '*Vouvoiement* and *tutoiement*: sociolinguistic reflections.' *Journal of French Language Studies* 20 (2): 127–50.

Crain, S. and P. Pietroski (2002) 'Why language acquisition is a snap.' *The Linguistic Review* 19: 163–83.

Croft, W. (2000) *Explaining language change*. London: Longman.

—— (2001) *Radical Construction Grammar*. Oxford: Oxford University Press.

Cuervo, R. J. (1907) *Apuntaciones críticas sobre el lenguaje bogotano con frecuente referencia al de los países de Hispano-América* (5th edn). París: Roger and Chernoviz. See Internet Archive, http://www.archive.org/ (home page), date accessed July 2011.

Culf, A. (1994) 'BBC radio seeks to reach parts cut-glass accents cannot reach.' *Guardian*, 27 January 1994.

Culicover, P. W. (1993) 'Evidence against ECP accounts of the *that*-t effect.' *Linguistic Inquiry* 24 (3): 557–61.

D' Alessandro, R. (2002) 'Agreement in Italian impersonal *si* constructions: a derivational analysis.' *Revista da Abralin* 1 (1): 35–72.

D'Alessandro, R. and I. Roberts (2008) 'Movement and Agreement in Italian past participles and defective phases.' *Linguistic Inquiry* 39 (3): 477–91.

Damourette, J. and E. Pichon (1911–39) *Essai de grammaire de la langue française* (7 vols). Paris: D'Artrey.

Davies, M. (2002–) Corpus del Español (100 million words, 1200s–1900s), http://www.corpusdelespanol.org, date accessed 2010–12.

—— (2008–) The Corpus of Contemporary American English: 425 million words, 1990–present, http://corpus.byu.edu/coca/, date accessed 2011–12.

Debray, R. (1992) *Contretemps: eloges des idéaux perdus*. Paris: Folio.

Dennett, D. (2006) *Breaking the spell. Religion as a natural phenomenon*. Harmondsworth: Penguin.

Déprez, V. (1998) 'Semantics effects of agreement: the case of French past participle agreement.' *Probus* 10: 1–65.

Derfel, R. J. (1897) *Musings for the masses*. Manchester: R. J. Derfel.

Detges, U. and R. Waltereit. (2008) *The paradox of grammatical change: perspectives from Romance* (Current issues in linguistic theory 293). Amsterdam: John Benjamins.

Dobrovie-Sorin, C. (1998) 'Impersonal *se* constructions in Romance and the passivization of unergatives.' *Linguistic Inquiry* 29 (3): 399–437.

Dufter, A. (2010) 'El *que* galicado: distribución y descripción gramatical.' In A. Zamorano Aguilar and C. Sinner (eds.), *La 'excepción' en gramática. Perspectivas de análisis* (Lingüística Iberoamericana 41). Frankfurt: Vervuert, pp. 255–80.

Durand, J., B. Laks and C. Lyche (eds.) (2009) *Phonologie, variation et accents du francais.* Paris: Hermes Science.

È Kiss, K. (1998) 'Identificational focus versus information focus.' *Language* 74 (2): 245–73.

Eagleton, T. (1991) *Ideology.* London: Verso.

Eckert, P. (1989) 'The whole woman: sex and gender differences in variation.' *Language Variation and Change* 1: 245–67.

—— (2000) *Linguistic variation as social practice: the linguistic construction of identity in Belten High.* Malden, MA, Oxford: Blackwell.

Emonds, J. E. (1986) 'Grammatically deviant prestige constructions.' In M. Brame, H. Contreras and F. J. Newmeyer (eds.), *Festschrift for Sol Saporta.* Seattle: Noit Amrofer, pp. 93–129.

Encrevé, P. (1988) *La liaison avec et sans enchaînement.* Paris: Seuil.

Fabricius, A. (2000) 'T-glottaling between stigma and prestige. A sociolinguistic study of modern RP.' PhD thesis, University of Copenhagen.

—— (2002) 'Ongoing change in modern RP: evidence for the disappearing stigma of t-glottalling.' *English World-Wide* 23 (1): 115–36.

Fasold, R. (1990) *The sociolinguistics of language.* Oxford: Blackwell.

Finer, S. E. (1962) *The man on horseback: the role of the military in politics.* London: Pall Mall.

Finkielkraut, A. (1987) *La défaite de la pensée.* Paris: Gallimard.

Fónagy, I. (1989) 'Le français change de visage?' *Revue Romane* 24 (2): 225–53.

Fontana, J. M. (1993) 'Phrase structure and the syntax of clitics in the history of Spanish.' PhD dissertation, University of Pennsylvania.

Fougeron, C. and C. Smith (1993) 'French.' *Journal of the International Phonetic Association* 23: 73–6.

Foulet, L. (1921) 'Comment ont évolué les formes de l'interrogation?' *Romania* 47: 243–348.

Foulkes, P. and G. Docherty (eds.) (1999) *Urban voices: accent studies in the British Isles.* London: Arnold.

Fowler, H. W. (1926) *A dictionary of modern English usage.* Oxford: Oxford University Press.

Fowler, H. W. and F. G. Fowler (1922) *The King's English* (2nd edn). Oxford: Clarendon Press. (Viewable at Google Books.)

Frankenberg, R. (1969) *Communities in Britain.* Harmondsworth: Penguin.

Fromkin, V. A., R. Rodman and N. Hyams (2010) *An introduction to language* (9th edn). Boston: Wadsworth.

Gadet, F. (1989) *Le français ordinaire.* Paris: Armand Colin.

—— (1992) *Le français populaire.* Paris: Presses Universitaires de France.

—— (2003) *La variation sociale en français.* Paris: Ophrys.

—— (2007) 'Identités françaises différentielles et linguistique de contact.' In W. Ayres-Bennett and M. Jones (eds.), *The French language and questions of identity.* London: Legenda, pp. 206–16.

Garmadi, J. (1981) *La sociolinguistique.* Paris: Presses Universitaires de France.

Giddens, A. (1992) *The transformation of intimacy: sexuality, love and eroticism in modern societies.* Stanford: Stanford University Press.

Giles, H. (1970) 'Evaluative reactions to accents.' *Educational Review* 22: 211–27.

Giles, H. and P. Powesland (1975) *Speech style and social evaluation.* London: Academic Press.

Gissing, G. (1892a) *Denzil Quarrier.* London: Lawrence & Bullen.

—— (1892b) *Born in exile*. London: Adam and Charles Black.

Grace, G. W. (1981) 'Indirect inheritance and the aberrant Melanesian languages.' In J. Hollyman and A. Pawley (eds.), *Studies in Pacific languages and cultures in honour of Bruce Biggs*. Auckland: Linguistic Society of New Zealand, pp. 255–68.

—— (1990) The 'aberrant' (vs. 'exemplary') Melanesian languages.' In P. Baldi (ed.), *Linguistic change and reconstruction methodology*. Berlin: Mouton de Gruyter, pp. 155–73.

—— (1991) 'How do languages change? (More on 'aberrant' languages).' Paper presented at the Sixth International Conference on Austronesian linguistics, Honolulu.

—— (1993) 'What are languages?' *Ethnolinguistic Notes* (Series 3, no. 45). Printout, University of Hawaii.

Grant, R. (2003) *Incompetence*. London: Gollancz.

Grevisse, M. (1977) *Nouveaux exercices français (livre du maître)*. Paris: Duculot.

—— (1986) *Le bon usage*. Paris: Duculot.

Gries, S. (2002) 'Preposition stranding in English: predicting speakers' behaviour.' In V. Samiian (ed.) *Proceedings of the Western Conference on Linguistics* (vol. 12). Fresno: California State University, pp. 230–41.

Guasti, M.-T. (1996) 'A cross-linguistic study of Romance and arbëresch causatives.' In A. Belletti and L. Rizzi (eds.), *Parameters and functional heads: essays in comparative syntax*. Oxford: Oxford University Press, pp. 209–38.

Haakonssen, K. (1981) *The science of a legislator: the natural jurisprudence of David Hume and Adam Smith*. Cambridge: Cambridge University Press.

Haegeman, L. (1995) *The syntax of negation*. Cambridge: Cambridge University Press.

Hall, D. (2011) 'Geographical variation in the French of Northern France: do we have the basic data?' Paper presented at the Final Conference on 'Language and social structure in urban France', Peterhouse, Cambridge, September 2011.

Hall, K. and M. Bucholtz (1995) *Gender articulated: language and the socially constructed self*. London: Routledge.

Hansen, A. B. (2000) 'Le E caduc interconsonantique en tant que variable sociolinguistique – une étude en région parisienne.' LINX 42 (1): 45–58.

Harrington, J., S. Palethorpe and C. I. Watson (2000) 'Monophthongal vowel changes in Received Pronunciation: an acoustic analysis of the Queen's Christmas broadcasts.' *Journal of the International Phonetic Association* 30 (1): 63–78.

Harris, M. (1988) 'French.' In M. Harris and N. Vincent (eds.), *The Romance languages*. London: Croom Helm, pp. 209–45.

Harris, A. and L. Campbell (1995) *Historical syntax in a cross-linguistic perspective*. Cambridge: Cambridge University Press.

Harris, J. and M. Halle (2005) 'Unexpected plural inflections in Spanish: reduplication and metathesis.' *Linguistic Inquiry* 36: 195–222.

Haugen, E. (1972) 'Dialect, language, nation.' In J. B. Pride and J. Holmes (eds.), *Sociolinguistics. Selected readings*. Harmondsworth: Penguin, pp. 97–111.

Healey, A., J. diPaolo, P. Wilkin and Xin Xiang (2011) Dictionary of Old English Web Corpus, http://www.doe.utoronto.ca/pages/pub/web-corpus.html, date accessed October–November 2011.

Heycock C. and A. Kroch (1998) 'Inversion and equation in copular sentences.' *ZAS Papers in Linguistics* 10: 71–87.

Hobson, D. (1999) *The national wealth*. London. HarperCollins.

Hockett, C. (1958) *A course in modern linguistics*. New York: Macmillan.

Hoffmann, T. (2011) *Preposition placement in English: a usage-based approach*. Cambridge: Cambridge University Press.

Hoggart, R. (1957) *The uses of literacy*. London: Chatto and Windus.

Holmes, J. (1997) 'Women, language and identity.' *Journal of Sociolinguistics* 1 (2): 195–223.

Holthausen, F. (ed.) (1888) *Vices and virtues: being a soul's confession of its sins with reason's description of the virtues: a middle-English dialogue of about 1200 A.D.* London: Trübner.

Honey, J. (1977) *Tom Brown's universe. The development of the Victorian public school.* London: Millington.

—— (1989) *Does accent matter? The Pygmalion factor.* London: Faber.

—— (1997) *Language is power. The story of Standard English and its enemies.* London: Faber.

Horn, L. R. (1989) *A natural history of negation*. Chicago: University of Chicago Press.

Hornsby, D. (2012) 'Getting it wrong: liaison, pataquès and repair in contemporary French.' In T. Pooley and D. Lagorgette (eds), *On linguistic change in French: socio-historical approaches. Studies in honour of R. Anthony Lodge. Le changement linguistique en français: aspects socio-historiques. Etudes en hommage au Professeur R. Anthony Lodge.* Chambéry: Editions de l'Université de Savoie, pp. 69–83.

Houdebine, A.-M. (2003) *L'imaginaire linguistique*. Paris: L'Harmattan.

Hudson, R. (1996) *Sociolinguistics*. Cambridge: Cambridge University Press.

Hughes, G. (1988) *Words in time: a social history of the English vocabulary*. Oxford: Blackwell.

Hume, D. (1777) *The natural history of religion*, ed. H. E. Root. Stanford, CA: Stanford University Press, 1957. Originally composed 1757; published posthumously 1777.

Incomes Data Services (undated) http://www.incomesdata.co.uk/ (homepage), date accessed 2010 (various times).

Jespersen, O. (1917) *Negation in English and other languages*. Copenhagen: Høst.

Johannessen, J. B. (1998) *Coordination*. Oxford: Oxford University Press.

Jones, D. (1956) *The pronunciation of English*. Cambridge: Cambridge University Press.

Jones, M. and E. Esch (2002) *Language change: the interplay of internal, external, and extra-linguistic factors*. Berlin, New York: Mouton de Gruyter.

Joseph, J. E. (1987) *Eloquence and power*. Pinter: London.

Juarros-Daussà, E. (2000) 'The syntactic operator *se* in Spanish: a contemporary account.' Paper presented at the Fourth Hispanic Linguistics Symposium. Indiana University, Bloomington, November 17th–19th.

Judge, A. (1993) 'French: a planned language?' In C. Sanders (ed.), *French today. Language in its social context*. Cambridge: Cambridge University Press, pp. 7–26.

Kallel, A. (2007) 'The loss of negative concord in Standard English: internal factors.' *Language Variation and Change* 19: 27–49.

Kayne, R. S. (1977) *Syntaxe du français: le cycle transformationnel*. Paris: Seuil.

—— (1981) 'ECP extensions.' *Linguistic Inquiry* 12 (1): 93–133.

—— (1984) *Connectedness and binary branching*. Dordrect: Foris.

—— (1989) 'Facets of Romance past participle agreement.' In P. Benincà (ed.), *Dialect variation and the theory of grammar*. Dordrecht: Foris, pp. 85–103.

—— (1994) *The antisymmetry of syntax*. Cambridge, MA: MIT Press.

Keller, R. (1994) *On language change: the invisible hand in language*. New York: Routledge.

Kelling, C. (2006) 'Spanish *se*-constructions: the passive and the impersonal construction.' In M. Butt and T. Holloway King (eds.), *Proceedings of the LFG06 Conference, Universität Konstanz*. Stanford: CSLI Publications, http://csli-publications.stanford.edu/LFG/11/lfg06kelling.pdf, date accessed 21 December 2011).

Kerswill, P. and A. Williams (2000) 'Creating a new town koiné: children and language change in Milton Keynes.' *Language in Society* 29: 65–115.

—— (2002) '"Salience" as an explanatory factor in language change: evidence from dialect levelling in urban England.' In M. C. Jones and E. Esch (eds.), *Language change. The interplay of internal, external and extra-linguistic factors*. Berlin: Mouton de Gruyter, pp. 81–110.

Krifka, M. (1995) 'The semantics and pragmatics of polarity items.' *Linguistic Analysis* 25: 209–57.

Kroch, A. S. (1989) 'Reflexes of grammar in patterns of language change.' *Language Variation and Change* 1: 199–244.

—— (1994) 'Morphosyntactic variation.' In K. Beals, J. Denton, R. Knippen, L. Melnar, H. Suzuki, and E. Zeinfeld (eds.), *Proceedings of the thirtieth annual meeting of the Chicago Linguistic Society, vol. 2: The parasession on variation in linguistic theory*. Chicago: Chicago Linguistic Society, pp. 180–201.

—— (1995) 'Dialect and style in the speech of upper class Philadelphia.' In G. R. Guy, C. Feagin, D. Schiffrin and J. Baugh (eds.), *Towards a social science of language, vol 1. Papers in honour of William Labov*. Amsterdam: John Benjamins, pp. 23–45.

—— (2001) 'Syntactic change.' In M. Baltin and C. Collins (eds.), *The handbook of contemporary syntactic theory*. Oxford: Blackwell, pp. 699–729.

Kroch, A. S. and A. Taylor. (2000a) 'Verb-complement order in Middle English.' In S. Pintzuk, G. Tsoulas and A. Warner (eds.), *Diachronic syntax: models and mechanisms*. Oxford: Oxford University Press, pp. 132–63.

—— (2000b) Penn-Helsinki Parsed Corpus of Middle English (2nd edn). http://www.ling.upenn.edu/hist-corpora/PPCME2-RELEASE-2/.

Kuiper, L. (2005) 'Perception is reality: Parisian and Provençal perceptions of regional varieties of French.' *Journal of Sociolinguistics* 9 (1): 28–52.

Kuroda, S. Y. (1968) 'English relativization and certain related problems.' *Language* 44: 244–66.

Labov, W. (1963) 'The social motivation of a sound change.' *Word* 19: 273–309.

—— (1972a) *Language in the inner city: Studies in the Black English Vernacular*. Philadelphia: University of Pennsylvania Press.

—— (1972b) *Sociolinguistic patterns*. Philadelphia: University of Pennsylvania Press.

—— (1972c) 'Negative attraction and negative concord in English grammar.' *Language* 48 (4): 773–818.

—— (1994) *Principles of linguistic change. Internal factors*. Oxford: Blackwell.

—— (1966) *The social stratification of English in New York City*. Washington, DC: Center for Applied Linguistics.

—— (1998) 'The intersection of sex and social class in the course of linguistic change.' In J. Cheshire and P. Trudgill (eds.), *The sociolinguistics reader. Vol. 2: Gender and discourse*. London: Arnold, pp. 7–52.

—— (2001) *Principles of linguistic change. Social factors*. Oxford: Blackwell.

Landau, I. (2007) 'EPP extensions.' *Linguistic Inquiry* 38 (3): 485–523.

Lapesa, R. (1981) *Historia de la Lengua española* (9th edn). Madrid: Gredos.

—— (2000) *Estudios de morfosintáxis histórica del español*. Madrid: Gredos.

Larrivée, P. and R. Ingham (eds.) (2011) *The evolution of negation. Beyond the Jespersen Cycle*. Berlin: Mouton de Gruyter.

Lasnik, H. and N. Sobin. (2000) 'The *who/whom* puzzle: on the preservation of an archaic feature.' *Natural Language and Linguistic Theory* 18 (2): 343–71.

Le Flem, C. D. (1992) 'Toujours les imbriquées en *que … qui*: retour à la piste scandinave.' *Revue Romane* 27 (2): 163–80.

Léon, M. (1984) 'Erreurs et normalisation: les liaisons fautives en français contemporain.' *Revue de Phonétique Appliquée*, 69: 1–9.

Le Page, R. B. (1989) 'What is a language?' In P. Livesey and M. K. Verma (eds.), *York papers in linguistics* 13: *Festschrift for R. B. Le Page*. York: University of York Department of Language and Linguistic Science, pp. 9–20.

Le Page, R. B. and A Tabouret-Keller (1985) *Acts of identity: creole-based approaches to language and ethnicity*. Cambridge: Cambridge University Press.

Lightfoot, D. (1979) *Principles of diachronic syntax*. Cambridge: Cambridge University Press.

—— (1991) *How to set parameters: arguments from language change*. Cambridge, MA: MIT Press.

—— (1999) *The development of language: acquisition, change and evolution*. Oxford: Blackwell.

—— (2006) 'Cueing a new grammar.' In A. van Kemenade and B. Los (eds.), *The handbook of the history of English*. Oxford: Blackwell, pp. 24–44.

Llamas, C. (1998) 'Language variation and innovation in Middlesbrough: a pilot study.' *Leeds working papers in linguistics and phonetics* 6: 97–114.

Lodge, R. A. (1993) *French: from dialect to standard*. London: Routledge.

—— (1998) 'French is a logical language.' In L. Bauer and P. Trudgill (eds.), *Language myths*. Harmondsworth: Penguin, pp. 23–31.

—— (2004) *A sociolinguistic history of Parisian French*. Cambridge: Cambridge University Press.

Longobardi, G. (2001) 'Formal syntax, diachronic minimalism and etymology: the history of French *chez*.' *Linguistic Inquiry* 32: 275–302.

Lowth, R. (1763) *A short introduction to English grammar: with critical notes* (2nd edn). London: Millar and Dodsley. (Viewable at Google Books.)

Lyons, J. (1977) *Semantics*. Cambridge: Cambridge University Press.

—— (1981) *Language and linguistics. An introduction*. Cambridge: Cambridge University Press.

Macaulay, R. and G. Trevelyan (1973). 'Language, education and employment in Glasgow.' Final report to the SSRC.

Maffesoli. M. (1988) *Le temps des tribus*. Paris: Klincksieck.

Malderez, I. (2000) 'L'analyse de la variation phonétique de corpus de français parlé: problèmes méthodologiques'. In L. Anderson and A. B. Hansen (eds.), *Le français parlé: corpus et résultats*. Copenhagen: Museum Tusculanum Press, pp. 65–89.

Malécot, H. (1976) 'The effect of linguistic and paralinguistic variables on the elision of the French mute-*e*.' *Phonetica* 33: 93–112.

Maling, J. and A. Zaenen (1985) 'Preposition-stranding and passive.' *Nordic Journal of Linguistics* 8: 197–209.

Marsh, G. P. (1865) *Lectures on the English language* (ed. W. Smith). London: John Murray.

Marshall, J. (2003) 'The changing sociolinguistic status of the glottal stop in Northeast Scottish English.' *English World-Wide* 24: 89–108.

Martineau, F. and R. Mougeon (2003) 'A sociolinguistic study of the origins of *ne* deletion in European and Quebec French.' *Language* 79 (1): 118–52.

Martinet, A. (1945) *La prononciation du français contemporain*. Paris: Droz.

—— (1969) 'C'est jeuli, le Mareuc!' In A. Martinet, *Le français sans fard*. Paris: Presses Universitaires de France, pp. 345–55.

Martinon, P. (1913) *Comment on prononce le français*. Paris: Larousse.

Mathieu E. (2004) 'The mapping of form and interpretation: the case of optional WH-movement in French.' *Lingua* 114 (9–10): 1090–1132.

Matthews, P. H. (1981) *Syntax*. Cambridge: Cambridge University Press.

—— (1991) *Morphology* (2nd edn). Cambridge: Cambridge University Press.

McDaniel, D., C. McKee and J. B. Bernstein (1998) 'How children's relatives solve a problem for minimalism.' *Language* 74 (2): 308–34.

McMahon. A. (1994) *Understanding language change*. Cambridge: Cambridge University Press.

Meillet, A. (1921) *Linguistique historique et linguistique générale*. Paris: Champion.

Merton, R. K. (1968) *Social theory and social structure*. Glencoe, IL: Free Press.

Milroy, J. (1992) *Linguistic Variation and Change*. Oxford: Blackwell.

—— (2001) 'Language ideologies and the consequences of standardization.' *Journal of Sociolinguistics* 5 (4): 530–55.

—— (2002) 'The legitimate language: giving a history to English.' In R. Watts and P. Trudgill (eds.), *Alternative histories of English*. London: Routledge, pp. 7–25.

—— (2003) 'When is a sound change? On the role of external factors in language change'. In D. Britain and J. Cheshire (eds.), *Social dialectology: in honour of Peter Trudgill*. Amsterdam: John Benjamins, pp. 209–21.

Milroy, J. and L. Milroy (1999) *Authority in language* (3rd edn). London: Routledge.

Milroy, J., L. Milroy, S. Hartley and D. Walshaw (1994) 'Glottal stops and Tyneside glottalization: competing patterns of variation and change in British English.' *Language Variation and Change* 6 (3): 327–57.

Milroy, L. (1987a) *Observing and analysing natural language*. Oxford: Blackwell.

—— (1987b) *Language and social networks*. Oxford: Blackwell.

—— (2003) 'Social and linguistic dimensions of phonological change. Fitting the pieces of the puzzle together.' In D. Britain and J. Cheshire (eds.), *Social dialectology: in honour of Peter Trudgill*. Amsterdam: John Benjamins, pp. 155–72.

Milward, A. (1984) *The economic effects of the two world wars on Britain*. Basingstoke: Macmillan.

Moland, L. (ed.) (1877–85) *Œuvres complètes de Voltaire* (vol. 19). Paris: Garnier.

Moré, B. (2000) 'The ideological construction of an empirical base: selection and elaboration in Andrés Bello's grammar.' In J. del Valle and L. Gabriel-Stheeman (eds.), *The battle over Spanish between 1800 and 2000: language ideologies and Hispanic intellectuals*. London: Routledge, pp. 42–63.

Moro, A. (1997) *The raising of predicates. Predicative noun phrases and the theory of clause structure*. Cambridge: Cambridge University Press.

Mülhäusler, P. (1996) *Linguistic ecology*. Oxford: Blackwell.

Müller, N. (1999) 'Past-participle agreement in Romance.' Habilitationsschrift, University of Hamburg.

Ohkado, M. (2010) 'On stylistic fronting in Middle English prose.' In M. Kytö, J. Scahill and H. Tanabe (eds.), *Language change and variation from Old English to Late Modern English*. Bern: Peter Lang, pp. 104–16.

Olson, G. A. and L. Faigley (1991) 'Language, politics and composition: a conversation with Noam Chomsky.' *Journal of Advanced Composition* 11: 1–35.

Orwell, G. (1959) *The road to Wigan pier*. Harmondsworth: Penguin. (First published 1937).

Pedersen, J. (2005) 'The Spanish impersonal se-construction. Constructional variation and change.' *Constructions*, Articles 2005,, http://elanguage.net/journals/constructions/index (homepage), date accessed 21 May 2012.

Penny, R. (2000) *Variation and change in Spanish*. Cambridge: Cambridge University Press.

—— (2002) *A history of the Spanish language* (2nd edn). Cambridge: Cambridge University Press.

Perkin, H. (2002) *The rise of professional society: England since 1880*. London: Routledge.

Perlmutter, D. M. (1971) *Deep and surface structure constraints in syntax*. New York: Holt, Rinehart and Winston.

Pesetsky, D. 1982. 'Complementizer-trace phenomena and the nominative island condition.' *The Linguistic Review* 1: 297–345.

Pesetsky, D. and E. Torrego (2001) 'T-to-C movement.' In M. Kenstowicz (ed.), *Ken Hale: a life in language*. Cambridge, MA: MIT Press, pp. 355–426.

Pintzuk, S. (1999) *Phrase structures in competition: variation and change in Old English word order*. New York: Garland.

—— (2005) 'Arguments against a universal base: evidence from Old English.' *English Language and Linguistics* 9 (1): 115–38.

Pintzuk, S. and A. Taylor (2006) 'The loss of OV order in the history of English.' In B. Los and A. van Kemenade (eds.), *The handbook of the history of English*. Oxford: Blackwell, pp. 249–78.

Pirvulescu, M. and I. Belzil. (2008) 'The acquisition of past participle agreement in Québec French L1.' *Language Acquisition* 15 (2): 75–88.

Poole, G. (2006) 'Interpolation and the left periphery in Old Spanish.' *Newcastle Working Papers in Linguistics* 13: 188–216.

Pooley, T. (2006) 'On the geographical spread of Oïl French in France.' *Journal of French Language Studies* 16 (3): 357–90.

Posner, R. (1996) *The Romance languages*. Cambridge: Cambridge University Press.

Pountain, C. (2001) *A history of the Spanish language through texts*. London: Routledge.

Preston, D. (1991) 'Sorting out the variables in sociolinguistic theory.' *American Speech* 66 (1): 33–56.

Price, G. (1984) *The French language: present and past* (2nd edn). London: Grant & Cutler.

Pullum, G. K. and R. Huddleston (2002) 'Prepositions and prepositional phrases.' In R. Huddleston and G. K. Pullum (eds.), *The Cambridge grammar of the English language*. Cambridge: Cambridge University Press, pp. 597–661.

Quattlebaum, J. A. (1994) 'A study of Case assignment in coordinate noun phrases.' *Language Quarterly* 32: 131–47.

Quirk, R. (1964) *The use of English*. London: Longman.

Quirk, R., S. Greenbaum, G. Leech and J. Svartvik (1985) *A comprehensive grammar of the English language*. London: Longman.

Radford, A. (1988) *Transformational grammar*. Cambridge: Cambridge University Press.

—— (2010) *An introduction to English sentence structure* (International student edition). Cambridge: Cambridge University Press.

Radford, A. and C. Felser (2011) 'On preposition copying and preposition pruning in *wh*-clauses in English.' *Essex Research Reports in Linguistics* 60 (4).

Radford, A. and M. Vincent (2007.) 'On past participle agreement in transitive clauses in French.' In A. Bisetto and F. E. Barbieri (eds.), *Proceedings of the XXXIII Incontro di grammatica generativa, Bologna, March 1–3, 2007*. Bologna: Università di Bologna, pp. 140–61.

Real Academia Española (1931) *Gramática de la lengua española (nueva edición, reformada)*. Madrid: Espasa-Calpe.
—— (2005) *Diccionario panhispánico de dudas*, http://buscon.rae.es/dpdI/html/cabecera. htm, date accessed 2011 (various times).
—— (undated (a)) *Corpus diacrónico del español*, http://corpus.rae.es/cordenet.html, date accessed 2011 (various times).
—— (undated (b)) *Corpus de referencia del español actual*, http://corpus.rae.es/creanet. html, date accessed 2011 (various times).
Reinhart, T. and T. Siloni (2004) 'Against an unaccusative analysis of reflexives.' In A. Alexiadou, E. Anagnostopoulou and M. Everaert (eds.), *The unaccusativity puzzle: explorations of the syntax–lexicon interface*. Oxford: Oxford University Press, pp. 159–80.
Richards, N. (1997) 'What moves where when in which Language?' PhD dissertation, Massachusetts Institute of Technology.
Rickard, P. (1974) *A history of the French language*. London: Hutchinson.
—— (1992) *The French language in the seventeenth century. Contemporary opinion in France*. Cambridge: Brewer.
Riemsdijk, H. van. (1978) *A case study in syntactic markedness: the binding nature of prepositional phrases*. Dordrecht: Foris.
Ritchie, R. and J. Moore (1914) *A manual of French composition*. Cambridge: Cambridge University Press.
Rivarol, A. de (1784) *De l'universalité de la langue française: discours qui a remporté le prix à l'Académie de Berlin*. Paris: Bailly et Dessenne.
Rivero, M. L. (1991) 'Clitic and NP climbing in Old Spanish.' In H. Campos and F. Martínez-Gil (eds.), *Current studies in Spanish linguistics*. Washington, DC: Georgetown University Press, pp. 241–82.
—— (1993) 'Long Head Movement versus V2, and null subjects in Old Romance.' *Lingua* 89: 217–45.
—— (2002) 'On impersonal reflexives in Romance and Slavic and Semantic variation.' In J. Camps and C. Wiltshire (eds.), *Romance syntax, semantics and L2 acquisition. Selected papers from the 30th Linguistic Symposium on Romance Languages, Gainesville, Florida, February 2000*. Amsterdam and Philadelphia: John Benjamins, pp. 169–95.
Rizzi, L. (1982) *Issues in Italian syntax*. Dordrecht: Foris.
—— (2001) 'Relativized minimality effects.' In M. Baltin and C. Collins (eds.), *The handbook of contemporary syntactic theory*. Oxford: Blackwell, pp. 89–110.
Roberts, I. (2007) *Diachronic syntax*. Oxford: Oxford University Press.
Romaine, S. (1984a) 'The status of sociolinguistic models and categories in explaining linguistic variation.' *Linguistische Berichte* 90: 25–38.
—— (1984b) *The language of children and adolescents*. Oxford: Blackwell.
Rouveret, A. and J.- R. Vergnaud. (1980) 'Specifying reference to the subject: French causatives and conditions on representations.' *Linguistic Inquiry* 11 (1): 97–202.
Ruwet, N. (1982) *Grammaire des insultes et autres etudes*. Paris: Seuil.
Sankoff, D. (1988) 'Sociolinguistics and syntactic variation.' In F. J. Newmeyer (ed.), *Linguistics: the Cambridge survey*. Vol. IV, *Language: the socio-cultural context*. Cambridge: Cambridge University Press, pp. 140–61.
Sankoff, G. and D. Vincent. (1977) 'L'emploi productif du *ne* dans le français parlé à Montréal.' *Le Français Moderne* 45 : 243–54.
Schütze, C. T. 1996. *The empirical base of linguistics: grammaticality judgments and linguistic methodology*. Chicago: University of Chicago Press.
Seabrook, J. (2000) *Nobrow: The culture of marketing, the marketing of culture*. London: Methuen.

Silverstein, M. (1979) 'Language structure and linguistic ideology.' In R. Cline, W. Hanks and C. Hofbauer (eds.), *The elements: a parasession on linguistic units and levels*. Chicago: Chicago Linguistic Society, pp. 193–247.

Singy, P. (1996) *L'image du français en Suisse romande*. Paris: L'Harmattan.

Smith, A. (1996) 'A diachronic study of French variable liaison.' MLitt dissertation, Newcastle University.

Smith, G. (ed.) (1969) *The letters of Aldous Huxley*. London: Chatto and Windus.

Smith, J. C. (1993) 'The agreement of the past participle conjugated with *avoir* and a preceding direct object – a brief history of prescriptive attitudes.' In R. Sampson (ed.), *Authority and the French language. Papers from a conference at the University of Bristol*. Münster: Nodus, pp. 87–125.

Sobin, N. (1987) 'The variable status of Comp-trace phenomena.' *Natural Language & Linguistic Theory* 5 (1): 33–60.

—— (1997) 'Agreement, default rules, and grammatical viruses.' *Linguistic Inquiry* 28: 318–43.

—— (2009) 'Prestige case forms and the Comp-trace effect.' *Syntax* 12 (1): 32–59.

Sornicola, R. 1988. '*It*-Clefts and *Wh*-clefts: two awkward sentence types.' *Journal of Linguistics* 24: 343–79.

Sportiche, D. (1988) 'A theory of floating quantifiers and its corollaries for constituent structure.' *Linguistic Inquiry* 19: 425–49.

Stewart, C. (Forthcoming) 'Mapping language ideologies in multiethnic urban Europe: the case of Parisian French.' *Journal of Multilingual and Multicultural Development*.

Strongman, K. and J. Woosley. (1967) 'Stereotyped reactions to regional accents.' *British Journal of Social and Clinical Psychology* 6: 164–7.

Stuart-Smith, J. (1999). 'Glottals past and present: a study of t-glottalling in Glaswegian.' In C. Upton and K. Wales (eds.), *Leeds Studies in English*, 30. Leeds: University of Leeds, pp. 181–204.

Sturtevant, E. H. (1947) *An introduction to linguistic science*. New Haven: Yale University Press.

Sunstein, C. (1994) *The partial constitution*. Cambridge, MA: Harvard University Press.

Tanase, E. (1976) 'L'accord du participe passé dans le français oral.' In M. Boudreault and F. Möhren (eds.), *Actes du XIIIe Congrès international de linguistique et philologie romanes: tenu à l'Université Laval (Québec, Canada) du 29 août au 5 septembre 1971*. Québec: Presses de l'Université Laval, pp. 475–82.

Thody, P. (1989) *French caesarism from Napoleon I to Charles de Gaulle*. Basingstoke: Macmillan.

Thody, P., with H. Evans and M. Pepratx-Evans (1995) *Le franglais: forbidden English, forbidden American: law, politics and language in contemporary France: a study in loan words and national identity*. London: Athlone.

Tremblay, A. (2005) 'The L2 acquisition of Spanish passive and impersonal *Se* by French- and English-speaking adults.' In L. Dekydtspotter *et al.* (eds.), *Proceedings of the 7th Generative approaches to second language acquisition conference* (GASLA 2004). Somerville, MA: Cascadilla Proceedings Project, pp. 251–68, www.lingref.com, document #1171, date accessed 22 December 2011.

Trudgill, P. (1974) *The social differentiation of English in Norwich*. Cambridge: Cambridge University Press.

—— (1986) *Dialects in contact*. Oxford: Blackwell.

—— (1988) 'Norwich revisited: recent linguistic changes in an English urban dialect.' *English World-Wide* 9 (1): 33–49.

—— (1990) *The dialects of England*. Oxford: Blackwell.

—— (1992) 'Series Editor's preface'. In J. Milroy, *Linguistic variation and change*. Oxford: Blackwell, pp. vi–vii.

—— (1995) *Sociolinguistics. An introduction to language and society* (3rd edn). Harmondsworth: Penguin.

—— (2002) *Sociolinguistic variation and change*. Washington, DC: Georgetown University Press.

Tuten, D. N. (2003) *Koineization in medieval Spanish*. Berlin: Mouton de Gruyter.

Ura, H. (1993) 'On feature-checking for *wh*-traces.' *MIT Working Papers in Linguistics* 18: 243–80.

Valdman, A. (1976) *Introduction to French phonology and morphology*. Rowley, MA: Newbury House.

—— (1982) 'Français standard et français populaire: sociolectes ou fictions?' *French Review* 56 (2): 218–27.

Vattimo, G. (1991) *The end of modernity: nihilism and hermeneutics in post-modern culture*, trans. J. R. Snyder. Cambridge: Polity Press.

Vaugelas, C. Favre de (1663) *Remarques sur la langue françoise: utiles à ceux qui veulent bien parler et bien escrire* (2nd edn). Paris: Lovis Billaine. (Viewable at Google Books.)

Veland, R. (1998) 'Une construction dite ne pas exister en français moderne: le passif suivi d'un infinitif nu.' *Journal of French Language Studies* 8: 97–113

Walden, G. (1996) *We should know better. Solving the education crisis*. London: Fourth Estate.

—— (1999) *Lucky George. Memoirs of an anti-politician*. London: Allen Lane.

—— (2006) *New elites. A career in the masses* (2nd edn). London: Gibson Square.

Watt, D. (1998) 'Variation and change in the vowel system of Tyneside English.' PhD thesis, Newcastle University.

Watt, D. and Milroy, L. (1999) 'Patterns of variation and change in three Newcastle vowels: is this dialect levelling?' In P. Foulkes and G. Docherty (eds.) *Urban voices: accent studies in the British Isles*. London: Arnold, pp. 25–46.

Waugh, E. (1964) *A little learning*. London: Chapman & Hall.

Wheatcroft, G. (2005) *The strange death of Tory England*. London: Allen Lane.

Willemyns, R. (2007) 'De-standardization in the Dutch territory at large.' In C. Fandrych and R. Salverda (eds.), *Standard, Variation und Sprachwandel in germanischen Sprachen*. Tübingen: Narr, pp. 265–279.

Williams, E. (1997) 'The asymmetry of predication.' *Texas Linguistic Forum* 38: 323–33.

Williams, R. (1958) *Culture and society, 1780–1950*. London: Chatto and Windus.

Wouters, C. (1986) 'Formalization and informalization: changing tension balances in civilizing processes.' *Theory, Culture & Society* 2 (2): 1–18.

Wright, R. (1999) 'Periodization and how to avoid it.' In R. J. Blake, D. L. Ranson, and R. Wright (eds.), *Essays in Hispanic linguistics dedicated to Paul M. Lloyd*. Newark: Juan de la Cuesta, pp. 25–41.

Wright Mills, C. (1956) *The power elite*. New York: Oxford University Press.

Wurff, W. van der (1999) 'Objects and verbs in modern Icelandic and fifteenth-century English: a word order parallel and its causes.' *Lingua* 109: 237–65.

Wyld, H. C. (1936) (ed.) *The universal dictionary of the English language*. London: Joseph.

Zribi-Hertz, A. (2011) 'Pour un modèle diglossique de description du français: quelques implications théoriques, didactiques et méthodologiques.' *Journal of French Language Studies* 21 (2): 231–56.

Index